ROUTLEDGE LIBRARY EDITIONS: ENERGY

Volume 1

ENERGY GUIDE

ENERGY GUIDE
A Directory of Information Resources

VIRGINIA BEMIS

Routledge
Taylor & Francis Group

LONDON AND NEW YORK

First published in 1977 by Garland

This edition first published in 2019
by Routledge
2 Park Square, Milton Park, Abingdon, Oxon OX14 4RN

and by Routledge
52 Vanderbilt Avenue, New York, NY 10017

Routledge is an imprint of the Taylor & Francis Group, an informa business

British Library Cataloguing in Publication Data
A catalogue record for this book is available from the British Library

ISBN: 978-0-367-21122-6 (Set)
ISBN: 978-0-429-26565-5 (Set) (ebk)
ISBN: 978-0-367-21109-7 (Volume 1) (hbk)
ISBN: 978-0-429-26553-2 (Volume 1) (ebk)

Publisher's Note
The publisher has gone to great lengths to ensure the quality of this reprint but points out that some imperfections in the original copies may be apparent.

Disclaimer
The publisher has made every effort to trace copyright holders and would welcome correspondence from those they have been unable to trace.

ENERGY GUIDE
A Directory of
Information Resources

Virginia Bemis
Department of English
Michigan State University

with the assistance of
Denton E. Morrison   Frederick H. Buttel
Frederick Frankena   Joseph Galin
Jay Cardinal   Judy Benjamin

GARLAND PUBLISHING, INC. • NEW YORK & LONDON
1977

Library of Congress Cataloging in Publication Data

Bemis, Virginia.
  Energy guide.

  (Garland reference library of social science ; v. 43)

  Includes index.

  1. Power resources—Bibliography. 2. Energy policy—Bibliography. 3. Power resources—Information services. 4. Energy policy—Information services. I. Title.
Z5853.P83B35   [TJ163.2]   016.3337   77-10471
ISBN 0-8240-9870-6

To Charles E. Seim,
librarian of East Lansing High School,
my first teacher of librarianship

CONTENTS

PREFACE

"The energy crisis." This phrase has become so common a part of our language as to be taken for granted. Energy demand increases daily, while our supplies of conventional fuels such as oil and natural gas are finite and will eventually be exhausted. From schoolchild to adult voter, we are all thinking about energy and debating energy-related questions.

Energy Guide's function is to act as an access-point for energy information. The book is not intended only for scholars and energy professionals. Every effort has been made to include a wide range of material so that the *Guide* will be useful for teachers, school librarians, public librarians, and any other readers interested in finding out more about energy. The chapters separate information according to the type of material (e.g., instructional aids, periodicals) or the issuing organization (e.g., government services). The index classifies according to type of energy (e.g., oil, solar, nuclear) or issue (e.g., policy, transportation).

A special feature of the *Guide* is the section of annotated listings of empirical social science studies on energy and the energy crisis. The annotations cover the methods, variables and findings of many research projects on attitudes, behavior, costs, policy and other energy-related matters.

At the time of writing (May 1977), President Carter's proposed national energy policy has been introduced and described, but not yet acted upon; a Federal Information Center or local library can provide information on the current status of the national energy policy. The program includes:

Establishment of a cabinet-level Department of Energy, consolidating Federal energy efforts which are now dispersed among many agencies and departments such as ERDA and FEA.

Stress on energy conservation and efficiency in all sectors of the economy. Homes, businesses and transportation authorities must cut back on both energy use and energy waste.

Tax rebates and credits to encourage energy-saving practices and technology in business and industry.

Promotion of insulation, alternative energy systems and efficiency standards for vehicles, buildings and appliances.

Encouragement of the use of coal instead of oil and natural gas, increased natural gas prices and partial decontrol of retail gasoline prices.

Reforms in utility company rate structures and energy delivery systems.

These proposals have not yet reached the floor of Congress, though the Department of Energy is nearest to being brought to a vote.

Readers looking for specific articles, books, papers and conference proceedings will find two other Garland publications useful. *Energy* (1975) and *Energy II* (1977), both compiled by Denton E. Morrison, are bibliographies of energy literature in social science and related fields. *Energy* lists items through December 1974, and *Energy II*'s listings run from December 1974 through October 1976. In both volumes, readers will find not only general energy information, but also much that was too advanced or specialized for inclusion in *Energy Guide.*

ACKNOWLEDGMENTS

The following individuals and organizations contributed material used in preparing *Energy Guide*. Highly technical material was used in *Energy II*. Any omissions from this list are inadvertent, and I apologize for any that may have occurred.

The Reference and Government Documents staffs of the Michigan State University Library

The East Lansing Public Library

The East Lansing Public Schools, particularly Mr. Charles Seim, Librarian of East Lansing High School; and the staff of the Instructional Media Center

Professors Richard Benvenuto and Larry Landrum of Michigan State University's English Department for their assistance and advice

The Department of Sociology and the Michigan Agricultural Experiment Station for the continuing support of several of the assistant compilers

Robert J. Bemis, without whose help and understanding this book would not have been possible

Also:

Stan L. Albrecht
Alternatives, Trent University
American Astronautical Society
American Enterprise Institute for Public Policy Research
American Political Science Association
American Society of Planning Officials
Association for the Study of Man-Environment Relations, Inc.
BDM Corporation
Roberta A. Baron
Robert B. Bechtel
Behavioral Studies Group, George Washington University

James S. Bowman
Gordon L. Bultena
Bureau of Social Science Research, Inc.
William S. Cain
Vary T. Coates
Albert E. Collins
Common Cause
The Conference Board
Congressional Research Service, Library of Congress
Desmond M. Connor
Peg Corwin
E. O. Derow
Steven Deutsch
Joseph F. Donnermeyer
Dorothy Dorren
Harvey A. Feit
Donald R. Field
Friends of the Earth
Charles Geisler
Scott Geller
Nicholas Georgescu-Roegen
Beth Givens
Mary R. Hamilton
Eliot R. Hammer
Howard Hammerman
Susan Hanson
Alice C. Hastings
John C. Hendee
Daryl Hobbs
Dorothy Huffman
Institute of Behavioral Science, University of Colorado
Institute of Electrical and Electronics Engineers
International City Management Association
Patrick C. Jobes
Sue Johnson
Brian Jones
Martha T. Jordan

Jill King
J. D. Kirschten
ElDean V. Kohrs
Daniel Lauber
C. Burgess Ledbetter
F. Larry Leistritz
Midwest Energy Alternative
Mitre Corporation
John A. Molino
Annabelle B. Motz
Stuart S. Nagel
National Opinion Research Center
National Research Council
National Science Foundation
National Technical Information Service
H. McIlvaine Parsons
Arthur H. Patterson
James R. Pease
Ronald E. Reinsel
William R. Renfro
Resources for the Future
J. S. Reynolds
Kent D. Shifferd
Sierra Club
David L. Sills
Richard C. Smodon
Kathleen Spangler
Mary D. Stearns
Erik J. Stenehjem
Ema Striner
Paul Tanner
Calvin W. Taylor
Michele M. Tetley
United Nations Association of the U.S.
United States Bureau of Land Management
United States Department of Agriculture
United States Federal Energy Administration

United States National Bureau of Standards
University of Utah, College of Law
Jon M. Veigel
Susan E. Wright
Hiroaki Yoshii

INSTRUCTIONAL AIDS

INSTRUCTIONAL AIDS

Introduction

While there are many sources of instructional aids, few deal solely and specifically with energy. For this reason, this section includes many general science and environmentally-oriented sources. Where possible, the listings have been annotated to indicate the types of aids available from each source and the level for which they were intended. Listings include material for all levels from primary to post-graduate. The sources include reviewing services, educational journals, commercial distributors, companies and organizations distributing materials, and government agencies. When ordering materials from a government agency, orders should be placed several months in advance, as these sources are used by a great many schools and community groups.

Materials in this section include films, filmstrips, charts, posters, video and audio tapes, cassettes, multi-media kits, games and simulations. Both United States and Canadian sources of educational materials are listed, with addresses. Price lists have not been included, as this information changes rapidly. For prices and detailed ordering instructions, contact the supplier or distributor.

Indexes, Guides, Periodicals

1. AN ANNOTATED BIBLIOGRAPHY OF 16MM FILMS USEFUL IN COLLEGE LEVEL GEOLOGY AND EARTH SCIENCE COURSES, Noel Potter, Jr., (ed.), American Geological Institute, 2201 M Street NW, Washington, D.C. 20037. 1971.

    Classifies approximately 300 films according to usefulness for undergraduate courses and annotates those suitable for college courses. Those listed as too elementary may be useful for high school students.

2. AUDIOVISUAL, P.O. Box 101, Croydon ENGLAND CR9 1QH. Monthly.

    Regular reviews of educational films, filmstrips and multimedia packages.

3. AUDIOVISUAL INSTRUCTION, National Education Association, 1201 16th Street NW, Washington, D.C. 20036. 10/year.

    Audiovisual instruction techniques and indexing of current reviews.

4. AUDIOVISUAL MARKETPLACE: A MULTIMEDIA GUIDE, R.R. Bowker, New York, NY 10036. Biennial.

Lists producers and distributors of audiovisual material, public radio and television program libraries, reference books, directories, periodicals. Subject index.

5. BASIC REFERENCE SHELF ON SIMULATION AND GAMING, ERIC Clearinghouse on Educational Media and Technology, Stanford University, Stanford, CA 94305.

Available in hard copy and microfiche, lists books, journals and other materials.

6. BIBLIOGRAPHY OF ENERGY EDUCATION MATERIALS, Center for Science in the Public Interest, Box E, 1757 S Street NW, Washington, D.C. 20009.

Reviews of more than 20 publications available for use in developing classroom curricula on energy and the environment in grades K-12.

7. BIBLIOGRAPHY OF SCIENCE COURSES OF STUDY AND TEXTBOOKS, National Science Teachers Association, 1201 16th Street NW, Washington, D.C. 20036.

Lists textbooks for grades K-12, and courses of study from state and local schools.

8. BIBLIO-JEUNES: NIVEAUX.PRESCOLAIRE ET ELEMENTAIRE, La Centrale des Biblioteques, Montreal, Quebec CANADA, 1971.

Elementary and preschool level books, arranged by Dewey decimal classification.

9. BLUEBOOK OF AUDIOVISUAL MATERIALS, Educational Screen and Audiovisual Guide, 434 S. Wabash Avenue, Chicago, IL 60605. Annual.

An annotated list of audiovisual materials at all levels, indexed by subject.

10. BOOKLIST, American Library Association, 50 East Huron Street, Chicago, IL 60611. Semi-monthly September-July, monthly in August.

Reviews books and educational media including films, filmstrips, cassettes and slides, indicating subject and grade level.

11. CANADIAN FILM INSTITUTE TITLE INDEX, Canadian Film Institute, 303 Richmond Road, Ottawa, Ontario K1Z 6X3 CANADA.

Catalog of over 6500 titles, covering the entire CFI film holdings. Annual updates.

12. CANADIAN MATERIALS, Canadian Library Association, Ottawa, Ontario CANADA.

Annual list of print and nonprint media for school resource centers.

4

13. CANADIAN SOURCEBOOK OF EDUCATIONAL MATERIALS, Vicki and D.
     Hillary (comps.), Canadian Educational Resources for
     Teachers, Calgary, Alberta CANADA, 1973.

     List of free, free-loan and inexpensive educational
     materials from Canadian and U.S. sources.

14. CATALOGUE OF INSTRUCTIONAL MEDIA AND MATERIALS, 2855 Shermer
     Road, Northbrook, IL 60062.

15. COURSE AND CURRICULUM IMPROVEMENT MATERIALS, National Science
     Foundation. Available from U.S. Government Printing
     Office, Washington, D.C.

     Lists films, books and instructional materials in the
     sciences for elementary, intermediate and secondary
     school classes.

16. EFLA EVALUATIONS, Educational Film Library Association, 17
     West 60th Street, New York, NY 10023.

     Approximately 300 reviews annually of 16mm educational
     films. Annotated, with synopsis, subject and age group.

17. EDUCATIONAL AND INDUSTRIAL TELEVISION, 607 Main Street,
     Ridgefield, CT 06877. Monthly.

     Articles and reviews on educational program series.

18. EDUCATIONAL SCREEN AND AUDIOVISUAL GUIDE, Educational Screen,
     Chicago, IL. Monthly

     Articles, news and reviews on all aspects of elementary
     and secondary audiovisual instruction.

19. EDUCATIONAL SIMULATION AND GAMING, ERIC Clearinghouse on
     Media and Technology, Stanford Center for Research and
     Development in Teaching, Stanford, CA 95305.

20. EDUCATIONAL SOUND AND FILMSTRIP DIRECTORY, Du Kane Corp.,
     Audiovisual Division, St. Charles, IL 60174.

21. EDUCATOR'S GUIDE TO MEDIA LISTS, Mary Robertson Sive (ed.),
     Libraries Unlimited, Littleton, Colorado, 1975.

22. EDUCATOR'S PROGRESS SERVICE, Randolph, WI 53956.

     Guides to free and free-loan material.
     EDUCATOR'S GUIDE TO FREE FILMS.
     EDUCATOR'S GUIDE TO FREE FILMSTRIPS.
     EDUCATOR'S GUIDE TO FREE SCIENCE MATERIALS.
     EDUCATOR'S GUIDE TO FREE SOCIAL STUDIES MATERIALS.
     EDUCATOR'S GUIDE TO FREE TAPES, SCRIPTS AND TRANSCRIP-
     TIONS. Materials include films, filmstrips, slides,
     transparencies, videotapes, charts, and records.

23.　EDUCATOR'S PURCHASING GUIDE, North American Publishing Co., Philadelphia, PA, 1974.

　　A publisher-producer directory to textbooks and printed materials, audiovisual materials, maps and accessories, educational equipment and supplies.

24.　8MM FILM DIRECTORY, Grace Ann Dane (ed.), Comprehensive Service Corp., 250 West 64th Street, New York, NY 10023.

　　Over 5000 films in all formats are listed by subject with descriptions.

25.　ENERGY AND ORDER, Mark Terry and Paul Witt, 1976.

　　A teacher's handbook for a unit on energy for high school students, with presentations, experiments and activities to show how energy works in the world we live in, and the concept of energy-intensiveness. Available from Environmental Action Reprint Service.

26.　THE ENVIRONMENT FILM REVIEW: A CRITICAL GUIDE TO ECOLOGY FILMS, Environment Information Center, 124 East 39th Street, New York, NY 10016. 1972.

　　Reviews films on environmental affairs. Catagories include air pollution, energy, environmental education, renewable and non-renewable resources, solid waste and transportation.

27.　ENVIRONMENTAL EDUCATION: AN ANNOTATED BIBLIOGRAPHY OF SELECTED MATERIALS AND SOURCES AVAILABLE, National Education Association, 1201 16th Street NW, Washington, D.C. 20036.

28.　ERIC CLEARINGHOUSE ON EDUCATIONAL MEDIA AND TECHNOLOGY, Stanford Center for Research and Development in Teaching, Stanford University, Stanford, CA 94305.

29.　FEDERAL PUBLICATIONS SELECTED FOR HIGH SCHOOL LIBRARIES, Information Canada, 171 Slater Street, Ottawa, Ontario CANADA K1A 0S9.

30.　FILM NEWS, 250 West 57th Street, New York, NY 10019. Bimonthly.

　　A primary source of media information through feature articles, previews and reviews on educational films, filmstrips and records.

31.　FILMS OF THE FUTURE: A SELECTIVE LISTING, World Future Society Book Service, 4916 St Elmo Avenue, Washington, D.C. 20014.

　　Groups films according to major subject areas, with descriptions, source and rental cost information.

32. FREE AND INEXPENSIVE LEARNING MATERIALS, Division of Surveys and Field Services, George Peabody College for Teachers, Nashville, TN. Biennial.

   Guide to pamphlets, offprints, prints, charts, maps and paperbound books available free or at low cost, with ordering information.

33. FREE AND INEXPENSIVE MATERIALS ON WORLD AFFAIRS, Teachers College Press, Columbia University, New York, NY 10027.

   Elementary and secondary level books, films, film-strips, periodicals, etc.

34. FREE LOAN EDUCATIONAL FILMS: SCHOOL CATALOG, Modern Talking Picture Service, Long Island, NY. Annual.

   Free loan films from associations, companies, etc. in science, social science and other fields. Rental catalog also available. A 1974-75 release is "Energy Versus Ecology: the Great Debate".

35. GUIDE BOOK 1975: TELEVISION INSTRUCTION, Agency for Instructional Television, Bloomington, Indiana, 1975. Also available from ERIC.

   Describes instructional television films from the elementary level up.

36. A GUIDE TO FILM AND TELEVISION COURSES IN CANADA, 1975, Canadian Film Institute, 303 Richmond Road, Ottawa, Ontario K1Z 6X3 CANADA.

   Lists films and television courses geographically by province and outlines curricula and courses of various colleges and universities.

37. GUIDE TO MICROFORMS IN PRINT, NCR Microcard Editions, Washington, D.C. Annual.

   Listing of microfilm, microcard and microfiche materials. Complemented by the biennial SUBJECT GUIDE TO MICROFORMS IN PRINT.

38. THE GUIDE TO SIMULATIONS AND GAMES, David W. Zuckerman and Robert E. Horn, Information Resources, Inc., Lexington, MA, 1975.

   Describes simulations and games, and discusses their use in instruction.

39. GUIDE TO FOREIGN GOVERNMENT LOAN FILMS IN THE U.S. Serina Press, 70 Kennedy Street, Alexandria, VA 22305.

40. GUIDE TO U.S. GOVERNMENT LOAN FILMS. Serina Press, 70 Kennedy Street, Alexandria, VA 22305.

41.   HANDBOOK OF GAMES AND SIMULATION EXERCISES, G.I. Gibbs (ed.), Sage Publications, 275 South Beverly Drive, Beverly Hills, CA 90212, 1974.

Describes 2000 games and simulations from the elementary through the post-graduate level.

42.   INDEPENDENT SCHOOL BULLETIN, National Association of Independent Schools, 4 Liberty Square, Boston, MA 02109. Quarterly.

Reviews and discusses films with classroom applications.

43.   INDEX TO COMPUTER ASSISTED INSTRUCTION, Helen A. Lekan (ed.); Harcourt, Brace, New York, NY, 3rd edition, 1971.

Information on 1264 programs in 70 subject areas from preschool to graduate education levels.

44.   INDEX TO INSTRUCTIONAL MEDIA CATALOGS: A MULTI-INDEXED DIRECTORY OF MATERIALS AND EQUIPMENT FOR USE IN INSTRUCTIONAL PROGRAMS, R.R. Bowker, 1180 Avenue of the Americas, New York, NY, 10036. 1974.

Deals with kits, posters, films, etc. on early childhood-primary, intermediate, Junior High, Senior High and adult levels.

45.   INSTRUCTOR, Instructor Publications, 7 Bank Street, Dansville, NY 14437. Monthly, September-June.

Regular feature, "Reviews of Instructional Media," classified either by topics such as science, or by form. Discusses films, filmstrips, records, tapes and other learning aids.

46.   INTERNATIONAL INDEX TO MULTI-MEDIA INFORMATION, Audio Visual Associates, 180 East California Blvd., Pasadena, CA 91108. Quarterly.

Indexes reviews and articles on nonprint media, films, charts, games, etc. Has subject index and distributor directory.

47.   INTERNATIONAL MICROFORMS IN PRINT 1974-75. Allen B. Veaner and Alan M. Meckler, (eds.), Microform Review, Weston, CT. 1974.

Microfilm, microcard and microfiche by non-U.S. publishers.

48.   JOURNAL OF COLLEGE SCIENCE TEACHING, 1742 Connecticut Avenue, NW, Washington, D.C. 20009. 5/year.

Reviews films, filmstrips, kits and transparencies.

49.   LANDERS FILM REVIEWS, P.O. Box 69760, Los Angeles, CA 90069.
      Monthly, no July and August issues.

      Reviews 16 mm instructional films, with synopsis of each
      and source directory. Announces new multimedia instruc-
      tional materials.

50.   LEARNING DIRECTORY, Westinghouse Learning Corp., 180 Park
      Avenue, New York, NY 10017. 1970-1971, supplement 1972.

      Volume I, Source Index, lists publishers and producers.
      Other volumes combine print and non-print media, lists
      books, films, games, videotapes, programmed material
      and other media, from preschool to the college and
      vocational level.

51.   LIBRARY JOURNAL/SCHOOL LIBRARY JOURNAL REVIEWS: NEWS AND
      REVIEWS OF NON-PRINT MEDIA, R.R. Bowker, 1180 Avenue of
      the Americas, New York, NY 10036. Monthly, September-
      May.

      Reviews 16 and 8mm films, filmstrips, slides, games,
      kits, maps and charts on all instructional levels.
      September, January and May issues have AUDIOVISUAL
      GUIDE: A MULTIMEDIA SUBJECT LIST, which gives new
      titles for release in the coming quarter.

52.   LIBRARY OF CONGRESS CATALOG: FILMS AND OTHER MATERIALS FOR
      PROJECTION; A CUMULATIVE LIST OF WORKS REPRESENTED BY
      LIBRARY OF CONGRESS PRINTED CARDS, Card Division,
      Library of Congress, Washington, D.C. Three quarterly
      issues, annual cumulation.

      Annotated list of films, filmstrips, etc. of educational
      value released in the U.S. and Canada. Subject Index
      and list of producers.

53.   MASS MEDIA, Mass Media Association, 2116 North Charles Street,
      Baltimore, MD 21218. Biweekly.

      Reviews educational and instructional films, filmstrips,
      television programs, cassettes and media packets.

54.   MEDIA AND METHODS, North American Publishing Co., 134 North
      13th Street, Philadelphia, PA 19107. Monthly, September-
      May.

      The section "Media and Methods Recommended," reviews
      educational films, filmstrips and kits. "Mediabag"
      describes new educational materials.

55.   MEDIA MIX, 145 Brentwood Drive, Palatine, IL 60067. Monthly,
      October-May, no December issue.

56.   MEDIA REVIEW DIGEST, (Formerly MULTI-MEDIA REVIEWS INDEX),
      Pierian Press, Ann Arbor, MI. Annual.

An index to reviews of non-print educational media:
Films, filmstrips, tapes, videotapes, games, kits.
Annotated, with grade levels and review source indicated.
Author-title index.

57. MICROFORM REFERENCE, Manlys Cybulski (comp.), Updata Publications, Santa Monica, CA. 1974.

58. MODERN MEDIA TEACHER, 33 West Fifth Street, Dayton, OH 45402.
Bimonthly during the school year.

Articles on instructional media, annotated lists
of films, tapes, etc. for elementary and secondary
teachers.

59. NATIONAL INFORMATION CENTER FOR EDUCATIONAL MEDIA, University of Southern California, University Park,
Los Angeles, CA 90007.

Indexes to nonbook media, with regular indexes for
each medium. Frequent updates and revisions
prepared from NICEM's computerized data base.
Individual indexes:
NICEM INDEX TO 16MM EDUCATIONAL FILMS.
NICEM INDEX TO 35MM FILMSTRIPS.
NICEM INDEX TO EDUCATIONAL VIDEO TAPES.
NICEM INDEX TO 8MM MOTION CARTRIDGES.
NICEM INDEX TO EDUCATIONAL OVERHEAD TRANSPARENCIES.
NICEM INDEX TO EDUCATIONAL SLIDE SETS.
NICEM INDEX TO EDUCATIONAL AUDIO TAPES.
NICEM INDEX TO EDUCATIONAL RECORDS.
NICEM INDEX TO ECOLOGY-MULTIMEDIA.
NICEM INDEX TO PRODUCERS AND DISTRIBUTORS.
NICEM UPDATE OF NON-BOOK MEDIA.

60. NATIONAL REGISTER OF MICROFORM MASTERS, Library of
Congress, Washington, D.C. 20541. Serial,
issued irregularly.

61. THE PHYSICS TEACHER, American Institute of Physics,
335 East 45th Street, New York, NY 10017. Monthly,
September-May.

62. PREVIEWS, R.R. Bowker Co., 1180 Avenue of the Americas,
New York, NY 10036. Monthly, September-May.

Each issue reviews approximately 100 non-print
items for classroom use: 16mm films, filmstrips,
slides, games, transparencies and kits.

63. RECORDED VISUAL INSTRUCTION, University of Nebraska,
Box 80699, Lincoln, NE 68501.

Descriptive catalog of materials from the Great
Plains National Instructional Television Library,
including videotapes, videocassettes and films.

64. RESEARCH IN EDUCATION, U.S. Government Printing Office, Washington, D.C. 20402. Monthly.

    Journal of abstracts on educational research, program reports, etc., with subject and author indexes.

65. SCHOOL MEDIA QUARTERLY, American Association of School Librarians, 50 East Huron Street, Worcester, MA 01608.

66. SERVICE SUPPLEMENT: VIDEO AND CABLE, Educational Film Library Association, 17 West 60th Street, New York, NY 10023.

    Lists videotapes for sale or exchange.

67. SCIENCE ACTIVITIES, Heldref Publications, 400 Albemarle Street NW, Washington, D.C. 20016. Bimonthly.

68. SCIENCE AND CHILDREN, National Science Teachers Association, 1742 Connecticut Avenue NW, Washington, D.C. 20009. 8/year, September-May.

    Reviews and evaluation of audiovisual materials, with selected grade levels.

69. SCIENCE BOOKS AND FILMS, American Association for the Advancement of Science, Subscription Department, 1515 Massachusetts Avenue NW, Washington, D.C. 20005. Quarterly.

    Lists trade and text books, reference materials and 16mm films from kindergarten through college.

70. SCIENCE NEWS, Science Service Inc., 1710 North Street NW, Washington, D.C. 20036. Weekly.

    Reviews 4 to 5 films in most issues.

71. SCIENCE TEACHER, National Science Teachers Association, 1742 Connecticut Avenue NW, Washington, D.C. 20009. Monthly, September-May.

    Column on audiovisual aids, approximately 3 reviews each issue.

72. SIMULATION AND GAMES, Sage Publications, 275 South Beverly Drive, Beverly Hills, CA 90212. Quarterly.

    Reviews and evaluates educational games and simulations.

73. 16MM FILMS AVAILABLE FOR PURCHASE AND RENTAL IN THE U.S. National Film Board of Canada, 16th Floor, 1251 Avenue of the Americas, New York, NY 10020.

    Listing and description of NFB films available in the U.S. through commercial distributors.

74. SOURCES OF FREE AND INEXPENSIVE EDUCATIONAL MATERIALS,
    P.O. Box 186, Grafton, WV 26334.

    Lists and supplies information on films, filmstrips
    slides and graphics on subjects including energy,
    science, conservation and transportation.

75. TEACHER, Macmillan Professional Magazines, Inc., One
    Fawcett Place, Greenwich, CT 06830. Monthly,
    September-May/June.

    Includes reviews of audiovisual materials and
    other educational media, mostly compiled from
    evaluations by classroom teachers.

76. TEACHERS GUIDES TO TELEVISION, P.O. Box 564, Lenox Hill
    Station, New York, NY 10021. 2/year.

    Reviews and guides to educational television programs.

77. TODAYS EDUCATION, National Education Association, 1201
    16th Street NW, Washington, D.C. 20036. Bimonthly,
    September-April.

    Reviews 16mm films and other audiovisual materials.

78. VIDEOPLAY PROGRAM SOURCE GUIDE, C.S. Tepfer, 607 Main
    Street, Ridgefield, CT 06877, 1974.

    Lists over 4100 videocassette programs.

79. WILSON LIBRARY BULLETIN, H.W. Wilson Co., New York, NY.
    Monthly except July and August.

    Reviews reference books and selected government
    publications, lists free materials.

Publishers and Distributors

80. AGENCY FOR INTERNATIONAL DEVELOPMENT, Radio-TV Films
    Services, Information Staff, Washington, D.C. 20523.

81. AIMS INSTRUCTIONAL MEDIA SERVICES, P.O. Box 1010,
    Hollywood, CA 90028.

82. ALL ATOMIC COMICS, Environmental Action Reprint Service,
    2239 East Colfax, Denver, Colorado 80206.

    Educational comic book on the nuclear industry,
    its problems and prospects, with a safety quiz and
    recommended reading.

83. AMERICAN ASSOCIATION FOR THE ADVANCEMENT OF SCIENCE
    FILM CATALOG, R.R. Bowker, 1180 Avenue of the
    Americas, New York, NY 10036, 1975.

    Lists films, including free-loan films, divided
    into Junior High-Adult and Primary-Intermediate
    classifications.

84. AMERICAN DOCUMENTARY FILMS, 335 West 23rd Street,
    New York, NY 10001.

85. AMERICAN BROADCASTING CO., 1330 Avenue of the Americas,
    New York, NY 10019.

86. AMERICAN GAS ASSOCIATION, 1515 Wilson Boulevard,
    Arlington, VA 22209.

    Catalog of publications, posters, filmstrips etc.
    FILMS ON GAS lists films from AGA or member
    companies.

87. AMERICAN MAP COMPANY, INC., 1926 Broadway, New York, NY 10023.

    Maps, charts and displays for classroom use.

88. AMERICAN PETROLEUM INSTITUTE, Committee on Public
    Affairs, 1271 Avenue of the Americas, New York, NY 10020.

89. ASSOCIATION-STERLING FILMS, 866 Third Avenue, New York,
    NY 10022.

    Distributes films by the Sierra Club, CBS, the
    American Iron and Steel Institute and others.

90. BFA EDUCATIONAL MEDIA, 2211 Michigan Avenue, Santa
    Monica, CA 90404.

91. BRIGHAM YOUNG UNIVERSITY, Educational Media Services,
    Provo, Utah 84602.

92. BUREAU OF MINES, Motion Pictures, 4800 Forbes Avenue,

Pittsburgh, PA 15213.

16mm films on mining and fossil fuels.

93.   CANADIAN BROADCASTING CORPORATION, CBC Learning Systems,
      Box 500, Station A, Toronto, Ontario CANADA M5W 1E6.

94.   CANADIAN FILM INSTITUTE, 303 Richmond Road, Ottawa,
      Ontario CANADA K1Z 6X3.

      Catalogues of films from the National Science
      Film Library in earth sciences, engineering and
      technology, engineering and physical sciences,
      history of science and scientific research,
      education, handicapped.

95.   CANADIAN FILM-MAKERS DISTRIBUTION CENTRE, 406 Jarvis
      Street, Toronto, Ontario CANADA M4Y 2G6.

      16mm films, senior high and college levels.

96.   CANFILM SCREEN SERVICE LTD., 522 11 Avenue SW, Calgary,
      Alberta, CANADA T2R 0C8.

      16 and 8mm films, audio tapes and multimedia
      kits on all levels.

97.   CARMAN EDUCATIONAL ASSOCIATES, Box 205, Youngstown, NY 14174.

      Slides, 16mm films, and filmstrips.

98.   CAROUSEL FILMS, 1501 Broadway, New York, NY 10036.

      16mm films, subjects include conservation and
      quality of life.

99.   CHARLES E. MERRILL PUBLISHING CO., 1300 Alum Creek
      Drive, Columbus, OH 43216.

100. CHURCHILL FILMS, 662 North Robertson Boulevard, Los
      Angeles, CA 90069.

      A four film series on energy use: Energy: The
      Dilemma; Energy: The Nuclear Alternative;
      Energy: New Sources; Energy: Less is More.

101. CORONET FILMS, 65 South Water Street, Chicago, IL 60601.

102. THE CREATIVE TEACHER, INC., P.O. Box 5187, Grand
      Central Station, New York, NY 10017.

      Multimedia kits for levels K-2, 3-5 and 6-9.

103. DOCUMENT ASSOCIATES, INC., 880 Third Avenue, New York,
      NY 10022.

      Rental and purchase of films on science, scientific
      impacts, futures, etc.

104. DOUBLEDAY MULTIMEDIA, Box 11607, 1371 Reynolds Avenue,
Santa Ana, CA 92705.

Environment-related films and filmstrips, levels K-12.

105. EARTH METABOLIC DES., Box 2016, Yale Station, New Haven,
CT 06526.

Tapes and slides.

106. ECOGRAPHIX, 13 Center Street, Rutland, VT 05701.

Set of 3 17 x 24" reference charts on nuclear
power, the nuclear fuel cycle and nuclear facilities.

107. EDMUND SCIENTIFIC COMPANY, 55 Edscorp Building,
Barrington, NY 08007.

Kits, slides, charts, lab equipment, games and
other science materials.

108. EDUCATIONAL IMAGES, P.O Box 367, Lyon Falls, NY 13368.

Slide sets on science.

109. EDUCATIONAL MATERIALS AND EQUIPMENT CO., P.O. Box 17,
Belham, NY 10803,

Solar energy outfit for science teachers and
experimenters.

110. EDUCATION MEDIA ASSOCIATES, P.O. Box 402, Peru, IL 61354.

111. EDUCATIONAL MODULES, INC., 266 Lyell Avenue, Rochester,
NY 14608.

Instructional modules on pollution, waste and
recycling, including experiment materials, slides
and teachers manuals.

112. EMBASSY OF AUSTRALIA, Office of Counsellor (Scientific)
1601 Massachusetts Avenue, Washington, D.C. 20036.

Films: Water from the Sun, Solar Heating, and
Design for Climate.

113. EMC CORPORATION, 180 East Sixth Street, St. Paul, MN 55101.

Suppliers of multi-media kits.

114. ENCYCLOPEDIA BRITANNICA EDUCATIONAL CORPORATION, 425 North
Michigan Avenue, Chicago, IL 60611.

Films: Energy for the Future (Middle-school up);
Learning About Nuclear Energy (**Middle School**);
Food From the Sun (Primary); Energy: A Matter of
Choices (junior high); Energy from the Sun (junior high
and high school); Atomic Energy (junior high-up).

115. ENERGY AND MAN'S ENVIRONMENT, 224 South West Hamilton, Suite 301, Portland, OR 97201.

     Energy Curriculum Inventory of curriculum materials and reference sources in all media for grades K-12. Lists reference sources and information collections on energy and energy related to the physical and social sciences.

116. ENVIRONMENTAL ACTION REPRINT SERVICE, 2239 East Colfax, Denver, CO 80206.

     Catalog of books, films, pamphlets, posters and equipment on solar energy, energy alternatives and nuclear power.

117. ENVIRONMENTAL AND NATURAL RESOURCES FILMS, U.S. Department of the Interior, Washington, D.C. 20240.

118. ENVIRONMENTAL EDUCATION GROUP, 1543 North Martel Avenue, Los Angeles, CA 90046.

     Environmental and energy education materials, including posters.

119. FILM ASSOCIATION OF CALIFORNIA, 11559 Santa Monica Boulevard, Los Angeles, CA 90025.

120. FILMS FOR EDUCATION, 21 Audio Lane, New Haven, CT 06500.

121. FILMS, INC., 1144 Wilmette Ave., Wilmette, IL 60091.

122. FILMSTRIP HOUSE, INC., 432 Park Avenue South, New York, NY 10016.

123. FISHER SCIENTIFIC COMPANY, Educational Materials Division, 1259 North Wood Street, Chicago, IL 60622.

     8mm films, overhead transparencies, slides and study prints for intermediate, junior and senior high and college levels.

124. FORD MOTOR COMPANY, Film Library, The American Road, Dearborn, MI 48121.

     Films on the automobile, transportation, etc.

125. FRIENDS OF THE EARTH, 505 Commercial Street, San Francisco, CA.

     Energy and Order: A Lesson Plan.

126. GENERAL ELECTRIC EDUCATIONAL FILMS, Corporations Park, Building 3705, Scotia, NY 12302.

127. GENERAL MOTORS EDUCATIONAL AIDS, Room 1-101, General Motors Building, Detroit, MI 48202.

128. GINN AND CO., 450 West Algonquin Road, Arlington Heights, IL 60005.

129. GLEN/KAYE FILMS, 100 East 21st Street, Brooklyn, NY 11226.

    Film: The Age of the Sun, describing the sun and how it affects life on earth.

130. GREAT PLAINS NATIONAL INSTRUCTIONAL TELEVISION LIBRARY, Box 80669, Lincoln, NE 68501.

    Films, videocassettes and tapes, slide sets and sound filmstrips from the preschool through adult levels.

131. HAMMOND, INC., Educational Division, 515 Valley Street, Maplewood, NY.

132. HAYES SCHOOL PUBLISHING CO., 321 Pennwood Avenue, Wilkinsburg, PA 15221.

133. HOLT, RINEHART, AND WINSTON, 383 Madison Avenue, New York, NY 10017.

134. HUBBARD EARTH SCIENCES, 2855 Shermer Road, Northbrook, IL 60062.

135. INDIANA UNIVERSITY, Audio-Visual Center, Bollomington, IN 47401.

    Distributes National Educational Television, Indiana University, Public Television Library and National Instructional Television Center films. Several films on energy; sources, conservation, alternatives and problems.

136. INFORMATION CANADA SELECTIONS: FEDERAL GOVERNMENT AND INTERNATIONAL PUBLICATIONS FOR EDUCATORS, 1975. Information Canada, 171 Slater Street, Ottawa, Ontario K1A QS9 CANADA.

    Secondary-school level materials, including audiovisual materials.

137. INSTRUCTIONAL AIDS, INC., P.O. Box 191, Mankato, MN 56001.

138. INSTRUCTIONAL SYSTEMS, INC., 21 East 26th Street, New York, NY 10010.

139. INTERNATIONAL ATOMIC ENERGY AGENCY FILM CATALOGUE, Unipub, Inc., P.O. Box 433, 650 1st Avenue, New York, NY 10016.

    Films on nuclear power, reactors and peaceful uses of atomic energy from international sources.

140. INTERNATIONAL FILM BUREAU, INC., 332 South Michigan Avenue, Chicago, IL 60604.

141. JAN HANDY SCHOOL SERVICE CENTER, School Education Division,

2781 East Grand Boulevard, Detroit, MI 48211.

142. JOHN WILEY AND SONS, Audio-Visual Department, 605 Third Avenue, New York, NY 10016.

143. LAB-AIDS, INC., 130 Wilbur Place, Bohemia, NY 11716.

Science kits and materials.

144. LANSFORD PUBLISHING CO., 10088 Lincoln Avenue, Box 8711, San Jose, CA 95155.

College and university level charts, cassettes, etc.

145. LEARNING CORPORATION OF AMERICA, 711 Fifth Avenue, New York, NY 10022.

146. THE LIBRARY OF FILMS, 267 West 25th Street, New York, NY 10001.

147. MACMILLAN FILMS, INC., 34 MacQuesten Parkway South, Mount Vernon, NY 10550.

148. MARATHON OIL COMPANY, Public Relations Film Library, 539 South Main Street, Findlay, OH 45840.

149. MASS MEDIA ASSOCIATES, 2116 North Charles Street, Baltimore, MD 21218.

150. MEDIA MASTERS, INC., 400 West Sixth Street, Tustin, CA 92680.

151. METASTASIS, P.O. Box 128T, Marblemount, WA 98267.

Stocks books and plans in appropriate technology and alternative energy. Many hard-to-get items can be found here. An ideal source for the person with limited access to bookstores.

152. MICHIGAN STATE UNIVERSITY, Instructional Media Center, East Lansing, MI 48824.

153. MILLIKEN PUBLISHING CO., 611 Olive Street, St. Louis, MO 63101.

154. MILTON-BRADLEY CO., Springfield, MA 01101.

155. MODERN TALKING PICTURE SERVICE, 2323 New Hyde Park Road, New Hyde Park, NY 11040.

Films on adult and K-12 levels.

156. MOODY INSTITUTE OF SCIENCE, Educational Film Division, 12000 East Washington Boulevard, Whittier, CA 90606.

157. NASCO-STIENHILBER, Fort Atkinson, WI 53538.

158. NATIONAL AUDIOVISUAL CENTER (GSA), Washington, D.C. 20409.

Films, slides, audio and video cassettes and tapes and multimedia kits for junior high, senior high and college levels. Handles most federal government produced audio-visual materials.

159. NATIONAL BROADCASTING COMPANY, 30 Rockefeller Plaza, Room 914, New York, NY 10022.

160. NATIONAL FILM BOARD OF CANADA, P.O. Box 6100, Montreal, Quebec CANADA H3C 3H5.

FILM CATALOGUE, 1974-75-76. Annotated listing of NFB films with information for borrowing and buying, and list of regional NFB offices.
MEDIA CATALOGUE 1974-75. Annotated listing of filmstrips, loops, kits, slide sets and transparencies. French versions of both catalogues are available.

161. NATIONAL INSTRUCTIONAL TV LIBRARY, 10 Columbus Circle, New York, NY.

162. NATIONAL RESEARCH COUNCIL OF CANADA, Montreal Road, Ottawa, Ontario CANADA K1A OR6.

Produces films and videotapes, available through National Film Board of Canada. Intended for Canadian audiences, though not limited to these audiences.

163. NATIONAL VOICE LIBRARY, Michigan State University, East Lansing, MI 48824.

Taped reproductions of speeches by statesmen, scientists, educators, etc. Tapes available on loan or exchange include Presidential addresses and crucial public speeches.

164. NEW YORK UNIVERSITY FILM LIBRARY, 41 Press Annex, Washington Square, New York, NY 10003.

165. OFFICE OF MEDIA SERVICES, Films Librarian, Room 5819A, Bureau of Public Affairs, Washington, D.C. 20520.

166. OHIO STATE UNIVERSITY, Film Distribution Supervisor, Department of Photography and Cinema, 156 West 19th Avenue, Columbus, OH 43210.

167. OKLAHOMA STATE UNIVERSITY, Audiovisual Center, Stillwater, Oklahoma 74074.

168. PRENTICE-HALL, INC., Educational Book Division, Customer Service-Science Equipment, P.O. Box 908, Englewood Cliffs, NJ 07632.

Textbooks, films and filmstrips for all levels.

169. PRENTICE-HALL OF CANADA, LTD., 1870 Birchmont Road, Scarborough, Ontario CANADA M1P 2J7.

8mm films and silent filmstrips from preschool and kindergarten through college level.

170. PRE-SCHOOL PUBLICATIONS, Box 272, Commerce TX 75428.

Films, filmstrips, models, study prints etc. for preschool, kindergarten and primary students.

171. PROGRAMMED LEARNING AID SERIES, Learning Systems Company, 1818 Ridge Road, Homewood, IL 60430.

Self-teaching module, THE ENERGY CRISIS, for high school and college students. A self-paced introduction to the energy problem, with programmed questions and answers for self-testing of progress.

172. RANDOM HOUSE, Singer School Division, 201 East 50th Street, New York, NY 10022.

173. SCHOLASTIC AUDIO-VISUAL MATERIALS, 904 Sylvan Avenue, Englewood Cliffs, NJ 07632.

174. SCIENCE KIT, INC., 777 East Park Drive, Tonawanda, NY 14150.

Charts, models, films, filmstrips and multimedia kits from kindergarten through junior college.

175. SCIENCE RELATED MATERIALS, Box 1422, Janesville, WI 53545.

Transparencies, charts and models for senior high and college levels.

176. SCIENCE RESEARCH ASSOCIATES, INC., 259 Erie, Chicago, IL 60611.

Films, filmstrips, audio tapes, multimedia kits and learning systems on all levels.

177. SCIENTIFIC FILM CO., 909 East 31st Street, LaGrange Park, IL 60525.

178. SCIENTIFIC SUPPLY COMPANY, 600 South Spokane Street, Seattle, WA.

179. SCIENTIFICOM, 708 North Dearborn Avenue, Chicago, IL 60610.

Films, filmstrips and slides for college level.

180. SCIENTISTS' INSTITUTE FOR PUBLIC INFORMATION, 30 East 68th Street, New York, NY 10021.

Workbooks on electric power and environmental impacts of nuclear power.

181. SCOTT, FORESMAN AND CO., Film Distribution Center, 305 East

45th Street, New York, NY 10016.

182. SCOTT SCIENTIFIC, INC., Box 2121, Fort Collins, CO 80521.

Charts, multimedia kits, pollution test kits and audio tapes on preschool through senior high levels.

183. SETUPS, Supplementary Empirical Teaching Units in Political Science, American Political Science Association, 1527 New Hampshire Avenue NW, Washington, D.C. 20036.

Modules, lesson materials and computer simulation models for college undergraduates. Includes one on U.S. ENERGY, ENVIRONMENT AND ECONOMIC PROBLEMS.

184. SHELL FILM LIBRARY, 450 North Meridian Street, Indianapolis, IN 46204.

Material on petroleum products and oil-related questions.

185. SMITHSONIAN INSTITUTION, Audio Visual Services, Office of Public Affairs, Museum of History and Technology, Washington, D.C. 20560.

186. STANLEY BOWMAR CO., 4 Broadway, Valhalla, NY 14174.

187. STERLING EDUCATIONAL FILMS, 241 East 34th Street, New York, NY 10016.

Film: Energy: Harnessing the Sun, deals with development and potential of solar energy for generating electricity.

188. STUART FINLEY, INC., 3428 Mansfield Road, Falls Church, VA 22041.

189. TENNESSEE VALLEY AUTHORITY, Film Services, Knoxville, TN 37902.

190. TIME LIFE MULTIMEDIA, District Center, 100 Eisenhower Drive, Paramus, NJ 07652.

Films include BBC TV's 1974 Energy Crunch Series of documentaries on the energy crisis and the world's future energy supplies.

191. TROLL ASSOCIATES, 320 Route 17, Mahwah, NJ 07420.

Elementary level tapes and filmstrips.

192. UNION CARBIDE CORPORATION, Sterling Forest Research Center, Educational Aids Department, P.O. Box 363, Tuxedo, NY 10987.

193. UNESCO FILMSTRIP CATALOGUE, Unipub, Inc., P.O. Box 433, 650 1st Avenue, New York, NY 10016.

194.   U.S. DEPARTMENT OF AGRICULTURE, Motion Pictures Service, Washington, D.C. 20250.

195.   U.S. ENERGY RESEARCH AND DEVELOPMENT ADMINISTRATION, Washington, D.C. 20545.

       16mm films and slides, intermediate through senior high, college and adult levels, focusing on atomic energy. The Energy-Environment Simulator is a simulation game giving an opportunity to provide solutions to future energy problems by projecting resources, energy demands, environmental effects and population growth rates. 65 of these "electronic time machines" travel throughout the U.S. under the direction of trained consultants.

196.   U.S. GOVERNMENT FILMS: A CATALOG OF AUDIO-VISUAL MATERIALS FOR RENT AND SALE BY THE NATIONAL AUDIO-VISUAL CENTER, National Audio-Visual Center, National Archives and Record Center, Washington, D.C. 20409

       Catalog of films, filmstrips and other media produced by U.S. Government agencies, with content descriptions.

197.   U.S. GOVERNMENT PRINTING OFFICE, Washington, D.C. 20402

       Many publications of government agencies, including "So What's New? Energy History of the U.S. 1776-1976" a full color wall chart and explanatory booklet on the U.S. energy experience.

198.   U.S. NATIONAL AERONAUTICS AND SPACE ADMINISTRATION, Public Affairs Office, Washington, D.C. 20409.

       Booklets, films and other educational material. Films include "Great Is the House of the Sun" and "Eclipse of the Quiet Sun".

199.   U.S. NATIONAL COMMISSION FOR UNESCO, Public Information Office, U.S. Department of State, Washington, D.C. 20520.

200.   UNITED STATES STEEL CORPORATION, Film Distribution Center, Room 2209, 525 William Penn Place, Pittsburgh, PA.

201.   UNITED TRANSPARENCIES, INC., P.O. Box 688, Binghamton, NY 13902.

202.   UNIVERSITY OF CALIFORNIA, Extension Media Center, 2223 Fulton Street, Berkeley, CA 94720.

       Series of films on energy conservation, sources and problems, including some for elementary students.

203.   UNIVERSITY OF ILLINOIS, Visual Aids Service, 1325 South Oak, Champaign, IL 61820.

204.   UNIVERSITY OF IOWA, Media Library, Audio-Visual Center,

C-5 East Hall, Iowa City, IA 52242.

205. UNIVERSITY OF NEBRASKA, Instructional Media Center, University Extension Division, Lincoln, NE 68508.

206. UNIVERSITY OF UTAH, Educational Media Center, Milton Bennion Hall 207, Salt Lake City, Utah 84110.

207. VALIANT INSTRUCTIONAL MATERIALS CORP., 237 Washington Ave., Hackensack, NJ 07602.

Upper elementary and high school level filmstrips on energy, recycling, pollution, etc.

208. VISUAL SCIENCES, Box 599RB, Suffern, NY 10901.

Silent filmstrips, intermediate through senior high, college and adult levels.

209. WARD'S NATURAL SCIENCE ESTABLISHMENT, INC., P.O. Box 1712, Rochester, NY.

210. WESTERN INSTRUCTION TELEVISION, INC., 1549 North Vine Street, Los Angeles, CA 90028.

Videocassettes and tapes, preschool through intermediate levels.

211. WORLD FUTURE SOCIETY, 4916 St. Elmo Avenue, Washington, D.C. 20014.

Tape series from the 1974 forum ENERGY: TODAY'S CHOICES, TOMORROW'S OPPORTUNITIES, on 60 and 90 minute tapes. Second General Assembly on the Next 25 Years tape series, 1975, includes tapes on conservation, planning and life-styles.

212. XEROX EDUCATIONAL SCIENCE, 191 Spring Street, Lexington, MA 02173.

213. ZOMEWORKS CORPORATION, P.O. Box 712, Albuquerque, NM 97103.

Solar slide set.

REFERENCE

REFERENCE

Introduction

This section contains directories, bibliographies, abstracts, catalogs, periodical indexes, checklists and other materials to be found in library reference rooms. In addition to works dealing with energy or some specific sub-catagory of energy, general science and environmental materials with some relationship to energy have been included. Publishers and distributors of specialized materials are listed in sections of the guide appropriate for the type of material they produce. Some reference material on energy alternatives and energy self-suficiency will be found in that section.

Reference Materials

214. AMERICAN ASSOCIATION FOR THE ADVANCEMENT OF SCIENCE BOOK LIST FOR CHILDREN, AAAS, 1515 Massachusetts Avenue NW, Washington, D.C. 20005.

Science books and periodicals for primary and middle school students. Modified Dewey decimal arrangement. 1972.

215. AMERICAN ASSOCIATION FOR THE ADVANCEMENT OF SCIENCE BOOK LIST, SECONDARY AND COLLEGE, AAAS, 1515 Massachusetts Avenue NW, Washington, D.C. 20005.

Evaluation and selection of science materials, with annotated book listings. For secondary school students and college undergraduates and the non-specialized reader. Third edition 1970. Update planned.

216. ANNUAL REVIEW OF ENERGY, Annual Reviews, Inc., Palo Alto, CA. 1976.

217. APPLIED SCIENCE AND TECHNOLOGY INDEX, H.W. Wilson Co., 950 University Avenue, Bronx, NY 10452. Monthly, no July issue. Annual cumulation.

Subject index to English-language scientific and technical periodicals in fields including chemistry, earth sciences, electricity and electronics, engineering and transportation.

218. BIBLIOGRAPHY OF THE SOCIAL EFFECTS OF NUCLEAR POWER: 1945-1973, Brian Coleman (comp.), British Columbia Hydro and Power Authority, Vancouver, British Columbia CANADA. 1974.

219. BUSINESS PERIODICALS INDEX, H.W. Wilson Co., 950 University
      Avenue, Bronx, NY 10452. Monthly, no August issue,
      yearly cumulation.

220. CANADIAN ANNUAL REVIEW OF POLITICS AND PUBLIC AFFAIRS, Uni-
      versity of Toronto Press, Toronto, Ontario CANADA.
      Annual.

      A review of issues and events in Canadian politics and
      public policy during the preceeding year.

221. CANADIAN EDUCATION INDEX, Canadian Education Association,
      Toronto. Quarterly, annual cumulation.

      Author and subject listings of selected educational
      periodicals, books, pamphlets.

222. CANADIAN PERIODICAL INDEX, Canadian Library Association,
      151 Sparks Street, Ottawa, Ontario CANADA K1P 5E3.
      Monthly, annual cumulation.

      Author and subject indexing of periodicals published
      in Canada.

223. CANADIAN REFERENCE SOURCES: A SELECTIVE GUIDE, Dorothy E.
      Ryder (ed.), Canadian Library Association, 151 Sparks
      Street, Ottawa, CANADA K1P 5E3, 1973. Supplement 1975.

224. CANADIAN SERIALS DIRECTORY, University of Toronto Press,
      Toronto, Ontario CANADA. Annual.

      Lists periodicals and serial publications published in
      Canada, indexed by title, author and subject.

225. CONGRESSIONAL INDEX, Commerce Clearing House, Inc., 4025
      West Peterson Avenue, Chicago, IL 60646. 2/week while
      Congress meets.

      Reports on activities, votes, bills, hearings, etc. in
      Congress. For quick research on status of legislation
      pending before Congress.

226. CIS INDEX TO PUBLICATIONS OF THE U.S. CONGRESS, Congressional
      Information Service, Inc., 7101 Wisconsin Avenue NW,
      Washington, D.C. 20014. Monthly.

      Abstracts of government documents, hearings reports and
      testimony.

227. CITIZEN ENERGY NEWSLETTERS, Center for Science in the Public
      Interest, P.O. Box E, 1757 S Street NW, Washington,
      D.C. 20009.

      Listing of 99 newsletters, most published by consumer
      and environmental groups, carrying news on energy issues.

228. CONSUMER INFORMATION: A CATALOG OF SELECTED FEDERAL PUBLI-

CATIONS OF CONSUMER INTEREST. Consumer Information
Center, Dept WM, Pueblo, Colorado 81009.

Information on saving gas, home energy conservation,
insulation, etc. examples: TIPS FOR ENERGY SAVERS,
MAKING THE MOST OF YOUR ENERGY DOLLARS. INFORMACION
PARA EL CONSUMIDOR, a catalog of selected Federal Publications in Spanish.

229. CURRENT CONTENTS: SOCIAL AND BEHAVIORAL SCIENCES, Institute for Scientific Information, 325 Chestnut Street,
Philadelphia, PA 19106. Weekly.

Contents pages from over 1250 journals (as they appear)
in social and behavioral sciences. Includes sociology,
law, education, economics, business, management, planning, political science and history. Subject index
and author address directory.

The Institute for Scientific Information also publishes
CURRENT CONTENTS: AGRICULTURE, BIOLOGY AND ENVIRONMENTAL
SCIENCES; CURRENT CONTENTS: ENGINEERING, TECHNOLOGY
AND APPLIED SCIENCES; and CURRENT CONTENTS: PHYSICAL
AND CHEMICAL SCIENCES.

230. CURRENT INDEX TO JOURNALS IN EDUCATION, Macmillan Information,
866 Third Avenue, New York, NY 10022. Monthly.

Product of ERIC. Covers major education and education-
related journals, annotated with subject and author
indexes. Semi-annual and annual cumulative indexes.

231. DIRECTORY OF ASSOCIATIONS IN CANADA, University of Toronto
Press, Toronto, Ontario CANADA

232. DIRECTORY OF CANADIAN SCIENTIFIC AND TECHNICAL PERIODICALS:
A GUIDE TO CURRENTLY PUBLISHED TITLES, National Science
Library, Ottawa, Ontario CANADA. 5th edition, 1973.

233. DIRECTORY OF CONSUMER PROTECTION AND ENVIRONMENTAL AGENCIES,
Marquis Who's Who, Inc., 200 East Ohio Street, Chicago,
IL 60611.

234. DIRECTORY OF NUCLEAR ACTIVISTS, Environmental Action Reprint
Service, 2239 East Colfax, Denver, Colorado 80206.

235. DIRECTORY OF STATE GOVERNMENT ENERGY-RELATED AGENCIES, U.S.
Federal Energy Administration, National Energy Information Center, Washington, D.C. 20461.

Listing of agencies in each state engaged in energy-
related activities. Revisions are planned to update
the September, 1975 version as state organizations change.

236. EDUCATION INDEX, H.W. Wilson Co., 950 University Avenue,
Bronx, NY 10452. Monthly, no July or August issues.

Annual cumulation.

237. EDUCATIONAL RESOURCES INFORMATION CENTER, (ERIC), Information Analysis Center for Science, Mathematics and Environmental Education, 400 Lincoln Tower, Ohio State University, Columbus, OH 43210.

Cataloging, indexing and abstracting of education literature, and computerized data bank. Includes RESEARCH IN EDUCATION, and CURRENT INDEX TO JOURNALS IN EDUCATION.

238. EL-HI TEXTBOOKS IN PRINT, R.R. Bowker, 1180 Avenue of the Americas, New York, NY 10036. Yearly.

Lists textbooks and series from grades K-12 in categories including environmental studies, general science, physical science and physics. Also includes maps and teaching aids. Subject and series indexes.

239. ERDA ENERGY RESEARCH ABSTRACTS, U.S. Energy Research and Development Administration. Available from National Technical Information Service, Information and Sales Center, 425 13th Street NW, Room 620, Washington, D.C. 20230.

240. ENERGY: A CONTINUING BIBLIOGRAPHY WITH INDEXES, National Aeronautics and Space Administration, Scientific and Technical Information Office, Washington, D.C. Quarterly.

241. ENERGY: A GUIDE TO ORGANIZATIONAL AND INFORMATION RESOURCES IN THE UNITED STATES, Center for California Public Affairs, Claremont, CA. 1974, addenda 1975.

Directory of Federal, state, city and local agencies and other organizations concerned with energy and energy policy.

242. ENERGY: A KEY-PHRASE DISSERTATION INDEX, University Microfilms International, Ann Arbor, MI. 1976.

An index to 6000 doctoral dissertations on energy research and development, 1866-1975.

243. ENERGY ABSTRACTS FOR POLICY ANALYSIS, Oak Ridge National Laboratory, P.O. Box X, Oak Ridge, TN 37830. Monthly.

Publicly available nontechnical literature on many energy areas. Abstracting and indexing of books, research reports, conference proceedings, etc. Both specific fields of energy such as efficiency, alternatives, and nuclear power and areas such as policy, supply and demand, etc. are included.

244. ENERGY CATALOG, Environmental Action Reprint Service, 2239 East Colfax, Denver, CO 80206.

Books, plans, posters, films, directories and surveys

on energy, conservation and alternatives. Descriptive
annotations and ordering information.

245. ENERGY CONSERVATION: A BIBLIOGRAPHY WITH ABSTRACTS, Edward
J. Lehmann (comp.), National Technical Information
Service, Springfield, VA. 1975.

246. ENERGY CONSERVATION IN THE FOOD SYSTEM: A PUBLICATIONS LIST,
U.S. Government Printing Office, Washington, D.C. 20402.

An annotated list of U.S. government publications on
energy conservation in the food system, for the use of
food wholesalers, food retailers and the cooking public.

247. ENERGY CRISIS, Volumes 1 and 2, Facts on File, Inc., 119
West 56th Street, New York, NY 10019.

Compilations of energy data and news reports from 1969-
1975. For high school, college and professional readers.

248. ENERGY CRISIS IN THE UNITED STATES, Nan C. Burg (comp.),
Council of Planning Librarians, Monticello, IL. Exchange Bibliography No. 550, 1974.

249. ENERGY DIRECTORY, Environment Information Center, Energy
Reference Department, 124 East 39th Street, New York,
NY 10016. Annual.

250. ENERGY-EFFICIENT PLANNING: AN ANNOTATED BIBLIOGRAPHY, Ef-
raim Gil (comp.), American Society of Planning Officials,
1313 East 60th Street, Chicago, IL 60637. Report No.
315, 1976.

251. THE ENERGY-ENVIRONMENT DILEMMA: A SELECTIVE BIBLIOGRAPHIC
GUIDE WITH ANNOTATIONS, Elizabeth Peters (comp.), Coun-
cil of Planning Librarians, Monicello, IL. Exchange
Bibliography No. 1111, 1976.

252. ENERGY/ENVIRONMENT/ECONOMY: AN ANNOTATED BIBLIOGRAPHY OF
SELECTED U.S. GOVERNMENT PUBLICATIONS CONCERNING UNITED
STATES ENERGY POLICY, Environment Information, Green
Bay, WI. 1973. 2 volumes.

253. ENERGY FOR THE FUTURE: A SELECTED BIBLIOGRAPHY, Nan C. Burg
(comp.), Council of Planning Librarians, Monticello, IL.
Exchange Bibliography No. 776, 1975.

254. ENERGY FOR THE FUTURE: AN UPDATE TO EXCHANGE BIBLIOGRAPHY NO.
776, Nan C. Burg (comp.), Council of Planning Librarians,
Monticello, IL. Exchange Bibliography No. 946, 1975.

255. ENERGY INDEX, Environment Information center, Energy Reference Department, 124 East 39th Street, New York, NY
10016.

Guide to energy information since 1970 from government,

academic and private sources.

256. ENERGY INFORMATION ABSTRACTS, Environment Information Center, 124 East 39th Street, New York, NY 10016. Bi-monthly.

Abstracts of current research and activity in energy.

257. ENERGY INFORMATION IN THE FEDERAL GOVERNMENT: A DIRECTORY OF ENERGY SOURCES IDENTIFIED BY THE INTERAGENCY TASK FORCE ON ENERGY INFORMATION, National Technical Information Service, Springfield, VA. 1975.

Description and user's guide to the Federal Energy Information Locator System. Federal energy agencies, publications, data sources.

258. ENERGY INFORMATION LOCATOR, Environment Information Center, Energy Reference Department, 124 East 39th Street, New York, NY 10016.

259. ENERGY MANAGEMENT, Commerce Clearing House, Inc., 4025 West Peterson Avenue, Chicago, IL 60646.

Digest of federal laws and regulations pertaining to energy, energy decisions and new developments in federal energy policy.

260. ENERGY RESEARCH AND TECHNOLOGY, National Technical Information Service, Information and Sales Center, 425 13th Street NW, Room 620, Washington, D.C. 20230.

Abstracts of National Science Foundation research results.

261. ENERGY RESEARCH INFORMATION SYSTEM, Old West Regional Commission, Hedden-Empire Building, Suite 228, Billings, Montana 59101.

ERIS issues quarterly reports on ongoing and recently completed energy-related research projects, with abstracts and cumulative indexes. Liason with other energy information clearing-houses. Computer search service.

262. THE ENERGY SITUATION, Eric Swanick (comp.), Council of Planning Librarians, Monticello, IL. Exchange Bibliography No. 742, 1975.

263. ENERGY STATISTICS, U.S. Department of Transportation, Office of the Secretary, Assistant Secretary for Policy, Plans and International Affairs, 400 Seventh Street SW, Washington, D.C. 20590. Annual.

264. ENERGY STATISTICS: A GUIDE TO SOURCES, Sarojini Balachandran (comp.), Council of Planning Librarians, Monticello, IL. Exchange Bibliography No. 1065, 1976.

265. ENGINEERING INDEX ENERGY ABSTRACTS, Engineering Index, Inc.,

345 East 47th Street, New York, NY 10017. 9/year.

Engineering Index, Inc. also publishes:
ENERGY CONSERVATION ABSTRACTS. 9/year.
ENERGY CONVERSION ABSTRACTS. 9/year.
ENERGY PRODUCTION, TRANSMISSION AND DISTRIBUTION AB-
STRACTS. 9/year.
ENERGY SOURCES ABSTRACTS. 9/year.
ENERGY UTILIZATION ABSTRACTS. 9/year.

266. ENVIRONMENT ENERGY CONTENTS MONTHLY, Environment Energy
Institute, P.O. Box 1450, Portland, OR 97207. Monthly.

Reproduces tables of contents from over 400 domestic
and foreign periodicals that carry articles on energy
and environmental subjects. A valuable reference tool
for keeping informed on current energy activity and
developments.

267. GOVERNMENT MANUAL, U.S. Government Printing Office, Washington, D.C.

The official handbook of U.S. government purposes and
programs of government agencies. Lists the top personnel in each agency.

268. GUIDE TO U.S. GOVERNMENT SERIALS AND PERIODICALS, Documents
Index, McLean, VA. Annual.

Volume I lists 2216 government agencies, committees,
etc. with a brief history of each. Volume II lists
publications of current government agencies. Volume
III lists publications of abolished or superseded
agencies.

269. INDEX OF CANADIAN CITIZENS' ENVIRONMENTAL ORGANIZATIONS,
Information Canada, 171 Slater Street, Ottawa, Ontario
CANADA K1A 0S9. 1973.

Directory of citizen groups in Canada, listed by province and community.

270. INDEX TO U.S. GOVERNMENT PERIODICALS, Infordata International,
Inc., Suite 4602, 175 East Delaware Place, Chicago,
IL 60611. Quarterly, annual cumulation.

Access to government periodicals and articles from
those periodicals. Indexed by title, author, subject
and agency.

271. INFORMATION ON INTERNATIONAL RESEARCH AND DEVELOPMENT AC-
TIVITIES IN THE FIELD OF ENERGY. U.S. Government
Printing Office, Washington, D.C. 1976.

Information on 1,766 ongoing or recently completed
energy research projects in France, Italy, Canada and
over 25 other countries.

33

272. INFORUM, 1747 Pennsylvania Avenue, Suite 1150, Washington, D.C. 20006.

A data bank including social impact data associated with the construction and operation of nuclear power plants.

273. MERES AND THE ANALYSIS OF ENERGY ALTERNATIVES, Council on Environmental Quality, 722 Jackson Place NW, Washington, D.C. 20006.

MERES stands for Matrix of Environmental Residuals for Energy Systems, a data bank on air and water emissions, solid wastes, land use and occupational health effects of present and future energy systems.

274. MINERAL AND ENERGY PRODUCTION IN A GEOGRAPHIC CONTEXT, Jerry E. Green (comp.), Council of Planning Librarians, Monticello, IL. Exchange Bibliography No. 1015, 1976.

275. MONTHLY CHECKLIST OF STATE PUBLICATIONS, U.S. Government Printing Office, Washington, D.C. 20402.

Listing of state publications received by the Library of Congress.

276. NUCLEAR ENERGY HOTLINE: DIRECTORY FOR MEDIA, American Nuclear Society, 244 East Ogden Avenue, Hinsdale, IL 60521.

277. PARK PROJECT ON ENERGY INTERPRETATION, National Recreation and Park Association, 1601 North Kent Street, Arlington, VA 22209.

List of citizen groups, university programs, organizations and corporations doing energy work which may be of educational value to citizens.

278. PERIODICALS THAT PROGRESSIVE SCIENTISTS SHOULD KNOW ABOUT, Progressive Technology, Inc., P.O. Box 20049, Tallahassee, Florida 32304.

As of September, 1976, listed over 200 periodicals.

279. PROCEEDINGS IN PRINT, P.O. Box 247, Mattapan, MA 02126. 6/year, annual cumulation.

Index to conference proceedings, symposia, hearings, colloquia, meetings, seminars, courses, etc. whose proceedings were published.

280. PRO FILE INDEX, MicroMedia Limited, Toronto, Ontario CANADA. Monthly.

Author and subject index to publications of Canadian provinces and municipalities.

281. PUBLIC AFFAIRS INFORMATION SERVICE BULLETIN, 11 West 40th

Street, New York, NY 10018. Weekly, except last 2 weeks of each quarter. Cumulated 5 times yearly.

Subject list of books, articles, pamphlets, government publications, etc., published in English, on economics and social conditions and international relations.

282. PUBLICATIONS OF THE UNITED NATIONS SYSTEM: A REFERENCE GUIDE, Harry M. Winton (comp.), R.R. Bowker, 1180 Avenue of the Americas, New York, NY. 1972.

283. RAW MATERIALS, CRISIS FOR THE '70S, John E. Dinsmore (comp.), Council of Planning Librarians, Monticello, IL. Exchange Bibliography No. 879, 1975.

284. SCIENCE CITATION INDEX, Institute for Scientific Information, 325 Chestnut Street, Philadelphia, PA 19106.

An international multi-disciplinary index to scientific and technical information.

285. SCIENCE FOR SOCIETY: A BIBLIOGRAPHY, Howard T. Bausum (comp.), American Association for the Advancement of Science, Washington, D.C. 3rd edition, 1972.

For lay readers and college undergraduates, focusing on social problems caused by scientific and technological advances.

286. SCIENCE, TECHNOLOGY, AND SOCIETY: A GUIDE TO THE FIELD, Ezra D. Heitowit (ed.), National Technical Information Service, 5285 Port Royal Road, Springfield, VA 22161.

Lists teaching and research activities of over 400 colleges and universities, including descriptions of over 2,000 courses and over 100 programs, institutions, centers, etc. Also lists periodicals, groups, organizations and companies with activities relating to science and its impact on society.

287. SCIENCE-TECHNOLOGY RESOURCES IN CANADA, National Research Council of Canada, Ottawa, Ontario CANADA.

Lists scientific and technological literature to be found in 48 Canadian institutions. Includes universities, public libraries and other organizations.

288. SCIENTIFIC AND TECHNICAL BOOKS IN PRINT, R.R. Bowker, 1180 Avenue of the Americas, New York, NY. Annual.

289. SCIENTIFIC AND TECHNICAL SOCIETIES OF CANADA, National Science Library, Ottawa, Ontario CANADA.

A directory to professional societies.

290. SELECTED U.S. GOVERNMENT PUBLICATIONS, Superintendent of Documents, U.S. Government Printing Office,

Washington, D.C. 20402.

291. SMITHSONIAN SCIENCE INFORMATION EXCHANGE, INC., Room 300, 1730 M Street NW, Washington, D.C. 20036.

Central data base for information about research in progress in the sciences, social sciences and inter-disciplinary fields. Over 1,300 organizations, U.S. and foreign, government, educational and private are included.

292. SOCIAL SCIENCES CITATION INDEX, Institute for Scientific Information, 325 Chestnut Street, Philadelphia, PA 19106.

An international multi-disciplinary index to social, behaviorial and related sciences.

293. STATE ENERGY ORGANIZATIONS, Federal Energy Administration, Washington, D.C.

Information on 39 state energy programs, with name, address and telephone number of each agency.

294. A SURVEY OF FUEL AND ENERGY INFORMATION SOURCES, Mitre Corporation. National Technical Information Service, Springfield, VA. 1970.

Fairly technical, for the advanced energy student.

295. TRANSPORTATION AND ENERGY: 170-March 1974, updated March 1976, Cynthia Jackson (comp.), Northwestern University Transportation Center, Evanston, IL. 1976.

296. TRANSPORTATION ENERGY CONSERVATION DATA BOOK, A.S. Loebl, et al., (comps.), Oak Ridge National Laboratory, Oak Ridge, TN.

Contains statistics on energy use in different modes of transportation and on other factors that influence energy consumption in the transportation sector. Issued in 1976, with annual updating.

297. UNITED NATIONS DOCUMENTS INDEX, United Nations Sales Section, New York, NY 10017. 11/year and annual cumulation.

Lists publications of the U.N. system.

298. U.S. GOVERNMENT PUBLICATIONS: MONTHLY CATALOG, Superintendent of Documents, U.S. Government Printing Office, Washington, D.C. 20402.

Comprehensive, current list of government publications. Non-annotated, annual cumulative index in December, periodical list in February.

299. WASHINGTON ENERGY DIRECTORY, Center for Policy Process, 1757 Massachusetts Avenue NW, Washington, D.C. 20036.

Summary of national energy research and development programs, list of key Washington personnel, synopsis of legislative basis for energy research and development. First published in 1975, periodically updated through supplements.

Publishers of Printed Material

300. ALBION PUBLISHING COMPANY, 1736 Stockton Street, San Francisco, CA 94133.

Series on energy for college and professional readers.

301. ARCO PUBLISHING COMPANY, INC., 219 Park Avenue South, New York, NY 10003.

Wide variety of history, technical, science and self-teaching titles. Records and tapes also available.

302. AVON BOOKS, 959 Eighth Avenue, New York, NY 10019.

Paperbound books in many areas, including D.D. Halacy's THE COMING OF THE SOLAR AGE.

303. BALLINGER PUBLISHING CO:, 17 Dunster Street, 4th Floor, Cambridge, MA 02138.

A wide variety of energy titles for undergraduate, graduate, business and professional readers. Publishes the reports of the Ford Foundation Energy Policy Project and The Environmental Law Institute State and Local Energy Conservation Project.

304. BOYD AND FRASER PUBLISHING COMPANY, 3627 Sacramento Street, San Francisco, CA 94118.

Books for college undergraduates on social impacts of energy and technology.

305. BROOKINGS INSTITUTION, 1775 Massachusetts Avenue NW, Washington, D.C. 20036.

Books on economics, government and foreign policy for advanced and scholarly readers.

306. CENTER FOR CALIFORNIA PUBLIC AFFAIRS, Affiliate of the Claremont Colleges, 1266 West Foothill Boulevard, Box 30, Claremont, CA 91711.

Environmental Studies Series for professional and academic readers. Who's Doing What Series for high school, college and educated lay readers. Directories, sourcebooks, etc. on energy policy. Reference works and studies on energy in California.

307. CONGRESSIONAL QUARTERLY, INC., 1414 22nd Street NW,

Washington, D.C. 20037.

Titles on the energy crisis, and reference material on government operations and policies.

308. CORNELL UNIVERSITY PRESS, 124 Roberts Place, Ithaca, NY 14850.

Scholarly publishing, titles on energy policy, supply and natural resources.

309. THOMAS Y. CROWELL COMPANY, INC., 666 Fifth Avenue, New York, NY 10019.

Adult and children's books and textbooks in many energy-related technical and non-technical areas by Crowell and its associated companies.

310. DARWIN PRESS, INC., P.O. Box 2202, Princeton, NJ 08540.

Material on energy economics and solar energy.

311. E.P. DUTTON AND CO., INC., 201 Park Avenue South, New York, NY 10003.

General and advanced books on energy issues, including MAN AND ATOM, a treatment of the nuclear power controversy.

312. ENERGY PROBE, 43 Queens Park Crescent East, Toronto, Ontario M5S 2C3 CANADA.

Books and pamphlets on energy alternatives and self-sufficiency. Material on Canadian energy concerns.

313. FACTS ON FILE, INC., 119 West 56th Street, New York, NY 10019.

Compliations of data from weekly news reports for high school, college and professional readers.

314. FEARON PUBLISHERS, INC., 6 Davis Drive, Belmont, CA 94002.

Textbooks, teaching aids and supplies for primary and high school.

315. FRANKLIN WATTS, INC., 845 Third Avenue, New York, NY 10022.

Books for levels from primary through high school on science, environment, economics, conservation, etc.

316. FREEMAN, COOPER AND CO., 1736 Stockton Street, San Francisco, CA 94133.

Comprehensive publications for energy-environment-resources fields.

317. GARDEN WAY PUBLISHING CO., Charlotte, VT 05445.

Books and pamphlets on energy self-sufficiency, alternative energy and low-cost energy sources. Quality paperback format.

318. GREENWOOD PRESS, 51 Riverside Avenue, Westport, CN 06880.

319. HARPER AND ROW, INC., 10 East 53rd Street, New York, NY 10022.

Trade and textbooks, including college texts.

320. D.C. HEATH AND COMPANY, 125 Spring Street, Lexington, MA 02173.

Lexington Books publishes for academics, policy-makers, researchers and those interested in energy policy matters. Many key titles on energy policy, planning, futures and alternatives.

321. HUMANITITES PRESS, INC., Hutchinson University Library, Atlantic Highlands, NH 07716.

Scholarly-professional publishing.

322. IMPORTED PUBLICATIONS, INC., 320 West Ohio Street, Chicago, IL 60610.

Books in English from U.S.S.R., Eastern Europe, and developing countries.

323. INSTITUTE OF ELECTRICAL AND ELECTRONICS ENGINEERS, INC., 345 East 47th Street, New York, NY 10017.

A few titles on technical and social energy problems.

324. INTERBOOK, INC., 545 Eighth Avenue, New York, NY 10018.

Publishes for non-profit organizations. Business, education, general and social studies books.

325. INTERMEDIATE TECHNOLOGY PUBLICATIONS, LTD., 9 Kings Street, London WC2E 8HN ENGLAND.

Journals and documents on appropriate technology for developing countries.

326. INTERNATIONAL SCHOLARLY BOOK SERVICES, INC., P.O. Box 555, Forest Grove, OR 97116.

Books on science, technology, medicine, social sciences etc.

327. IOWA STATE UNIVERSITY PRESS, Ames, IA 50010.

Agriculture and health sciences, for college and professional readers.

328. LEARNING SYSTEMS COMPANY, 1818 Ridge Road, Homewood, IL 60430.

Programmed Learning Aid Series for high school, college, training programs and self-study. Includes ENVIRONMENTAL SCIENCE, and THE ENERGY CRISIS.

329. J.B. LIPPINCOTT COMPANY, East Washington Square, Philadelphia, PA 19105.

General and scholarly books on energy, the environment
and the future.

330. LITTLE, BROWN AND CO., 34 Beacon Street, Boston, MA 02106.

Texts for basic courses in Environmental Science, none
exclusively on energy or energy-related issues.

331. DAVID MCKAY COMPANY, INC., 750 Third Avenue, New York, NY
10017.

College texts in economics, political science and
sociology. Some related to environmental issues.

332. MIT PRESS, 28 Carleton Street, Cambridge, MA 02142.

Many scholarly and professional books and reports on
energy-related questions including energy policy,
technology and futures.

333. MONTHLY REVIEW PRESS, 62 West 14th Street, New York, NY 10011.

Books on energy politics and economics, particularly
international. General, college and graduate readers.

334. NEW YORK UNIVERSITY PRESS, Washington Square, New York, NY
10003.

Advanced and general books on history, politics and
economics.

335. NORTHWESTERN UNIVERSITY PRESS, 1735 Benson Avenue, Evanston,
IL 60201.

Scholarly books on economics, business, politics and
geography.

336. NOYES DATA CORPORATION, Mill Road at Grand Avenue, Park Ridge,
NJ 07656.

Series of Energy Technology Reviews for engineering
undergraduates and graduates. Generally highly technical.

337. OHIO STATE UNIVERSITY PRESS, 2070 Neil Avenue, Columbus, OH
43210.

Social science and technical books for the advanced
reader. Suitable for graduate, business and professional use.

338. OPEN COURT PUBLISHING COMPANY, Box 599, LaSalle, IL 61301.

Mainly scholarly books for professionals.

339. OREGON STATE UNIVERSITY PRESS, P.O. Box 689, Corvallis, OR
97330.

Emphasis on biological sciences at the college and

professional level.

340. OXFORD UNIVERSITY PRESS, 200 Madison Avenue, New York, NY
10016.

Many titles suitable for undergraduate courses. Books
on energy and environment.

341. PENGUIN BOOKS, INC., 72 Fifth Avenue, New York, NY 10011.

Many energy-related titles, including THE ENERGY BALLOON,
POWER PLAY, and OIL AND WORLD POWER.

342. PERGAMON PRESS, INC., Maxwell House, Fairview Park, Elsmford,
NY 10523.

Technical and scholarly books and journals in energy and
related fields. Wide variety of materials on energy
sources and technology. ENERGY SOURCES, a sequence of
reprints from the collection of the Engineering
Societies Library of New York. Microforms or full-size
electrostatic copies. Special concentration on out of
print materials. Solar, hydrocarbons, wind, hydro, geothermal, electricity, etc.

343. PLENUM PUBLISHING CORPORATION, 227 West 17th Street, New York,
NY 10011.

Books on environment, ecology, natural resources and the
future.

344. PRAEGER PUBLISHERS, INC., 111 Fourth Avenue, New York, NY
10003.

Books for professionals in sociology, economics, and
political science, academic, business and government
specialists.

345. PRENTICE-HALL, INC., Englewood Cliffs, NJ 07632.

Textbooks, readers, etc. on energy politics, economics
and technology.

346. PRINCETON UNIVERSITY PRESS, Princeton, NJ 08540.

Books for advanced undergraduates, graduate students
and scholars in energy-related fields. Several items
on energy-efficient design.

347. PUBLISHING SCIENCES GROUP, INC., 545 Great Road, Littleton,
MA 01460.

Primarily medical textbooks, though with several titles
related to energy and environmental fields.

348. PUTNAM'S - COWARD, MCCANN AND GEOGHEGAN, INC., 200 Madison
Avenue, New York, NY 10016.

Energy titles for high school and adult readers. New Conservation series for ages 12-16.

349.   RANDOM HOUSE, INC., 201 East 50th Street, New York, NY 10022.

Hardcover and paperbound books on evergy policy, energy politics, the future of energy and energy alternatives.

350.   RESOURCES FOR THE FUTURE, 1755 Massachusetts Avenue NW, Washington, D.C. 20036.

Publishes results of RFF research in the social sciences.

351.   RODALE PRESS, INC., 33 East Minor Street, Emmaus, PA 18049.

Books for the general reader on alternative energy, energy conservation and low-impact lifestyles.

352.   RUNNING PRESS, 38 South 19th Street, Philadelphia, PA 19103.

Books on energy alternatives and conservation, including ENERGYBOOK #2.

353.   ST. MARTIN'S PRESS, 175 Fifth Avenue, New York, NY 10010.

College and educated general readership books on energy politics and policy.

354.   SCOTT, FORESMAN AND COMPANY, INC., Glenview, IL.

Trade and textbooks, including science texts, many on energy-related subjects.

355.   HOWARD W. SAMS AND CO., INC., 4300 West 62nd Street, Indianapolis, IN 46206.

How-to and do-it-yourself books on electricity, heating, refrigeration, etc.

356.   TAPLINGER PUBLISHING CO., 200 Park Avenue South, New York, NY 10003.

Publishing and distributing of books on economics and social science.

357.   SIMON AND SCHUSTER, INC., 630 Fifth Avenue, New York, NY 10020.

Young adult and adult books on energy, energy futures and science.

358.   UNIVERSE BOOKS, INC., 381 Park Avenue South, New York, NY 10016.

Appropriate technology, self-sufficiency, policy and planning, for general or college level readers.

359.   UNIVERSITY OF CHICAGO PRESS, Chicago, IL 60637.

Energy policy, economics and politics, for graduate, professional and college readers.

360. UNIVERSITY OF MICHIGAN PRESS, Ann Arbor, MI   48106.

Books on energy for university and professional level readers. Solar, atomic, geothermal and environmental protection.

361. UNIVERSITY OF NORTH CAROLINA PRESS, Chapel Hill, NC   27514.

Scholarly and advanced books.

362. UNIVERSITY OF TORONTO PRESS, Front Campus, University of Toronto, Toronto, Ontario CANADA.

Energy policy and economics, geography and environment. For university-educated audience, particular focus on Canadian problems.

363. UNIVERSITY OF WASHINGTON PRESS, Seattle, WA   98105.

College and technical books on energy policy and technology.

364. VIKING PRESS, INC., 625 Madison Avenue, New York, NY   10022.

Publications for advanced readers include THE SEVEN SISTERS, an account of the major oil companies.

365. H.W. WILSON CO., 950 University Avenue, Bronx, NY   10452.

Library reference materials and periodical indexes.

366. XEROX EDUCATIONAL PUBLICATIONS, Lexington, MA.

Science Tutor Books for grades 6-9, include LEARN ABOUT ATOMS and LEARN ABOUT ENERGY CONVERSIONS.

PUBLISHED SOURCES, TEXTS, READERS, MANUALS, ETC.

PUBLISHED SOURCES, TEXTS, READERS, MANUALS, ETC.

Introduction

This section includes books from the primary to post-graduate
and professional level. It is intended to be a basic overview and
introduction to energy problems and the literature on energy.
Material more advanced or specialized than falls within the scope of
ENERGY GUIDE can be found in the bibliographies ENERGY and ENERGY
II, compiled by Denton E. Morrison and others and published by
Garland. Most of the material in this section was published since
1970, though a few useful books with earlier dates have been
included.

367.   Abelson, Philip H., ENERGY FOR TOMORROW, Seattle: University
        of Washington Press, 1975.

        Non-technical summary of the causes of the energy crisis
        and possible ways for coping with it. U.S. energy
        policy discussed in a global context, suggested conser-
        vation programs.

368.   Abir, Mordechai, OIL, POWER AND POLITICS: CONFLICT IN
        ARABIA, THE RED. SEA AND THE GULF, London: Cass, 1975.

369.   Abraham, Norman, et al., INTERACTION OF MATTER AND ENERGY:
        INQUIRY IN PHYSICAL SCIENCE, Chicago: Rand McNally,
        1973.

        Text for grades 7-9.

370.   Alexander, Sidney S., PAYING FOR ENERGY, New York: McGraw-
        Hill, 1975.

371.   Allune, Fred C., and James M. Patterson, HIGHWAY ROBBERY: AN
        ANALYSIS OF THE GASOLINE CRISIS, Bloomington: Indiana
        University Press, 1974.

372.   Arad, Uzi B., et al., ENERGY AND SECURITY: IMPLICATIONS FOR
        AMERICAN POLICY, New York: Hudson Institute, 1974.

373.   Belknap, Richard H., (ed.), ENERGY: FUTURE ALTERNATIVES AND
        RISKS, Cambridge: Massachusetts, Ballinger, 1974.

374.   Berger, John, Jr., NUCLEAR POWER: THE UNVIABLE OPTION, A
        CRITICAL LOOK AT OUR ENERGY ALTERNATIVES, New York:
        Ramparts Press, 1976.

375.   Berger, Melvin, ENERGY FROM THE SUN, New York: Thomas Y.
        Crowell, 1976.

A Let's-Read-and-Find-Out-Science Book for ages 4-8 on the importance of solar energy, with illustrations and easy to do projects.

376. Blanpied, William A., and Gretchen Vermilye, (eds.), CASE STUDIES IN REGIONAL ENERGY PLANNING, Washington, D.C.: American Association for the Advancement of Science, 1976.

377. Bloustein, Edward J. (ed.), NUCLEAR ENERGY, PUBLIC POLICY AND THE LAW, Dobbs Ferry, New York: Oceana, 1964.

378. Braker, W.P., et al., EXPLORING AND UNDERSTANDING MATTER AND ENERGY, Winchester, IL: Benetic Press, n.d.

Set of books for grades 4-9, including workbooks and resource kits.

379. Brinkworth, B.J., SOLAR ENERGY FOR MAN, Somerset, NJ: John Wiley and Sons, 1973.

380. Burkman, Ernest, HOUSEHOLD ENERGY, Lexington, MA: Ginn, 1976.

Text for grades 9-12, with annotated teacher's edition.

381. Canada, Ministry of Energy, Mines, and Resources, AN ENERGY POLICY FOR CANADA, 2 volumes, Ottawa: Ministry of Energy, Mines, and Resources, 1973.

382. Clark, Peter, NATURAL ENERGY WORKBOOK, Berkeley, CA: Visual Purple, 1974.

383. Clark, Wilson, ENERGY FOR SURVIVAL: THE ALTERNATIVE TO EX-TINCTION, Garden City, NY: Doubleday, 1974.

Up-to-date non-technical information of the history, sociology and politics of energy and its use, and a guide to sources (over 1,000 references). Also available from Environmental Action Reprint Service.

384. Commoner, Barry, THE POVERTY OF POWER: ENERGY AND THE ECONOM-IC CRISIS, New York: Knopf, 1976.

Links energy policy to our political and economic system, and shows that complete socio-economic and power use restructuring is necessary for survival.

385. Conservation Foundation, (eds.), ENERGY CONSERVATION TRAINING MANUAL, Washington, D.C.: Conservation Foundation, 1976.

386. Cook, E.F., MAN, ENERGY, SOCIETY, San Francisco: W.H. Freeman, 1976.

387. Cottrell, William Frederick, ENERGY AND SOCIETY: THE RELA-TIONSHIP BETWEEN SOCIAL CHANGE AND ECONOMIC DEVELOPMENT,

New York: McGraw-Hill, 1955; reprinted by Greenwood
Press, Westport, CN, 1970.

388. Crawley, Gerard M., ENERGY, New York: Macmillan, 1975.

389. Darmstadter, Joel, Perry D. Teitelbaum, and Jaroslav G.
Polach, ENERGY IN THE WORLD ECONOMY: A STATISTICAL RE-
VIEW OF TRENDS IN OUTPUT, TRADE, AND CONSUMPTION SINCE
1925, Baltimore: Johns Hopkins University Press, 1971.

390. Davis, David Howard, ENERGY POLITICS, New York: St. Martin's
Press, 1974.

College level discussion of the energy crisis, and its
impact on U.S. and international policies and politics.

391. Dawson, Frank G., NUCLEAR POWER: DEVELOPMENT AND MANAGEMENT
OF A TECHNOLOGY, Seattle: University of Washington
Press, 1976.

History of U.S. nuclear power development, conflicts,
politics and considerations. Stress on key government
actions on the development, management and regulation of
nuclear power. College and technical readers.

392. Duffy, Joseph, POWER: PRIME-MOVER OF TECHNOLOGY, New York:
Taplinger, 1972.

Text for grades 11 and 12.

393. Dumas, Lloyd, ENERGY ALTERNATIVES, Lexington, MA: Lexington
Books, 1976.

394. Eblen, William R., and Richard Rink, ABCS OF THE TOTAL EN-
VIRONMENT, Austin, TX: Steck-Vaughn, n.d.

Grades 4-9, multi-media kit with records or cassettes.
Teacher's manual and activity manual.

395. Education Research Council of America, MAN AND THE ENVIRON-
MENT, Boston: Houghton Mifflin, 1974.

Grades 9-12. Lab supplies, learning games and teacher's
guide available.

396. Educational Research Council of America, YOU AND THE ENVIRON-
MENT: AN INVESTIGATIVE APPROACH, Boston: Houghton
Mifflin, 1976.

Grades 7-9, with annotated teacher edition, lab supplement and chapter tests.

397. Elkana, Yehuda, THE DISCOVERY OF THE CONSERVATION OF ENERGY,
Cambridge, MA: Harvard University Press, 1974.

398. Engineering Concepts Curriculum Project, MAN AND HIS TECH-
NOLOGY: PROBLEMS, ISSUES, New York: McGraw-Hill, 1971.

Grades 11-12. Classroom equipment and teacher manual available.

399. Environmental Law Institute, STATE AND LOCAL ENERGY CONSER-
VATION PROJECT REPORT, 8 volume series, Cambridge, MA:
Ballinger, 1977.

   8 volumes on energy impacts, feasibility and equity of
   energy conservation measures, taxation, government operations, pricing, industry, transportation, land-use,
   the food system and many other areas.

400. Eppen, Gary D. (ed.), ENERGY: THE POLICY ISSUES, Chicago:
University of Chicago Press, 1975.

   Readings on the energy problems, with viewpoints on
   possible energy policy.

401. Erickson, Edward W., and Leonard Waverman, (eds.), THE ENERGY
QUESTION: AN INTERNATIONAL FAILURE OF POLICY, 2 volumes,
Toronto: University of Toronto Press, 1974.

402. Fabun, Dan, ENERGY: TRANSACTIONS IN TIME, New York: Macmillan, 1971.

   1 part of a four-volume series DIMENSIONS OF CHANGE,
   which also includes FOOD: AN ENERGY EXCHANGE SYSTEM.
   Grades 10-12.

403. Fisher, John C., ENERGY CRISIS IN PERSPECTIVE, New York:
Wiley, 1974.

404. Foley, Gerald, THE ENERGY QUESTION, Baltimore: Penquin
Books, 1976.

405. Fowler, John M., ENERGY AND THE ENVIRONMENT, New York:
McGraw-Hill, 1974.

   Impacts and consequences of energy use on the environment.

406. Freeman, S. David, ENERGY: THE NEW ERA, New York: Random
House, 1974.

   A guide to the energy crisis, energy conservation and
   alternatives, and energy policy. Suggestions for
   national energy policy, and incentives and controls for
   energy conservation and innovation.

407. Freeman, S. David, et al., A TIME TO CHOOSE: AMERICA'S
ENERGY FUTURE, Cambridge, MA: Ballinger, 1974.

408. Gabel, Medard, ENERGY, EARTH AND EVERYONE: A GLOBAL STRATEGY
FOR SPACESHIP EARTH, New York: Simon and Schuster, 1975.

   For young adult and adult audiences.

409. Garvey, Gerald, ENERGY, ECOLOGY, ECONOMY: A FRAMEWORK FOR ENVIRONMENTAL POLICY, New York: Norton, 1972.

Grades 11 and up.

410. Gray, John E., ENERGY POLICY: INDUSTRY PERSPECTIVES, Cambridge, MA: Ballinger, 1975.

411. Gross, Jesse and Seymour Kopilow, STUDY LESSONS IN GENERAL SCIENCE, Chicago: Follett, n.d.

For slow learners in grades 7-9, including two books on energy, with teacher guides and workbooks.

412. Halacy, D.S., THE COMING AGE OF SOLAR ENERGY, New York: Harper and Row, 1973.

A basic overview of the history, development and future of solar energy, for the interested lay reader.

413. Harrah, Barbara K., and David Harrah, ALTERNATE SOURCES OF ENERGY: A BIBLIOGRAPHY OF SOLAR, GEOTHERMAL, WIND AND TIDAL ENERGY AND ENVIRONMENTAL ARCHITECTURE, Metuchen, NJ: Scarecrow, 1975.

414. Hartshora, J.E., POLITICS AND WORLD OIL ECONOMICS (Revised Edition), New York:' Praeger, 1967.

415. Healy, Timothy J., ENERGY AND SOCIETY, San Francisco: Boyd and Fraser, 1976.

College text on energy conservation, sources, and alternatives. Material on government, industry, the public interest and economics. Also contains lists of additional readings, general and mathematical problems, and advanced study problems.

416. Hellman, Hal, ENERGY IN THE WORLD OF THE FUTURE, Philadelphia: J.B. Lippincott, 1973.

For grades 7-12, a basic introduction to our energy future.

417. Hepple, Peter (ed.), OUTLOOK FOR NATURAL GAS, New York: Halstead, 1973.

418. Herrera, Phil, and John Holdren, ENERGY: A CRISIS IN POWER, Totowa, NJ: Sierra Club Books, 1971.

419. Holdren, John and Phillip Herrera, ENERGY, New York: Sierra Club, 1973.

One of the basic books on the energy situation.

420. Israel, Elaine, THE GREAT ENERGY SEARCH, New York: Simon and Schuster, 1974.

Grades 4 and up.

421. Jensen, Walter G., ENERGY IN EUROPE, Henley-on-Thames, ENGLAND: Foulis, 1967.

422. Jequier, Nicolas (ed.), APPROPRIATE TECHNOLOGY PROBLEMS AND PROMISES, Paris: OECD, 1976.

    Reader of essays and case histories by experienced persons in the AT field.

423. Kahn, Herman, et al., THE NEXT 200 YEARS: A SCENARIO FOR AMERICA AND THE WORLD, New York: Morrow, 1976.

424. Kalter, Robert J., and William A. Vogely, (eds.), ENERGY SUPPLY AND GOVERNMENT POLICY, Ithaca: Cornell University Press, 1976.

425. Kennan, J., et al., ENERGY: DEMAND, CONSERVATION AND IN-STITUTIONAL PROBLEMS, Cambridge, MA: MIT Press, 1974.

426. Landsberg, Hans H., et al., ENERGY AND THE SOCIAL SCIENCES: AN EXAMINATION OF RESEARCH NEEDS, Baltimore: Johns Hopkins Press, 1974.

427. Lapp, Ralph R., AMERICA'S ENERGY, Greenwich, CT: Reddy Communications, 1976.

428. Laxer, James, CANADA'S ENERGY CRISIS, Toronto: James Lewis and Samuel, 1974.

    Of particular interest to Canadians and students of Canada's energy failure.

429. Lenihan, John, and William W. Fletcher, (eds.), ENERGY, RE-SOURCES AND THE ENVIRONMENT, New York: Academic Press, 1976.

430. Lindberg, Leon N. (ed.), ENERGY POLICY: EAST-WEST NORTH-SOUTH, Lexington, MA: D.D. Heath, 1976.

431. Lindsay, R. Bruce (ed.), ENERGY: HISTORICAL DEVELOPMENT OF THE CONCEPT, Stroudsburg, PA: Dowden, Hutchinson and Ross, 1975.

432. Lovins, Amory B., WORLD ENERGY STRATEGIES: FACTS, ISSUES AND OPTIONS, San Francisco: Friends of the Earth, 1975.

    Assesses the constraints on our energy resources, discusses long-term options and short-term action to preserve those options.

433. Lovins, Amory B., and John Price, NONNUCLEAR FUTURES: THE CASE FOR AN ETHICAL ENERGY STRATEGY, Cambridge, MA: Ballinger, 1975.

    Economic and ethical concerns of nuclear power and its alternatives. For both the concerned citizen and the intelligent energy executive.

434. MacDonald, Angus J., POWER: MECHANICS OF ENERGY CONTROL, New York: Taplinger, n.d.

Text for grades 9-12, with teacher guide and workbook.

435. McNall, Preston E., and Harry B. Kircher, OUR NATURAL RESOURCES, Danville, IL: Interstate, 1970.

Illustrated, for grades 7-12.

436. Macrakis, Michael (ed.), ENERGY: DEMAND, CONSERVATION AND INSTITUTIONAL PROBLEMS, Cambridge, MA: MIT Press, 1974.

437. Marshall, James, GOING, GOING, GONE? THE WASTE OF OUR ENERGY RESOURCES, New York: Coward, McCann and Geoghegan, 1976.

Energy resources, conservation and the energy crisis for ages 12-16.

438. Messell, H., and S.T. Butler, (eds.), SOLAR ENERGY, Elmsford, NY: Pergamon Press, 1975.

Selected lectures on solar energy prepared specifically for high school students, especially 12th grade.

439. Metzger, Norman, ENERGY: THE CONTINUING CRISIS, New York: Thomas Y. Crowell, 1976.

Supply and demand, government energy policies, options for closing the energy supply-demand gap.

440. Meyer, Leo, NUCLEAR POWER IN INDUSTRY, Chicago: American Technical Society, 1974.

Illustrated text for grades 11 and up.

441. Michelsohn, David Reuben, ATOMIC ENERGY FOR HUMAN NEEDS, New York: Simon and Schuster, 1973.

For junior and senior high schools, a report on present and projected uses of atomic energy.

442. Millard, Reed, HOW WILL WE MEET THE ENERGY CRISIS? POWER FOR TOMORROW'S WORLD, New York: Simon and Schuster, 1974.

The energy crisis and energy futures, bringing together economic, technological and environmental concerns. Discusses atomic power, energy alternatives, etc. For junior and senior high school readers.

443. Mitchell, Edward J., U.S. ENERGY POLICY: A PRIMER, Washington, D.C.: American Enterprise Institute for Public Policy Research, National Energy Study 1, 1974.

444. Morgan, Richard, and Sandra Jerabek, HOW TO CHALLENGE YOUR LOCAL UTILITY, Washington, D.C.: Environmental Action Foundation, 1974.

How utilities operate, set rates, etc., what citizens can do, detailed reference list.

445. Morgan, Richard, Tom Riesenberg, Michael Troutman, TAKING CHARGE: A NEW LOOK AT PUBLIC POWER, Washington, D.C.: Environmental Action Foundation, 1976.

Workings of public power, private utilities, citizen action. Legal history, list of references.

446. Morrison, Denton E., ENERGY: A GUIDE TO SOCIAL SCIENCE AND RELATED LITERATURE, New York: Garland, 1975.

Unannotated listings of energy and energy-related literature in many social science areas. Most items are from the 1960's and early 1970's. Concerned with the social and social-science implications of world energy problems.

447. Morrison, Denton E., ENERGY II, New York: Garland, 1977.

An update to the 1975 ENERGY, listing social-science and related literature since 1974. May be used separately or as a companion volume to ENERGY.

448. Mosley, Leonard, POWER PLAY: OIL IN THE MIDDLE EAST, Baltimore: Penguin, 1974.

Political and economic background and history of the oil industry in the Middle East, the rise of OPEC, etc.

449. Murphy, Arthur W. (ed.), THE NUCLEAR POWER CONTROVERSY, Englewood Cliffs, NJ: Prentice-Hall, 1976.

Casebook of readings for the educated non-technical reader on the problems and prospects of nuclear energy.

450. Nakamura, Leonard I. (ed.), ENERGY FORUM, New York: Conference Board, 1974.

451. National Education Association, ENERGY CHOICES FOR NOW: SAVING, USING, RENEWING, Washington, D.C.: National Education Association, 1974.

Grades 9-12, student and teacher manuals.

452. Navarra, John G., et al., ENERGY AND THE ATOM: THE PHYSICAL SCIENCES, New York: Harper and Row, 1966.

Text, guidebook, tests and teacher's edition. Grades 7-9.

453. Odell, Peter R., OIL AND WORLD POWER: BACKGROUND TO THE OIL CRISIS, (4th edition), Baltimore: Penguin, 1975.

454. O'Toole, James, ENERGY AND SOCIAL CHANGE, Cambridge, MA:

MIT Press, 1976.

455. Palmer, Nelson P., et al., MATTER, LIFE AND ENERGY, Chicago: Rand McNally, 1972.

Grade 9 manual for laboratory and classroom investigation.

456. Patterson, Walter C., NUCLEAR POWER, Baltimore: Penguin, 1976.

Not exclusively technical, discussion of nuclear technology, social impacts and the future of nuclear energy.

457. Penner, S.S., and L. Icerman, ENERGY: DEMANDS, RESOURCES, IMPACT, TECHNOLOGY, AND POLICY, 3 volumes, Reading, MA: Addison-Wesley, 1974.

458. Polach, Jaroslav G., THE DEVELOPMENT OF ENERGY IN EAST EUROPE, Washington, D.C.: Resources for the Future, 1970.

459. Portola Institute, ENERGY PRIMER, Menlo Park, CA: Portola Institute, 1974.

A fairly technical reader on renewable energy for individuals, small groups and communities. Original articles, book reviews and sources of equipment.

460. Prenis, John (ed.), ENERGYBOOK #I: NATURAL SOURCES AND BACK-YARD APPLICATIONS, Philadelphia: Running Press, 1975.

Collection of information, instructions and bibliography on wind, solar, biogas and other alternative energy sources. Sequel, ENERGYBOOK #II, may be used either with ENERGYBOOK #I or separately.

461. Priest, Joseph, et al., ENERGY FOR A TECHNOLOGICAL SOCIETY: PRINCIPLES, PROBLEMS, ALTERNATIVES, Reading, MA: Addison-Wesley, 1975.

462. Ridgeway, James, and Bettina Conner, NEW ENERGY: UNDERSTANDING THE CRISIS AND A GUIDE TO AN ALTERNATIVE ENERGY SYSTEM, Boston: Beacon Press, 1975.

An historical perspective on the energy crisis, with plans for an alternative system of decentralization and local control.

463. Rocks, Lawrence, and Richard P. Runyon, THE ENERGY CRISIS, New York: Crown, 1972.

Basic introduction to the energy crisis, one of the key introductory works in the field.

464. Rodgers, Kay, ENERGY CRISIS: AN OVERVIEW, Washington, D.C.: U.S. Library of Congress, Science and Technology Division, 1974.

465. Rosen, Stephen, FUTURE FACTS, New York: Simon and Schuster, 1976.

    For young adult and adult readers, a look at the future in energy and other areas.

466. Ruedisili, Leon C., and Morris W. Firebaugh, PERSPECTIVES ON ENERGY: ISSUES, IDEALS AND ENVIRONMENTAL DILEMMAS, New York: Oxford University Press, 1975.

    Illustrated, for grade 12 and up, on energy, equity and environmental impacts.

467. Rybczynski, T.M., THE ECONOMICS OF THE OIL CRISIS, New York: Holmes and Meiser, 1976.

468. Saperstein, Alvin M., PHYSICS: ENERGY IN THE ENVIRONMENT, Boston: Little, Brown, 1975.

    Text for college freshmen or interested adults on energy and its environmental and social impacts.

469. Scheffer, Walter F. (ed.), ENERGY IMPACTS ON PUBLIC POLICY AND ADMINISTRATION, Normon, OK: University of Oklahoma Press, 1974.

470. Schurr, Sam H. (ed.), ENERGY, ECONOMIC GROWTH AND THE EN-VIRONMENT, Baltimore: Johns Hopkins University Press, 1972.

    Collection of Resources for the Future Papers, reaching the general conclusion that the growth of energy consumption as it now is cannot be compatible with desirable environmental objectives.

471. Seifert, William (ed.), ENERGY AND DEVELOPMENT, Cambridge, MA: MIT Press, 1973.

472. Smith, Craig B. (ed.), EFFICIENT ELECTRICITY USE: A PRACTI-CAL HANDBOOK FOR AN ENERGY CONSTRAINED WORLD, Elmsford, NY: Pergamon Press, 1976.

    Guide to energy-saving techniques that can be implemented immediately with little or no capital expenditure, and also to near and long-term methods that require some capital expenditure. Includes diagrams, tables.

473. Soutin, Harry, and D.S. Halacy, EXPERIMENTS WITH SOLAR ENERGY, New York: Grossett and Dunlap, 1969.

    Science text for grades 5-12 on applications of solar energy.

474. Szulc, Tad, THE ENERGY CRISIS, New York: Watts, 1974.

    Good basic introduction to the subject.

475.   Stoker, H. Stephen, Spencer L. Seager, and Robert L. Capener,
        ENERGY: FROM SOURCE TO USE, Glenview, IL: Scott,
        Foresman, 1975.

        College text on the energy crisis, current and proposed
        energy sources, conservation and alternatives, with lists
        of suggested readings. Can be used by advanced high
        school students.

476.   Stork, Joe, MIDDLE EAST OIL AND THE ENERGY CRISIS, New York:
        Monthly Review Press, 1975.

        Analysis of oil development and politics in the Middle
        East from World War II to the present.

477.   Szylowicz, Joseph S., and Bard E. O'Neill, (eds.), THE ENERGY
        CRISIS AND U.S. FOREIGN POLICY, New York: Praeger, 1975.

        How U.S. energy needs and future demands affect our for-
        eign policy and relations with other countries.

478.   Tanzer, Michael, THE ENERGY CRISIS: WORLD STRUGGLE FOR POWER
        AND WEALTH, New York: Monthly Review Press, 1974.

        Operation and structure of the oil industry, import, ex-
        port, supply and demand of energy, the energy crisis and
        the oil industry.

479.   Townsend, R., et al., ENERGY: MATTER AND CHANGE, Glenview,
        IL: Scott, Foresman, 1973.

        Text for grades 7-9, with lab book and teacher's handbook.

480.   Udall, Stewart, Charles Conconi, and David Osterhout, THE
        ENERGY BALLOON, Baltimore: Penguin Books, 1975.

        Explains the energy crisis and shows the complexity of
        the situation. Stress on conservation, restructuring
        lifestyles for the end of the era of abundant energy,
        national energy policy.

481.   U.S. Citizens' Advisory Committee on Environmental Quality,
        ENERGY IN SOLID WASTE: A CITIZEN GUIDE TO SAVING,
        Washington, D.C.: U.S. Government Printing Office, 1975.

        Guide for individuals and groups in reducing solid waste
        and saving energy in the home and the community. Encour-
        ages citizen action and stresses practices that can be
        initiated readily and rapidly.

482.   U.S. Congress, House, Committee on Interstate and Foreign
        Commerce, Subcommittee on Energy and Power, MIDDLE AND
        LONG-TERM ENERGY POLICIES AND ALTERNATIVES, 7 parts,
        Washington, D.C.: U.S. Government Printing Office, 1976.

        Comprehensive overview of the energy question, from
        hearings conducted by the committee.

483. U.S. Congress, House, Committee on Science and Astronautics, Subcommittee on Energy, ENVENTORY OF CURRENT ENERGY RESEARCH AND DEVELOPMENT (with lists of Research Projects), 3 volumes, Washington, D.C.: U.S. Government Printing Office, 1974.

484. U.S. Department of Commerce, National Bureau of Standards, ENERGY CONSERVATION PROGRAM GUIDE FOR INDUSTRY AND COM-MERCE, Washington, D.C.: National Bureau of Standards, Handbook 115, 1974.

485. U.S. Department of the Interior, ENERGY PERSPECTIVES, A PRE-SENTATION OF MAJOR ENERGY AND ENERGY RELATED DATA, Washington, D.C.: U.S. Government Printing Office, 1975.

486. Vexiroglu, T. Nejat (ed.), HYDROGEN ENERGY, New York: Plenum, 1975.

   Somewhat technical collection of readings on hydrogen as an alternative energy source.

487. Wagstaff, H. Reid, A GEOGRAPHY-OF ENERGY, Dubuque: W.C. Brown, 1974.

488. Wells, Malcolm, ENERGY ESSAYS, 1976. Available from Environ-mental Action Reprint Service.

   An illustrated idea pack on solar energy, nuclear power, energy conservation and waste management.

489. Wood, David, ENERGY: CONSERVATION AND ALTERNATIVE SOURCES, Toronto: Energy Probe, University of Toronto, 1975.

490. World Future Society, ENERGY: TODAY'S CHOICES, TOMORROW'S POLICY, Washington, D.C.: World Future Society, 1974.

491. Willrich, Mason, ENERGY AND WORLD POLITICS, New York: The Free Press, 1975.

492. Wright, Denis (ed.), OIL PRODUCERS AND CONSUMERS: CONFLICT OR COOPERATION, New York: American Universities Field Staff, 1974.

PERIODICALS

PERIODICALS

Introduction

    Magazines and newsletter often have the most recent information on a particular energy topic. If you are interested in the latest energy developments, periodicals should be your starting point.
    The magazines and journals in this section cover a wide range of science, social science and education topics. Environmentally-oriented magazines often publish articles on energy. Some of these magazines specialize in energy, or in some specific sub-area of energy. Others have a broader orientation, but publish either regular features or occasional energy articles. This section includes magazines for the general reader, and scholarly or technical journals in energy-related fields. Subscription prices have not been included, as these are subject to sudden change as postal rates, paper and other costs increase. For this information, apply to the editor or publisher of the periodical.
    Newsletters tend to reflect the particular interests of the sponsoring group, and so are often more specialized than magazines. Many state energy offices have newsletters on state energy developments. Your state energy office can inform you on this.

493.   AGRICULTURAL EDUCATION, RD2, Box 639, Halifax, PA 17032. Monthly.

        Journal for teachers of agriculture and related subjects.

494.   AGRICULTURAL ENGINEERING, 2950 Niles Road, St. Joseph, MI 49085. Monthly.

        Professional journal of the American Society of Agricultural Engineers.

495.   AGRICULTURAL HISTORY, University of California, Agricultural History Center, David, CA 95616. Quarterly.

496.   AGROLOGIST, Agricultural Institute of Canada, Suite 107, 151 Slater Street, Ottawa K1P 5H4 CANADA. Quarterly.

        Occasional articles on energy and agricultural topics.

497.   AIR POLLUTION CONTROL ASSOCIATION JOURNAL, Air Pollution Control Association, 4400 Fifth Avenue, Pittsburgh, PA 15213. Monthly.

        Technical-professional journal.

498.   AIR POLLUTION NOTES, Cook College, Rutgers University, New Brunswick, NY 08903. Bi-monthly.

499. ALTERNATIVES: PERSPECTIVES ON SOCIETY AND ENVIRONMENT, Trent University, Peterborough, Ontario CANADA. Quarterly.

Discusses environmental issues and controversial projects in Canada and the U.S. Also provides bibliographies in many areas, including energy and Canadian topics.

500. AMBIO: A JOURNAL OF HUMAN ENVIRONMENT, RESEARCH AND MANAGE-MENT, Universitetsforlaget, P.O. Box 307, Blindem, Oslo 3, NORWAY. Bi-monthly.

International scholarly journal, in English, on environmental management, technology, and natural science.

501. AMERICAN ASSOCIATION OF PETROLEUM GEOLOGISTS BULLETIN, Box 979, Tulsa, OK 74101. Monthly.

Professional journal of the American Association of Petroleum Geologists. Discusses oil, gas and other petroleum products.

502. AMERICAN GAS ASSOCIATION MONTHLY, American Gas Association, Inc., 1515 Wilson Boulevard, Arlington, VA. 22209. Monthly, bi-monthly in July-August.

503. AMERICAN JOURNAL OF AGRICULTURAL ECONOMICS, University of Kentucky, Lexington, KY 40506.

Topics in agricultural and resource economics for the post-graduate and professional reader. Professional journal of the American Agricultural Economics Association.

504. AMERICAN SCIENTIST, 345 Whitney Avenue, Hew Haven, CT 06511. Bi-monthly.

College level, published by Sigma Xi scientific research society. Articles, book reviews, color illustrations.

505. AMERICAN SECONDARY EDUCATION, College of Education, University of Akron, Akron, OH 44304. Quarterly.

506. ASHRAE JOURNAL, 345 East 47th Street, New York, NY 10017. Monthly.

Professional-technical journal of the American Society of Heating, Refrigerating and Air-Conditioning Engineers.

507. ANNALS OF NUCLEAR ENERGY (Incorporating JOURNAL OF NUCLEAR ENERGY), Pergamon Press, Fairview Park, Elmsford, NY 10523. Monthly.

International scholarly journal on various aspects of nuclear power.

508. ANNALS OF THE AMERICAN ACADEMY OF POLITICAL AND SOCIAL SCIENCE, 3937 Chestnut Street, Philadelphia, PA 19104. Bi-monthly.

509. ARCHITECTURE PLUS, Informat Publishing Corp., 1345 6th Avenue, New York, NY 10019. Bi-monthly.

Articles on energy-efficient building design and energy alternatives.

510. ARCHIVES OF ENVIRONMENTAL HEALTH, American Medical Association, 535 North Dearborn Street, Chicago, IL 60610. Monthly.

Scholarly journal on impacts of environmental factors on human health. College, graduate and professional students.

511. ATLANTIC COMMUNITY QUARTERLY, Atlantic Council of the United States, 1616 H Street NW, Washington, D.C. 20006.

512. ATOMIC ENERGY LAW JOURNAL, 210 South Street, Boston, MA 02111. Quarterly.

For lawyers, law students and those interested in legal principles and developments relating to atomic energy and nuclear power.

513. AWARE, Suite 12, 2038 Pennsylvania Avenue, Madison, WI 53704. Monthly.

Concerned with the environment and the electric power industry, power generation and future energy prospects.

514. BELL JOURNAL OF ECONOMICS, American Telephone and Telegraph Company, 195 Broadway, Room C 1800, New York, NY 10007. 2/year.

Articles on a variety of economic policy issues. Frequent articles on aspects of energy and economic policy.

515. BIG FARMER, 131 Lincoln Highway, Frankfort, IL 60423. 10/year.

Articles on agriculture and business, large-scale farming operations.

516. BIO SCIENCE, American Institute of Biological Science, 1401 Wilson Boulevard, Arlington, VA 22209. Monthly.

517. BULLETIN OF THE ATOMIC SCIENTISTS, 1020-24 East 58th Street, Chicago, IL 60637. 10/year, no July or August issues.

Stresses science and public affairs. Features on world energy news, nuclear power, nuclear safety, technology and socity, etc.

518. CALIFORNIA ENGINEER, 9 Northgate Hall, University of California, Berkeley, CA 94720. Quarterly.

519. CANADIAN GEOGRAPHICAL JOURNAL, 488 Wilbrod Street, Ottawa, Ontario K1N 6M8 CANADA. Monthly, combined July-August

issues.

520. CANADIAN TECHNICAL AND SCIENTIFIC INFORMATION NEWS JOURNAL, Suite 2A, 1509 Sherbrooke West, Montreal, Quebec H3C 1L7 CANADA. Bi-weekly.

News, current events and documentation in technology, science and industry.

521. CATALYST FOR ENVIRONMENTAL QUALITY, 274 Madison Avenue, New York, NY 10016. Quarterly.

Regular energy features, with a focus on energy conservation.

522. CHILTON'S OIL AND GAS ENERGY, (Formerly ENERGY PIPELINES AND SYSTEMS), Chilton Co., Chilton Way, Radnor, PA 19089. Monthly.

523. CHINESE SCIENTIFIC JOURNALS, Plenum Publishing Company-- China Program, 227 West 17th Street, New York, NY 10011.

524. CITY PROBLEMS. U.S. Conference of Mayors, 1707 H Street, N.W. Washington, D.C. 20066. Annual.

525. CLEAN AIR AND WATER NEWS, Commerce Clearing House, Inc., 4025 West Peterson Ave., Chicago, IL 60646. Weekly.

526. COLUMBIA JOURNAL OF WORLD BUSINESS, 407 Uris Hall, Columbia University, New York, NY 10027. Quarterly.

527. CONFERENCE BOARD RECORD, Conference Board, Inc., 845 Third Avenue, New York, NY 10022. Monthly.

Reports to management on business and economic affairs. Fairly frequent articles on energy and energy economics.

528. CONGRESSIONAL DIGEST, 3231 P Street NW, Washington, D.C. 20007. Monthly, combined June-July, August-September issues.

Reports on controversies in Congress, with viewpoints on both sides.

529. CONGRESSIONAL QUARTERLY SERVICE, 1414 22nd Street NW, Washington, D.C. 20037. Weekly.

News research service, reporting on recent developments in politics, legislation and national policy.

530. CURRENT HISTORY, 4225 Main Street, Philadelphia, PA 19127. Monthly.

Review and discussion on current world affairs.

531. DAEDALUS, American Academy of Arts and Sciences, 7 Linden Street, Cambridge, MA 02138. Quarterly.

Scholarly journal of arts and sciences, published by
Harvard for the American Academy of Arts and Sciences.

532. DEVELOPMENT AND CHANGE, Sage Publications, Inc., 275 South
      Beverly Drive, Beverly Hills, CA 90212.

533. EARTH SCIENCE, Box 1815, Colorado Springs, CO 80901. Bi-
      monthly.

534. ECOLOGIST, 73 Molesworth Street, Wadebridge, Cornwall PL21
      7DS ENGLAND.

      Stresses ecology and the conserver society. Somewhat
      technically-oriented, but not beyond the lay reader.

535. ECOLOGY, Duke University Press, P.O. Box 6697, College Sta-
      tion, Durham, NC 27708. Bi-monthly.

      The official publication of the Ecological Society of
      America.

536. EDUCATION AND URBAN SOCIETY, Sage Publications, 274 South
      Beverly Hills Drive, Beverly Hills, CA 90212.
      Quarterly.

537. EKISTICS, Athens Center for Ekistics, 24 Strat Syndesmore
      Street, Athens 136 GREECE. Monthly.

      Scholarly journal dealing with the problems and science
      of human settlements.

538. ELECTRICAL WORLD, McGraw-Hill, 1221 Avenue of the Americas,
      New York, NY 10020. Semi-monthly.

      Articles and features of interest to the electric utility
      industry.

539. THE ELEMENTS, Institute for Policy Studies, 1901 Q Street
      NW, Washington, D.C. 20009. Monthly.

      Journal on resource issues, with occasional articles
      on public ownership of energy.

540. ENERGY, Business Communications Company, 471 Glenbrook Road,
      Stamford, CT 06906. Quarterly.

541. ENERGY, League of Women Voters Education Fund, 1730 M Street
      NW, Washington, D.C. 20036.

542. ENERGY: THE INTERNATIONAL JOURNAL, Pergamon Press, Inc.,
      Fairview Park, Elmsford, NY 10523. Bi-monthly.

      Multidisciplinary scholarly journal on energy technology,
      resources, reserves, demands, conservation, management
      and policy.

543. ENERGY ANALECTS, Corpus Publishers Services, 6 Crescent Road,

Toronto, Ontario CANADA. Weekly.

544. ENERGY AND HUMAN WELFARE, Macmillan Information, 866 Third
     Avenue, New York, NY 10022.

     Articles on energy's effects on society, energy and the
     quality of life and related issues.

545. ENERGY COMMUNICATIONS, M. Dekker, 270 Madison Avenue, New
     York, NY 10016. Bi-monthly.

546. ENERGY CONTROLS, Prentice-Hall, Inc., Englewood Cliffs,
     NJ 07631.

547. ENERGY CONVERSION, Pergamon Press, Inc., Fairview Park,
     Elmsford, NY 10523. 2/year.

     An international technical journal, in English, for
     an advanced scholarly readership.

548. ENERGY DEVELOPMENT, Institute of Electrical and Electronics
     Engineers, 345 East 47th Street, New York, NY 10017.

     Fairly technical, for the advanced reader.

549. ENERGY DIGEST, Scope Publications, 1067 National Press Build-
     ing, Washington, D.C. 20004. 2/month.

     Review of recent energy events.

550. ENERGY FINANCE WEEK, 1239 National Press Building, Washington,
     D.C. 20045. Weekly.

     Reports on the effects of energy trends on the economy.

551. ENERGY FORUM, P.O. Box EF, Espanola, NM 87532. Monthly.

552. ENERGY INTERNATIONAL, Miller Freeman Publications, Inc.,
     500 Howard Street, San Francisco, CA 94105. Monthly.

     Journal on worldwide energy production and use.

553. ENERGY MANAGEMENT REPORT, P.O. Box 1589, Dallas, TX 75221.
     13/year.

     Topics in management of oil and gas companies.

554. ENERGY POLICY, IPC Science and Technology, King's Reach Tower,
     Stamford Street, London SE1 9LS ENGLAND.

     National and international energy policy, politics and
     planning.

555. ENERGY PROCESSING/CANADA, Sanford Evans Publ., Calgary,
     Alberta CANADA. Bi-monthly.

     Energy processing and technology in Canada.

556. ENERGY REPORTER, Federal Energy Administration, Office of
     Communications and Public Affairs, Washington, D.C.
     20461. Monthly.

557. ENERGY RESEARCH REPORTS, Advanced Technology Publications,
     P.O. Box 530, Newton, MA 02161. Monthly.

     Technical news on energy and energy research.

558. ENERGY RESOURCES REPORT, Business Publishers, Inc., P.O. Box
     1067, Blair Station, Silver Springs, MD 20910.

     Supply and demand in energy and the economy.

559. ENERGY REVIEW, Energy Research Corporation, 6 East Valerio
     Street, Santa Barbara, CA 93101. Bi-monthly.

     Information clearing house and coverage of recent energy
     research.

560. ENERGY SOURCES, Crane, Russak and Co., 347 Madison Avenue,
     New York, NY 10017.

561. ENERGY SYSTEMS AND POLICY, Crane, Russak and Co., 347 Madison
     Avenue, New York, NY 10017. Quarterly.

     Scholarly journal on energy policy, supply, demand and
     production. International and interdisciplinary.

562. ENERGY TODAY, Trends Publications Inc., National Press Build-
     ing, Washington, D.C. 20004. Semi-monthly.

     Current events and recent energy-related developments.

563. ENERGY USERS REPORT, Bureau of National Affairs, Inc., 1231
     25th Street NW, Washington, D.C. 20037. Weekly.

     A review of energy policy, supply and technology.
     Also includes statistics, and a weekly compilation of
     bills and energy policy maggers. Reference file on
     policies, programs, and statutes and a directory of
     government officials in energy-related fields.

564. ENERGY WORLD, Institute of Fuel, London, ENGLAND.

565. ENGINEERING AND MINING JOURNAL, McGraw-Hill, 1221 Avenue of
     the Americas, New York, NY 10020. Monthly.

566. ENVIRONMENTAL ACTION, 1346 Connecticut Avenue NW, Suite 731,
     Washington, D.C. 20036. Bi-weekly.

     Features on energy policy, nuclear power and risks,
     with particular concentration of the ecological impacts
     of energy.

567. ENVIRONMENT AND BEHAVIOR, Sage Publications, Inc., 275 South
     Beverly Drive, Beverly Hills, CA 90212. Quarterly.

568. ENVIRONMENT AND CHANGE, Blackburn Times Press, Maddox Editorial Ltd., 20 Ludor Street, London EC4 ENGLAND. Monthly.

569. ENVIRONMENT REPORT, Trends Publishing Inc., National Press Building, Washington, D.C. 20004. 2/month.

570. ENVIRONMENTAL AFFAIRS, Environmental Law Center, Boston College Law School, 855 Centre St., Newton Centre, Mass. 02159. Quarterly.

For college and professional readers interested in science and the law. Articles on legal aspects of energy and energy policy.

571. ENVIRONMENTAL COMMENT, Urban Land Institute, 1200 19th Street NW, Washington, D.C. 20036. Monthly.

572. ENVIRONMENTAL EDUCATION, Dembar Educational Research Services, P.O. Box 1605, Madison, WI 53701. Quarterly.

573. ENVIRONMENTAL QUALITY MAGAZINE, Environmental Awareness Association, 10658 Burbank Boulevard, North Hollywood, CA 91601.

574. ENVIRONMENTAL RESEARCH, Academic Press, Inc., 111 Fifth Avenue, New York, NY 10003.

575. ENVIRONMENTAL SCIENCE AND TECHNOLOGY, Membership and Subscription Service, American Chemical Society, P.O. Box 3337, Columbus, OH 43210. Monthly, additional issue in October, annual index.

Articles on science and technology and environmental impacts, for a technical-scholarly readership.

576. ENVIRONMENTAL TECHNOLOGY AND ECONOMICS, Environmental Science Services, Division of Environmental Research and Applications, P.O. Box 100, Briarcliff Manor, NY 10510.

577. FACTS ON FILE, 119 West 57th Street, New York, NY 10019. Weekly.

Digest of world news and events. Also publishes reference books collecting items on particular topics from weekly issues. 2 volumes on the energy crisis are available, one for 1969-73, and one for 1974-75.

578. FARM JOURNAL, 230 West Washington Square, Philadelphia, PA 19105. Monthly, semi-monthly February and March, bi-monthly June-July.

For families producing major crops or livestock. Editions differ slightly for different types of farming. Occasional articles on energy and the family farm.

579. F.A.S. PUBLIC INTEREST REPORT, Federation of American Scien-

tists, 307 Massachusetts Avenue NE, Washington, D.C. 20002.

580. FORBES, 60 Fifth Avenue, New York, NY 10011. Semi-monthly.

Articles on finance, management, industry and business. Reports on energy as it affects these areas.

581. FOREIGN AFFAIRS, Council on Foreign Relations, Inc., 58 East 68th Street, New York, NY 10021. Quarterly.

Discussion of international relations and policy issues with world impact.

582. FUTURES CONDITIONAL, P.O. Box 5296, Spokane, WA 99205.

583. THE FUTURIST, World Future Society, 4916 St. Elmo Avenue, Washington, D.C. 20014. Bi-monthly.

Developments and future trends in education and science.

584. GEOS, 588 Booth Street, Ottawa, Ontario K1A OE4 CANADA. Quarterly.

Articles on earth's resources, sponsored by Canada's Department of Energy, Mines and Resources.

585. GREEN REVOLUTION, School for Living, P.O. Box 3233, York, PA 17402.

586. IMPACT OF SCIENCE ON SOCIETY, Unipub-Xerox Educational Company, P.O. Box 433, Murray Hill Station, New York, NY 10016. Quarterly.

Articles on effects of scientific and technological developments on society, international relations, etc. A publication of UNESCO. Not heavily technical, editions available in English, French, Spanish and Arabic.

587. IMPASCIENCE, Editions SOLIN, 1, Rue des Fosse Saint-Jacques, 75005 Paris, FRANCE.

588. INTERCHANGE: A JOURNAL OF EDUCATIONAL STUDIES, Publication Sales, Ontario Institute for Studies in Education, 252 Bloor Street West, Toronto, Ontario CANADA. Quarterly.

589. INTERCIENCIA, P.O. Box 19315, Washington, D.C. 20036.

Articles on science and technology for development, with occasional discussion of energy technology.

590. INTERMEDIATE TECHNOLOGY, 556 Santa Cruz Avenue, Menlo Park, CA 94025.

Articles on alternatives to conventional technology and energy systems, including conservation and efficiency.

591.   INTERNATIONAL ATOMIC ENERGY AGENCY BULLETIN, Unipub, Inc.,
        P.O. Box 433, 650 1st Avenue, New York, NY 10016.
        6/year.

        Current information on IAEA activities in nuclear power
        and promotion of the peaceful use of atomic energy.

592.   INTERNATIONAL JOURNAL OF ENVIRONMENTAL STUDIES, Gordon and
        Breach Science Publishers Inc., One Park Avenue, New
        York, NY 10016. Quarterly.

        For advanced technical and scholarly readers.

593.   INTERNATIONAL WATER POWER AND DAM CONSTRUCTION, IPC Maga-
        zines Ltd., King's Reach Tower, Stamford Street, London
        SE1 9LS ENGLAND. Monthly.

        A technical journal, for advanced readers, with articles
        on water power and hydroelectric systems.

594.   JOURNAL OF COLLEGE SCIENCE TEACHING, 1742 Connecticut Avenue
        NW, Washington, D.C. 20009. 5/year.

        Useful information for science teachers at the college
        level. Material on aids, texts, lessons, and new scien-
        tific developments.

595.   JOURNAL OF ENERGY AND DEVELOPMENT, 216 Economics Building,
        University of Colorado, Boulder, CO 80309. 2/year.

        Energy conservation, development, resources, the environ-
        ment, domestic and international issues, the producer-
        consumer relationship. Book reviews.

596.   JOURNAL OF ENVIRONMENTAL EDUCATION, Heldref Publications,
        4000 Albemarle Street NW, Washington, D.C. 20016.
        Quarterly.

        For teachers in secondary schools and colleges. Re-
        search articles, project reports and critical essays
        intended to advance scientific study and the practice
        of environmental communication and education.

597.   JOURNAL OF ENVIRONMENTAL HEALTH, National Environmental
        Health Association, 1600 Pennsylvania, Denver, CO
        80203. Bi-monthly.

        Scholarly journal, with an emphasis on the effects of
        the environment on human health.

598.   JOURNAL OF ENVIRONMENTAL QUALITY, American Socity of Agronomy,
        677 South Segoe Road, Madison, WI 53711. Quarterly.

        Technical-professional journal with the objective of
        protecting and improving environmental quality.

599.   JOURNAL OF ENVIRONMENTAL SCIENCE AND HEALTH, (Formerly
        ENVIRONMENTAL LETTERS), Marcel Dekker Journals, P.O.

Box 11305 Church Street Station, New York, NY 10249.

Technical journal, for college and professional readers. Published in 3 parts, readers may subscribe separately or together.
Part A: ENVIRONMENTAL SCIENCE AND ENGINEERING, 12/year.
Part B: PESTICIDES, FOOD CONTAMINANTS AND AGRICULTURAL WASTES, 4/year.
Part C: ENVIRONMENTAL HEALTH SCIENCES, 2/year.

600. JOURNAL OF ENVIRONMENTAL SCIENCES, Institute of Environmental Sciences, 940 East Northwest Highway, Mount Prospect, IL 60056. Bi-monthly.

601. JOURNAL OF SOCIAL ISSUES, Society for the Psychological Study of Social Issues, Edwards Brothers, Inc., 2400 South State Street, Ann Arbor, MI 48104. Quarterly.

Scholarly journal on human behavior and social questions.

602. JOURNAL OF SOIL AND WATER CONSERVATION, 7515 Northeast Ankeny Road, Ankeny, IA 50021. Bi-monthly.

603. JOURNAL OF THE AMERICAN INSTITUTE OF PLANNERS, 917 15th Street NW, Washington, D.C. 20005. Bi-monthly.

604. LASER, 33 St. John's Avenue, Burgess Hill, West Sussex, RH15 8HJ ENGLAND.

605. MAN-ENVIRONMENT SYSTEMS, P.O. Box 57, Orangeburg, NW 10962. 6/year.

Communications on design and management of the environment, research in behavioral and social sciences.

606. MAN/SOCIETY/TECHNOLOGY, American Industrial Arts Association, National Education Association Headquarters, 1201 16th Street NW, Washington, D.C. 20036. Monthly, September-April, combined May/June.

Journal primarily for secondary school teachers, though applicable to other levels.

607. MOSAIC, U.S. Government Printing Office, Washington, D.C. 6/year.

A general interest magazine of science education, with illustrations. Published by the National Science Foundation.

608. NATIONAL JOURNAL REPORTS, 1730 M Street NW, Washington, D.C. 20036. Weekly.

Frequent articles on recent political developments relating to energy, both within the U.S. and in international relations. Particular focus on federal government activities.

609. NATURAL HISTORY, American Museum of Natural History, New York, NY 10024. Monthly, October-May, bi-monthly, June-September.

Illustrated articles for a general readership.

610. NATURAL RESOURCES JOURNAL, University of New Mexico School of Law, 1117 Stanford NE, Albuquerque, NM 87131. Quarterly.

International interdisciplinary journal for college and professional readers, with the stress on law and economics.

611. NATURE, Macmillan Journals Ltd., Brunel Road, Basingstoke, Hants, RG21 2XS ENGLAND. Weekly.

Fairly technical, for the working scientist. Largely short articles on the latest developments in various scientific fields, with occasional longer articles, usually in geology or biology.

612. NEW ENVIRONMENT BULLETIN, c/o H. Schwarzlander, 270 Fenway Drive, Syracuse, NY 13224.

613. NEW SCIENTIST, IPC Magazines Ltd., King's Reach Tower, Stamford Street, London SE1 9LS ENGLAND. Weekly.

Short features and news reports on current events and changes in the world of science and technology, and the impacts of technology on society. Not heavily technical.

614. NORTHWEST TECHNOCRAT, 7531 Greenwood Avenue North, Seattle, WA 98103.

615. NUCLEAR TIMES, Friends of the Earth, 9 Poland Street, London W1V 3DG ENGLAND.

616. OIL AND GAS JOURNAL, Petroleum Publishing Co., P.O. Box 1260, Tulsa, OK 74101. Weekly.

Covers oil and gas production, exploration and processing. Also reports on general energy questions, energy policies and current events in energy.

617. PEOPLE'S ENERGY DIGEST, P.O. Box 423, Lawrence, Kansas 66044.

Energy conservation, efficiency, self-sufficiency and alternatives.

618. THE PHYSICS TEACHER, American Institute of Physics, 335 East 45th Street, New York, NY 10017. Monthly, September-May.

619.   POPULAR SCIENCE, 380 Madison Avenue, New York, NY 10017.
       Monthly.

       General readership, industrial ideas and adventures in
       alternative energy.

620.   PROFESSIONAL ENGINEER, National Society of Professional
       Engineers, 2029 K Street NW, Washington, D.C. 20006
       Monthly.

       Professional-technical journal for the graduate engineer
       and those preparing for careers in engineering.

621.   PROGRESS IN ENERGY AND COMBUSTION SCIENCE, Pergamon Press,
       Fairview Park, Elmsford, NY 10523. Quarterly.

       An international review journal on scientific and
       technological developments, for the professional-tech-
       nical reader.

622.   PUBLIC INTEREST, 10 East 53rd Street, New York, NY 10022.
       Quarterly.

       Economics, politics and sociology, major trends and
       recent developments.

623.   PUBLIC POWER, American Public Power Association, 2600 Virginia
       Avenue NW, Washington, D.C. 20037. Bi-monthly.

       Focus on public owned utilities, with articles on power
       supply, rates and energy alternatives. January-February
       issue includes a directory of all municipal and public
       utility districts and their associations.

624.   PUBLIC UTILITIES FORTNIGHTLY, Suite 500, 1828 L Street NW,
       Washington, D.C. 20036. Bi-weekly.

       Articles on energy policy, supply and demand and other
       energy developments of interest to those dealing with
       public utilities.

625.   RESOURCES, Resources for the Future, 1755 Massachusetts Ave-
       nue NW, Washington, D.C. 20036. 3/year.

       Social science and technology articles on energy, futures,
       impacts and resources by leaders in various fields

626.   RURAL ELECTRIFICATION, National Rural Electric Cooperative
       Association, 2000 Florida Avenue NW, Washington, D.C.
       20009. Monthly.

       Activities of rural electric cooperatives. July issue
       includes a directory of all U.S. rural electric coopera-
       tives.

627.   SCIENCE, American Association for the Advancement of Science,
       1515 Massachusetts Avenue NW, Washington, D.C. 20005.
       Weekly.

Reports on academic research and on political and economic events of concern to scientists. College and up readership.

628. SCIENCE ACTIVITIES, Heldref Publications, 4000 Albemarle Street NW, Washington, D.C. 20016. Bi-monthly.

629. SCIENCE AND CHILDREN, National Science Teachers Association, 1742 Connecticut Avenue NW, Washington, D.C. 20009. 8/year, September-May.

630. SCIENCE AND GOVERNMENT REPORT, P.O. Box 6226A, NW Station Washington, D.C. 20015.

An independent bulletin on developments in government science policy.

631. SCIENCE DIGEST, Hearst Corporation, 224 West 57th Street, New York, NY 10019. Monthly.

General science articles for the non-technical reader.

632. SCIENCE FOR THE PEOPLE, 897 Main Street, Cambridge, MA 02139.

633. SCIENCE DIMENSION, National Research Council of Canada, Ottawa, Ontario K1A OR6 CANADA. 6/year.

Science articles for a general readership, with a Canadian orientation. Articles in English and French.

634. SCIENCE FORUM: A CANADIAN JOURNAL OF SCIENCE AND TECHNOLOGY, University of Toronto Press, Toronto, Ontario M5S 1A6 CANADA. Bi-Monthly.

Interdisciplinary science magazine for a college-level readership.

635. SCIENCE TEACHER, National Science Teachers Association, 1742 Connecticut Avenue NW, Washington, D.C. 20009. Monthly, September-May.

For the secondary-school science teacher.

636. THE SCIENCES, New York Academy of Sciences, 2 East 63rd Street, New York, NY 10021.

Interdisciplinary, with articles in many scientific and related fields.

637. SCIENTIFIC AMERICAN, 415 Madison Avenue, New York, NY 10017. Monthly.

Not heavily technical, comprehensive, for high school graduates though qualified younger readers can use it. Illustrated.

638. SELF RELIANCE. Institute for Local Self-Reliance, 1717 18th

Street NW, Washington, D.C. 20009. Bi-monthly.

Research and projects to make neighborhoods and communities self-reliant in many ways, including energy.

639. SIERRA CLUB BULLETIN, 1050 Mills Tower, San Franciso, CA 94104. 10/year.

Focus on environmental quality, opposition to energy waste and nuclear power.

640. SMALL FARMER'S JOURNAL, P.O. Box 197, Junction City, OR 97448. Quarterly.

Non-mechanized family farming, including animal-powered farm machinery.

641. SOCIAL SCIENCE QUARTERLY, University of Texas Press, P.O. Box 7819, Austin, TX 78712.

Scholarly articles in economics, political science, sociology, management, business and history.

642. STATE GOVERNMENT, Council of State Governments, Iron Words Pike, Lexington, KY 40511. Quarterly.

Policy, planning and legislative concerns of state governments, discussion of model legislation.

643. SURVEY RESEARCH, Survey Research Laboratory, University of Illinois, 414 David Kinley Hall, Urbana, IL 61801. 3 or 4/year.

Describes current and forthcoming social science research projects and publications on research methology.

644. TECHNICAL EDUCATION NEWS, McGraw-Hill Book Co., 330 West 42nd Street, New York, NY 10036.

645. TECHNOLOGY AND CULTURE, University of Chicago Press, 5801 Ellis Avenue, Chicago, IL 60637. Quarterly.

646. TECHNOLOGY REVIEW, Massachusetts Institute of Technology, Room E 19-430, Cambridge, MA 02139. 8/year.

Semi-technical magazine for college-level readers in engineering and the sciences.

647. THIS MAGAZINE, Suite 408, 56 Esplanade Street East, Toronto, Ontario M5E 1A8 CANADA. Bi-monthly.

Canadian education, politics and culture.

648. TODAY'S EDUCATION, National Education Association, 1201 16th Street, Washington, D.C. 20036. Bi-monthly, September-April.

For primary and secondary teachers, with information on

materials and trends in current education.

649. URBAN AFFAIRS QUARTERLY, Sage Publications, Inc., 275 South
Beverly Drive, Beverly Hills, CA 90212. Quarterly.

Scholarly journal on the concerns of cities, city policy-
makers and urban dwellers.

650. URBAN EDUCATION, Sage Publications, Inc., 275 South Beverly
Drive, Beverly Hills, CA 90212. Quarterly.

651. VIRGINIA ENERGY REVIEW, State Energy Office, 823 East Main
Street, Richmond, VA 23219. Monthly.

652. VITAL SPEECHES OF THE DAY, City News Publishing Co., P.O. Box
606, Southold, NY 11971. Semi-monthly.

Reproduces the text of speeches by leading figures in
government, economics, business and education.

653. WATER POLLUTION CONTROL FEDERATION JOURNAL, 3900 Wisconsin
Avenue NW, Washington, D.C. 20016. Monthly.

654. WEEKLY GOVERNMENT ABSTRACTS: ENERGY, National Technical
Information Service, P.O. Box 1553, Springfield, VA
22161.

Abstracts of results and access information on all aspects
of nonclassified federally funded energy research.

655. WORKING PAPERS FOR A NEW SOCIETY, Institute for Policy Studies,
1520 New Hampshire Avenue NW, Washington, D.C. 20036.

656. WORLD OIL, P.O. Box 2608, Houston, TX 77001. Monthly, semi-
monthly in February and August.

657. YALE SCIENTIFIC MAGAZINE, 244-A Yale Station, New Haven, CT
06520. 7/year.

Alternative Energy and Energy Self-Sufficiency Periodicals

658. APPROPRIATE TECHNOLOGY, IT Publications, 9 King Street,
      London WC2 8HN ENGLAND. Quarterly.

      Technical journal on appropriate technology for devel-
      oping countries, though most information could be ap-
      plied on small-scale basis in over-developed countries.

659. COEVOLUTION QUARTERLY, P.O. Box 428, Sausalito, CA 94965.

      Successor to the WHOLE EARTH CATALOG. Articles and
      book reviews on energy alternatives (solar, wind, etc.),
      and energy conservation.

660. COMPOST SCIENCE: JOURNAL OF WASTE RECYCLING, Rodale Press,
      Inc., 33 East Minor Street, Emmaus, PA 18049.
      Bi-monthly.

      Articles on methane 'and other resource recovery tech-
      niques.

661. CONSERVER SOCIETY NEWS, 512 Wilfred Lavigne Boulevard,
      Aylmer, Quebec L0H 3W3 CANADA.

      Articles and news items on appropriate technology and
      renewable energy in Canada.

662. COUNTRYSIDE, 312 Portland Road, Highway 19 East, Waterloo,
      WI 53594. Monthly.

      For small farmers in North America, includes alternative
      energy information.

663. DOING IT! A MAGAZINE OF PRACTICAL ALTERNATIVES FOR HUMANIZING
      CITY LIFE, P.O. Box 303, Worthington, OH 43085.
      Bi-monthly.

      City self-sufficiency and conservation in all areas,
      including energy.

664. ENERGIES, Solar Energy Society of America, P.O. Box 4264
      Torrance, CA 90510. 6/year.

      Articles on solar and related energy knowledge and man-
      agement, exploring new ideas and life styles.

665. FAMILY FOOD GARDEN, P.O. Box 1014, Grass Valley, CA 95945.
      10/year.

      Newspaper format magazine for the home and family

gardener. Regular column on solar energy and family
food production, features in other energy areas.

666. FARMSTEAD, P.O. Box 392, Blue Hill, ME 04614.

For gardeners and small farmers. Focus on conservation
and energy alternatives.

667. GEOTHERMAL ENERGY, 18014 Sherman Way #169, Reseda, CA 91335.

668. GEOTHERMAL RESOURCES COUNCIL BULLETIN, P.O. Box 1033, Davis,
CA 95616.

669. GEOTHERMICS, Pergamon Press, Fairview Park, Elmsford, NY
10523. Quarterly.

Technical-scholarly journal on geothermal energy and
technology.

670. THE GEYSER. P.O. Box 1525, Beverly Hills, CA 90213. Bi-
weekly.

News and articles on geothermal heating and geothermal
energy.

671. HARROWSMITH, Camden East, Ontario K0K 1J0 CANADA. Bi-monthly.

Focus on country living and gardening in cold climates,
particularly Canada and the northern United States.
Articles on energy alternatives and conservation, special Canadian features.

672. INTERNATIONAL JOURNAL OF HYDROGEN ENERGY, Pergamon Press, Inc.,
Fairview Park, Elmsford, NY 10523. Quarterly.

Technical journal sponsored by the International Association for Hydrogen Energy, dealing with theory and
applications of hydrogen energy.

673. JOURNAL OF THE NEW ALCHEMISTS, New Alchemy Institute, P.O.
Box 432, Woods Hole, MA 02543.

Energy alternatives and conservation, low-impact lifestyles.

674. MOTHER EARTH NEWS, P.O. Box 70, Hendersonville, NC 28739.
Bi-monthly.

Articles on alternative energy, ecology, doing more with
less. Research reports on solar energy, wind power,
biogas, etc. Experiments in new modes and methods of
energy production and conservation. "Energy Flashes"
column reports recent events, lists books and meetings
in energy field. Focus on energy self-sufficiency.

675. NATURAL ENERGY, Conservation Tools and Technology, Ltd.,
143 Maple Road, Surbiton, Surrey KT6 4BH ENGLAND.

676. NATURAL LIFE, Box 640, Jarvis, Ontario NOA 1J0 CANADA.
      Monthly.

      Journal of natural living and appropriate technology,
      including articles on wood heat, solar appliances,
      solar heating, wind power and heat pumps.

677. NEW EARTH TIMES, P.O. Box 252, Winchester, MA 01890.

678. ORGANIC GARDENING AND FARMING, Rodale Press, 33 East Minor
      Street, Emmaus, PA 18049. Monthly.

      Regular features on energy conservation and alter-
      natives. Lists of meetings include some on energy.
      Also has book reviews and ads for books and equipment.

679. PRACTICAL SELF-SUFFICIENCY, Broad Leys Jouse, Widdington,
      Saffron Walden, Essex CB11 3SP ENGLAND.

680. RAIN: JOURNAL OF APPROPRIATE TECHNOLOGY, 2270 N.W. Irving,
      Portland, OR 97210. Monthly.

      Information access journal and reference network.
      Reports on current projects, groups, events and
      publications.

681. SOLAR AGE, Rt. 515, Box 288, Vernon, NJ 07462. Monthly.

      Coverage of latest information and techniques in solar
      energy and wind power.

682. SOLAR ENERGY, c/o R.W. Klein, Smithsonian Radiation
      Biology Laboratory, 12441 Parklawn Drive, Rockville,
      MD 20852.

      Journal of the International Solar Energy Society.
      Professional-technical.

683. SOLAR ENERGY, Pergamon Press, Fairview Park, Elmsford, NY
      10523. Bi-monthly.

      Technical journal, mainly for the advanced reader
      in the sciences or social sciences.

684. SOLAR ENERGY DIGEST, P.O. Box 17776, San Diego, CA 92117.
      Monthly.

685. SOLAR ENERGY INTELLIGENCE REPORT, P.O. Box 1067, Silver
      Spring, MD 20910. Bi-weekly.

      Comprehensive reporting on federal issues, current
      events, budgets, codes and laws.

686. SOLAR ENGINEERING, Solar Engineering Publishers, Inc.,
      8435 North Stemmons Freeway, Suite 880, Dallas, TX
      75247. Monthly.

      Semi-technical publication of the Solar Energy

Industries Association. Reader inquiry service, manufacturers' listings.

687. SOLAR TECHNOLOGY REPORT, EIP, 2132 Fordem Avenue, Madison, WI 53701. Monthly.

688. SOLAR UTILIZATION NEWS, Alternative Energy Institute, P.O. Box 3100, Estes Park, CO 80517. Monthly.

News, patents and publications in solar energy.

689. SUNWORLD, Sunworld-International Solar Energy Society, 320 Vassar Avenue, Berkeley, CA 94708. Quarterly.

Published by the International Solar Energy Society, covers solar technology, design and engineering.

690. SYNERGY, P.O. Box 4790 Grand Central Station, New York, NY 10017. Semi-annual, January, July.

Directory of energy alternatives, listing books, pamphlets, government publications, articles, current research, manufacturers and distributors of equipment. Discusses solar energy, geothermal and other steam power, wind power, biogas, electrical energy, water power and various modes of energy storage.

691. TOTAL LIFESTYLE: THE MAGAZINE OF NATURAL LIVING, P.O. Box 1137-N, Harrison, Arkansas, 72601. Monthly.

Energy conservation, solar energy and wind power.

692. UNDERCURRENTS, 275 Finchley Road, London, N.W. 3, ENGLAND.

Alternative technology, especially British.

693. WIND POWER DIGEST, P.O. Box 489, Bristol, IN 46507.

News and know-how on wind energy. Plans, research reports, etc.

694. WOOD BURNING QUARTERLY, 8009 34th Avenue South, Minneapolis, MN 55420.

All aspects of wood heat, with articles on energy conservation, solar energy and wind power.

695. WOOD HEAT JOURNAL, Room MN7, Box 2302, Norwalk, CT 06851.

Wood lot management, heating and cooking with wood.

696. WOOD'N ENERGY, 5 South State Street, Concord, NH 03301. Quarterly.

News on wood heating, forest land management, energy conservation and related subjects, with bibliographies on subjects covered.

Newsletters

697. ACORN, Governors State University, Park Forest South, IL
      60466. Bi-monthly.

      Newsletter of the Midwest Energy Alternatives Network.
      Essays, field reports, information sources, conference
      listings, directory of Midwest energy activities.
      Includes national and world information with a bearing
      on energy events in the Midwest.

698. ADVANCED SOLAR ENERGY TECHNOLOGY NEWSLETTER, 1609 West
      Windrose, Phoenix, AZ 85029.

699. AIR AND WATER POLLUTION REPORT, Business Publishers, Inc.,
      P.O. Box 1067, Blair Station, Silver Spring, MD 20910.
      Weekly.

700. ALTERNATIVE ENERGY SOURCES, 143 Maple Road, Surbiton,
      Surrey, KT6 4BH ENGLAND.

      Quarterly newsletter on alternatives to conventional
      energy systems.

701. ALTERNATIVE SOURCES OF ENERGY, Rt 2, Box 90A, Milaca,
      MN 56353. Bi-monthly.

      Magazine-format newsletter on small scale environ-
      mentally appropriate energy systems and decentralized
      energy production. Contains how-to information and
      listings of information sources.

702. CHINA EXCHANGE NEWSLETTER, 2101 Constitution Avenue,
      Washington, D.C. 20418.

      Published by the National Academy of Sciences Com-
      mittee on Scholarly Communication with the People's
      Republic of China.

703. CONCERNED E.E.S., P.O. Box 19, Massapequa Park, NY 11762.

      Newsletter of the Concerned Electronics Engineers.

704. THE CONCRETE OPPOSITION, Highway Action Coalition, 1346
      Connecticut Avenue NW, Room 731, Washington, D.C. 20036.

      Mass transit and alternatives to the automobile.

705. CONSERVATION FOUNDATION LETTER, Conservation Foundation,
      1717 Massachusetts Avenue NW, Washington, D.C. 20036.

Monthly.

706. CONSTRUCTIVE CITIZEN PARTICIPATION, Development Press, Box 1016, Oakville, Ontario CANADA. Quarterly.

Newsletter containing information, reports etc. on citizen participation in government planning in the U.S. and Canada.

707. CRITICAL MASS, P.O. Box 1538, Washington, D.C. 20013. Monthly.

Newsletter of the Citizens Movement for Safe and Efficient Energy. Articles on energy policy and politics, current energy events, with particular focus on nuclear power and risks.

708. CURRENT SCIENCE, American Education Publications, Science Division, 245 Long Hill Road, Middletown, CT 06457. Weekly during the school year.

Newspaper on current developments in science and science education.

709. EARTHMIND NEWSLETTER, 5246 Boyer Road, Mariposa, CA 95338.

How-to information on "low technology" home-scale energy systems, with particular focus on wind-electric systems.

710. THE ELEMENTS, The Transnational Institute, 1901 Q Street NW, Washington, D.C. 20009.

Newsletter on world resources and related topics, including the nuclear power debate.

711. ENERGY, American Institute of Architects, 1735 New York Avenue, Washington, D.C. 20006. 10/year.

Newsletter on energy and the built environment, with emphasis on energy-efficient buildings.

712. ENERGY ACTION: NEWS AND VIEWS, Citizens for Energy Conservation and Solar Development, P.O. Box 49173, Los Angeles, CA 90049.

Newsletter devoted to solar energy promotion and energy conservation.

713. ENERGY CONSERVATION REPORT, Energy Conservation Project, Environmental Law Institute, 1346 Connecticut Avenue NW, Washington, D.C. 20036.

Newsletter of a research project on energy conservation laws and regulations at state and local levels. Discusses existing and proposed conservation measures.

714. THE ENERGY DAILY, (Formerly WEEKLY ENERGY REPORT),

1239 National Press Building, Washington, D.C. 20045.
Monday-Friday.

A newsletter on current events in energy and energy
policy, with particular focus on the actions of the
U.S. government. Also covers international energy
events, with editors in Brussels, London and Ottawa.

715.   ENERGY LEGISLATION, Council of State Governments Energy
       Project, Iron Works Pike, Lexington, KY 40511.
       Bi-weekly.

       Lists energy legislation introduced and enacted
       in the states.

716.   ENERGY PERSPECTIVES, Battelle Memorial Institute, 505
       King Avenue, Columbus, OH 43201. Monthly.

       Newsletter of the Battelle Energy Program. Covers
       energy issues and current energy news.

717.   ENERGY STUDIES, Center for Energy Studies, University of
       Texas At Austin, Engineering Science Building 143,
       Austin, TX 78712. Bi-monthly.

718.   ENVIRONMENT, 560 Trinity Avenue, St. Louis, MO 63130.
       10/year.

       Official publication of the Scientists Institute for
       Public.Information. Articles on environmental problems
       and solutions for a general audience. Unbiased
       scientific information for informed consent on politi-
       cal and social issues.

719.   ENVIRONMENT ACTION BULLETIN, Rodale Press, 33 East Minor
       Street, Emmaus, PA 18049. Bi-weekly.

       Newsletter focusing on environmental protection and
       conservation, low-impact and "organic" living.

720.   ENVIRONMENTAL CONSERVATION, 15 Chemin F. Lehmann, 1218
       Grand-Saconnex, Geneva, SWITZERLAND.

       International journal exposing and countering environ-
       mental deterioration from population pressure and
       unwise technology.

721.   ENVIRONMENTAL EDUCATION REPORT, Environmental Educators
       Inc., 1621 Connecticut Avenue NW, Washington, D.C.
       20009. Monthly.

       Newsletter with articles, book reports, current
       events, conferences, legislation, etc., in the environ-
       ment and environmental education.

722.   HIGH COUNTRY NEWS, Box K, Larder, WY 82520. Bi-weekly.

Reports on renewable energy action in the Rocky Mountain states.

723. IOWA ENERGY BULLETIN, Energy Policy Council, 300 Fourth Street, Des Moines, IA 50319. Monthly.

724. JUST ECONOMICS, Movement for Economic Justice, 1611 Connecticut Avenue NW, Washington, D.C. 20009.

Monthly newsletter for community organizers. Frequent articles on utility issues, including public power.

725. LAND NEWSLETTER, League Against Nuclear Dangers, Route 5, Box 176, Stevens Point, WI 54481.

Information and articles on nuclear power and nuclear risks.

726. NATURAL HAZARDS OBSERVER, Natural Hazards Research and Applications Information Center, Institute of Behavioral Science #6, University of Colorado, Boulder, CO 80309. Quarterly.

Weather, earthquakes, etc. Occasional articles on nuclear power and risks, errects of natural hazards on power systems, etc.

727. NECNP NEWSLETTER, New England Coalition Against Nuclear Pollution, P.O. Box 637, Brattleboro, VT 05301.

Nuclear energy, risks and impacts. Political and policy news related to nuclear energy.

728. NEWSLETTER ON SCIENCE, TECHNOLOGY AND HUMAN VALUES, Aiken Computation Laboratory 231, Harvard University, Cambridge, MA 02138. Quarterly during the academic year.

Impacts of technology, science and social issues, equity and ethics, news items and communications.

729. NORTH COUNTRY ANVIL, P.O. Box 37, Millville, MN 55957.

730. NOT MAN APART, Friends of the Earth, 529 Commercial, San Francisco, CA 94111. Monthly.

Articles on alternative energy and energy conservation. Column, "The Nuclear Blowdown", discusses risks and impacts. Anti-nuclear power.

731. NUCLEAR OPPONENTS, Citizens Energy Council, P.O. Box 285, Allendale, NJ 07401.

732. OREGON ENERGY NEWSLETTER, Oregon Department of Energy, 528 Cottage Street, Salem, OR 97310.

733. PEOPLE AND ENERGY, Center for Science in the Public
     Interest, 1757 S Street NW, Washington, D.C. 20009.
     Monthly.

     Articles and features on what citizens are and can
     be doing to influence local and national energy
     policy decisions. Information on oil, natural gas,
     nuclear power, conservation and related issues.
     Focuses on the social, environmental and economic
     aspects of local, regional and national energy policy
     development.

734. THE POWER LINE, Environmental Action Foundation, 724
     Dupont Circle Building, Washington, D.C. 20036.
     Monthly.

     Newsletter for utility activists, with current news
     on the electric utility industry, emphasizing citizen
     challenges to utility companies.

735. SCIENCE EDUCATION NEWS, AAAS Office of Science Education,
     1776 Massachusetts Avenue NW, Washington, D.C. 20036.

     Newsletter on materials and programs for science
     teachers, published by the American Association for
     the Advancement of Science.

736. SCIENCE NEWS, Science Service, Inc., 1719 N Street NW,
     Washington, D.C. 20036. Weekly.

     General interest articles in all science areas.

737. STPP NEWS, Program in Science, Technology and Public
     Policy, Department of Political Science, Purdue
     University, West Lafayette, IN 47907.

     Interdisciplinary newsletter on science, technology,
     public policy and society. Includes book reviews,
     lists of congressional publications, and meeting
     notices.

738. SOCIAL IMPACT ASSESSMENT, C.P. Wolf, 441 N Street SW,
     Washington, D.C. 20024. Monthly.

     Newsletter including news update, course outline
     and bibliographies.

739. SOLAR ENERGY INDUSTRY REPORT, 1001 Connecticut Avenue,
     Washington, D.C. 20036. Weekly.

740. SOLAR ENERGY WASHINGTON LETTER, 1001 Connecticut Avenue,
     Washington, D.C. 20036. Weekly.

741. SPARK, 475 Riverside Drive, New York, NY 10027.

     Newsletter of the Committee for Social Responsibility
     in Engineering.

742. SSRS REVIEW, Society for Social Responsibility in Science, 86 Lennox Hill Station, New York, NY 10021.

743. SUN PAPER, New Mexico Solar Energy Association, P.O. Box 2004, Santa Fe, NM 87501. Bi-monthly.

    Newsletter on solar heating, cooling, equipment and solar energy systems.

744. SUN TIMES, Alternative Energy Resources Organization, 435 Stapleton Street, Billings, Montana 59101. Monthly.

    Newsletter on energy alternatives, solar, wind and biogas. News features, book listings and reviews, practical information on renewable energy.

745. SUNERGY! NEWSLETTER, P.O. Box 643, La Quinita, CA 92253.

746. SUNPAPER: NEWSLETTER AND JOURNAL, New Mexico Solar Energy Association, P.O. Box 2004, Santa Fe, NM 87501.

    Most of America's direct-solar pioneers and experts belong to NMSEA.

747. TENNESSEE ENERGY NEWSLETTER, Tennessee Energy Office, 250 Capitol Hill Building, Nashville, TN 37219.

748. TEXAS ENERGY REPORT, Governor's Energy Advisory Council, 411 West 13th Street, Austin, TX 78701. Monthly.

749. TRANET, c/o William Ellis, 7410 Vernon Square Drive, Alexandria, VA 22306.

    Newsletter-directory of the Transnational Network for Appropriate/Alternative Technologies. Lists books, centers, programs, resources and current alternative energy news. Also offers a calendar of energy current events, conferences and meetings.

750. VERMONT ENERGY NEWSLETTER, State Energy Office, State Office Building, Montpelier, VT 05602.

751. VIRGINIA ENERGY NEWS, State Energy Office, 823 East Main Street, Richmond, VA 23219. Weekly.

752. WASHINGTON ENERGY NEWSLETTER, Department of Emergency Services, 4220 East Martin Way, Olympia, WA 98504.

753. WEEKLY BULLETIN, Environmental Study Conference, 2456 Rayburn House Office Building, U.S. House of Representatives, Washington, D.C. 20515.

754. WORLD ENVIRONMENT REPORT, United Nations Association of the United States, 345 East 46th Street, New York, NY 10017. Bi-weekly.

Newsletter of the U.S.Association of the U.S. Center for
International Environment Information.

NON-GOVERNMENT ORGANIZATIONS, ASSOCIATIONS AND COMPANIES

NON-GOVERNMENT ORGANIZATIONS, ASSOCIATIONS AND COMPANIES

Introduction

Many professional societies, national, regional and local groups are interested in energy. Many organizations specialize in some energy area. Environmental groups often have energy information. Some organizations specializing in alternative energy have been listed in the section on energy alternatives.

This section is devoted to organizations not part of a governmental unit. Companies, professional societies, citizens groups, lobbying and informational groups and some non-profit research organizations are included.

755. AIR POLLUTION CONTROL ASSOCIATION, 4400 Fifth Avenue, Pittsburgh, PA 15213.

756. ALLIANCE FOR ENVIRONMENTAL EDUCATION, INC., Department of Public Education, 126 Langdon Street, Madison, WI 53702.

   A group of organizations working to improve school and public education at all levels on environmental protection and quality.

757. AMERICAN ASSOCIATION FOR THE ADVANCEMENT OF SCIENCE, 1515 Massachusetts Avenue NW, Washington, D.C. 20005.

   Works to increase public understanding of science and scientific work, and assist scientists and science teachers. Publishes science education materials on levels from kindergarten through post-graduate, and SCIENCE, a weekly journal.

758. AMERICAN ASSOCIATION OF PETROLEUM GEOLOGISTS, P.O. Box 979, Tulsa, OK 74101.

759. AMERICAN CONSERVATION, INC., 30 Rockefeller Plaza, New York, NY 10020.

   Non-profit organization for the promotion of conservation knowledge and the wise use of our natural resources.

760. AMERICAN GAS ASSOCIATION, 1515 Wilson Boulevard, Arlington, VA 22209.

   Information association of privately owned segments of the natural gas industry. Publishes the AMERICAN GAS ASSOCIATION MONTHLY, and GAS FACTS, an annual compilation of information on the state of natural gas production and distribution.

761. AMERICAN INSTITUTE OF ARCHITECTS, 1735 New York Avenue NW, Washington, D.C. 20006.

Building design for energy conservation, promotion of construction and remodeling to produce energy-efficient buildings. A significant publication is "A Nation of Energy-Efficient Buildings by 1990."

762. AMERICAN INSTITUTE OF PHYSICS, 335 East 45th Street, New York, NY 10017.

Publishes THE PHYSICS TEACHER, a journal for secondary school and college teachers of physics.

763. AMERICAN INSTITUTE OF PLANNERS, 1776 Massachusetts Avenue NW, Washington, D.C. 20036.

A national professional society for urban and regional planners, most of whom work for local, state and national government organizations. Concerned with economic, social and physical development issues.

764. AMERICAN MINING CONGRESS, 1100 Ring Building, Washington, D.C. 20036.

765. AMERICAN NUCLEAR SOCIETY, 244 East Ogden Avenue, Hinsdale, IL 60521.

Annual catalog of publications on nuclear power, power plants and impacts.

766. AMERICAN PETROLEUM INSTITUTE, 1801 K Street NW, Washington, D.C. 20006.

767. AMERICAN POLITICAL SCIENCE ASSOCIATION, 1527 New Hampshire Avenue NW, Washington, D.C. 20036.

Publishes SETUPS, a series of instructional materials for college undergraduates, including one on energy.

768. AMERICAN PUBLIC POWER ASSOCIATION, 2600 Virginia Avenue NW, Suite 212, Washington, D.C. 20037.

An informational organization of local publicly owned electric utilities, with many publications, including the magazine PUBLIC POWER. Packets on solar energy, energy conservation and public power.

769. AMERICAN SOCIETY OF AGRICULTURAL ENGINEERS, 2950 Niles Road, St. Joseph, MI 49085.

National professional society for agricultural engineers. Educational efforts on the college level, provides publications and educational information for its members.

770. AMERICAN SOCIETY OF PLANNING OFFICIALS, 1313 East Sixtieth Street, Chicago, IL 60637.

Organization of persons working toward a better planned environment, composed of planners, elected officials, developers, teachers and students.

771. AMERICAN WATER RESOURCES ASSOCIATION, 206 East University Avenue, Urbana, IL 61801.

Interdisciplinary organization for research, planning and management in water resources areas. Membership includes scientists and social scientists.

772. APPROPRIATE TECHNOLOGY PROJECT, Volunteers in Asia, Box 4543, Stanford, CA 94305.

Publishes APPROPRIATE TECHNOLOGY SOURCEBOOK, listing plans abailable from many AT design centers on small-scale and low-impact technology.

773. ASSOCIATION FOR THE STUDY OF MAN-ENVIRONMENT RELATIONS, INC., P.O. Box 57, Orangeburg, NY 10962.

774. ATOMIC INDUSTRIAL FORUM, INC., 475 Park Avenue South, New York, NY 10016.

International organization for the promotion of peaceful applications of nuclear energy in business and industry.

775. BATTELLE MEMORIAL INSTITUTE, 505 King Avenue, Columbus, OH 43201.

Conducts research on energy use, production and conservation. A large energy research program on coal, solar, nuclear and geothermal power. Publishes the monthly newsletter ENERGY PERSPECTIVES.

776. BIOMASS ENERGY INSTITUTE, 310-870 Cambridge Street, Winnipeg, Manitoba R3M 3H5 CANADA.

777. BUREAU OF NATIONAL AFFAIRS, INC., Environmental and Safety Research Service, 1231 25th Street NW, Washington, D.C. 20037.

Subscribers to ENERGY USERS REPORT may use these information-research facilities. For a fee, BNA staff will perform special projects, including reports, legislative analysis, document searches, presentation of seminars, etc., in the energy field.

778. BUREAU OF SOCIAL SCIENCE RESEARCH, INC., 1990 M Street NW, Washington, D.C. 20036.

Annotated bibliography of Reports and Staff Member Publications, with annual cumulative revisions. Analyses on attitudes and economics of energy consumption, attitudes and behavior relating to transportation, and concern with population and environmental questions. Examples: "Energy Consumers' Awareness and Preferences in New Hampshire: A Comparative Assessment;" "Attitudes Toward Metrorail in the Washington Area."

779. BUSINESS AND PROFESSIONAL PEOPLE FOR THE PUBLIC INTEREST, 109 North Dearborn, Chicago, IL 60602.

780. CALIFORNIANS FOR NUCLEAR SAFEGUARDS, 405 Shrader Street, San Francisco, CA 94117.

Information and organizing for nuclear safety, attention to nuclear risks and impacts.

781. CENTER FOR CALIFORNIA PUBLIC AFFAIRS, 226 West Foothill Boulevard, Box 30, Claremont, CA 91711.

Books and information, including the Environmental Studies Series for the college and professional reader, and the Who's Doing What series for the high school, college and educated lay reader.

782. CENTER FOR ENERGY INFORMATION, 340 East 51st Street, New York, NY 10022.

Alternate sources of energy.

783. CENTER FOR NEW CORPORATE PRIORITIES, 1516 Westwood Boulevard, Suite 202, Los Angeles, CA 90024.

784. CENTER FOR SCIENCE IN THE PUBLIC INTEREST, Box E, 1757 S Street NW, Washington, D.C. 20009.

Publications on citizen energy action, laws and energy education. Practical information on low-impact lifestyles, reprints from the monthly newsletter PEOPLE AND ENERGY.

785. CENTER FOR THE STUDY OF RESPONSIVE LAW, P.O. Box 19367, Washington, D.C. 20036.

786. CENTRAL ATLANTIC ENVIRONMENTAL CENTER, 1717 Massachusetts Avenue NW, Washington, D.C. 20036.

Regional environment information center for Maryland, Virginia, Delaware and the District of Columbia. Publishes a monthly newsletter.

787. CHARLES F. KETTERING FOUNDATION, 5335 Far Hills Avenue, Dayton, OH 45429.

Publishes NEW WAYS, a quarterly report on Kettering research on many subjects including energy.

788. CITIZENS ENERGY COALITION, 5395 East 38th Street, Indianapolis, IN 46218.

789. CITIZENS FOR CLEAN AIR, 502 Madison Avenue, New York, NY 10022.

790. CITIZENS MOVEMENT FOR SAFE AND EFFICIENT ENERGY, P.O. Box 1538, Washington, D.C. 20013.

    Information on nuclear power and nuclear risks. Concentration on alternatives to nuclear energy.

791. COALITION OF CONCERNED UTILITY USERS, P.O. Box 10006, Columbus, OH 43201.

792. COMMISSION ON INTERNATIONAL RELATIONS, U.S. National Academy of Sciences, 2101 Constitution Avenue NW, Washington, D.C. 20418.

    Publishes a series of reports, including ENERGY FOR RURAL DEVELOPMENT, METHANE GENERATION, and APPROPRIATE TECHNOLOGIES FOR DEVELOPING COUNTRIES.

793. COMMITTEE FOR ENVIRONMENTAL INFORMATION, 438 North Skinker Boulevard, St. Louis, MO 63130.

    Organization of scientists and citizens concerned with environmental problems and protecting the environment. Originates and distributes instructional aids and information packages for schools, community groups and the news media.

794. COMMITTEE FOR A NONNUCLEAR FUTURE, P.O. Box 924, Tempe, Arizona 85281.

    Organization of educators and other professional people opposed to the construction of nuclear power generating stations.

795. COMMON CAUSE, 2030 M Street NW, Washington, D.C. 20036.

    Studies on energy and industry, links between energy industry and government policy, energy regulation.

796. CONCERN, INC., 2233 Wisconsin Avenue NW, Washington, D.C. 20007.

    Provides consumer education on the environmental impacts of household products and practices, and on energy conservation and alternatives. Publishes a series of consumer guides to environmental and energy issues.

797. CONSERVATION EDUCATION ASSOCIATION, University of Wisconsin-Green Bay, Green Bay, WI 54301.

    Promotes conservation in school and community, from elementary level up. Publishes a quarterly newsletter on conservation education.

798. CONSERVATION FOUNDATION, 1717 Massachusetts Avenue NW,

Washington, D.C. 20036.

Research, information and education on environmental quality for the public and private sectors. Publishes research reports and the monthly CONSERVATION FOUNDATION LETTER.

799. CONSERVER SOCIETY PRODUCTS, LTD., P.O. Box 5516, Station F, Ottawa, Ontario CANADA.

A co-operative company which markets and provides information on appropriate technology equipment. Also conducts research in appropriate technologies.

800. CONSUMER FEDERATION OF AMERICA, Energy Policy Task Force, 1012 14th Street NW, Washington, D.C. 20005.

801. COUNCIL OF PLANNING LIBRARIANS, P.O. Box 229, Monticello, IL 61856.

A group of librarians, faculty, planners, public and private planning organizations and others interested in research problems and in spreading informations pertinent to city and regional planning. Publishes comprehensive Exchange Bibliographies with academic, business, government and citizen-action oriented material. Titles include THE ENERGY SITUATION and ENERGY FOR THE FUTURE.

802. COUNCIL OF STATE GOVERNMENTS, P.O. Box 11910, Lexington, KY 40511.

Research on programs and problems of all states. Has a variety of publications.

803. CURE, Citizens United for Responsible Energy, East Sixth and Grand, Des Moines, IA 50309.

804. EASTERN FEDERATION OF NUCLEAR OPPONENTS AND SAFE ENERGY PROPONENTS, 433 Orlando Avenue, State College, PA 16801.

A coalition of east-coast groups trying to phase out nuclear power. Acts as an information clearing-house and liason between groups in an effort to promote environmentally sound energy sources.

805. EDUCATIONAL FOUNDATION FOR NUCLEAR SCIENCE, Kent Chemical Laboratory, 1020 East 58th Street, Chicago, IL 60637.

Research and publications on the implications of civilian uses of nuclear power, and on impacts of technology on society.

806. ELECTRIC ENERGY ASSOCIATION, 90 Park Avenue, New York, NY 10016.

Represents the privately owned/"investor owned"

electrical utility industry.

807. ELECTRIC POWER RESEARCH INSTITUTE, 3412 Hillview Avenue, P.O. Box 10412, Palo Alto, CA 94304.

808. ENERGY ACTION OF WASHINGTON, P.O. Box 4244, Seattle, WA 98104.

Energy library, lobbying and displays.

809. ENERGY POLICY COUNCIL, 300 Fourth Street, Des Moines, IA 50309.

810. ENERGY PROBE, 43 Queens Park Crescent East, Toronto, Ontario M5S 2C3 CANADA.

Helps groups and individuals across Canada concerned about energy issues. Special interest in long-term solutions to Canadian energy policy issues. Publications on energy conservation, renewable energy and nuclear energy.

811. ENERGY RESEARCH CORPORATION, 6 East Valerio Street, Santa Barbara, CA 93101.

Maintains a library of energy materials and a computerized data base for information searches. Publishes the bi-monthly ENERGY REVIEW.

812. ENERGY RESEARCH INFORMATION SYSTEM, Old West Regional Commission, Fratt Building, Suite 306A, Billings, MT 59101.

Data bank and information clearing-house for ongoing and recently completed energy research in the Old West Region. Lists complete research dating from January 1974, ongoing research from January 1975.

813. ENVIRONMENT INFORMATION CENTER, Energy Reference Department, 292 Madison Avenue, New York, NY 10017.

Publishes many energy indexes and abstracts, including a bi-monthly guide to scientific/technical and socio-economic energy developments. The annual ENERGY INDEX reviews energy events, research and publications in the preceeding year. ENERGY DIRECTORY UPDATE is a guide to factual energy information such as names, addresses and dates, with bi-monthly updates and an annual cumulative index. ENERGY INFORMATION LOCATOR is a guide to information sources. ENERGYLINE, an on-line data base, is the computerized counterpart of ENERGY INFORMATION ABSTRACTS. The Environment Information Center is an excellent source of comprehensive, detailed and up to date energy information.

814. ENVIRONMENTAL ACTION, Room 724, Dupont Circle Building, Washington, D.C. 20036.

Information gathering and lobbying information on energy conservation, solid waste and electric utilities. Aids activist groups in conservation. Publishes film list, bibliography and assorted fact sheets.

815. ENVIRONMENTAL ACTION COALITION, Educational Services, 235 East 49th Street, New York, NY 10017.

816. ENVIRONMENTAL ACTION OF COLORADO, University of Colorado at Denver, 1100 14th Street, Denver, CO 80202.

Projects to increase public awareness of solar energy include: NDF-sponsored solar energy exhibition, and directory of information sources on solar energy.

817. ENVIRONMENTAL LAW INSTITUTE, Suite 614 1326 Connecticut Avenue NW, Washington, D.C. 20036.

Research and information distribution on law and the environment.

818. ENVIRONMENTAL POLICY CENTER, 342 C Street SE, Washington, D.C. 20003.

Concerned with energy policy, land use, strip mining and water resources. Works with local and regional groups to influence environmental policy.

819. ENVIRONMENTAL RESEARCH AND DEVELOPMENT FOUNDATION, Suite 116, 2030 East Speedway, Tucson, AZ 85719.

Publications on social science research related to human welfare, and the relation between environment and human behavior. Some publications have energy-related components.

820. FEDERATION OF AMERICAN SCIENTISTS, 307 Massachusetts Avenue NE, Washington, D.C. 20002.

821. FRIENDS OF THE EARTH, INC., 529 Commercial Street, San Francisco, CA 94111.

Energy conservation and alternatives, opposition to nuclear power, development of less hazardous energy technologies. Affiliates in many foreign countries. Extensive list of publications, including the monthly newsletter, NOT MAN APART.

822. HIGHWAY ACTION COALITION, 1346 Connecticut Avenue NW, Room 731, Washington, D.C. 20036.

A non-profit public interest transportation group, working for mass transit and alternatives to the auto-mobile.

823. HUDSON INSTITUTE, Quaker Ridge Road, Croton-on-Hudson, NY 10520.

A non-profit research center, conducting energy policy

research for government agencies and private corporations. A list of energy-related publications is available.

824. INDEPENDENT PETROLEUM ASSOCIATION OF AMERICA, 1101 16th Street NW, Washington, D.C. 20036.

Grouping of oil and natural gas producers other than the major oil and gas companies.

825. INSTITUTE FOR LOCAL SELF-RELIANCE, 1717 18th Street NW, Washington, D.C. 20009.

Research and development on politically independent, economically self-sustaining and ecologically sound urban communities. Energy especially as related to food production. How-to booklets and charts.

826. INSTITUTE FOR POLICY STUDIES, 1520 New Hampshire Avenue NW, Washington, D.C. 20036.

Publishes WORKING PAPERS FOR A NEW SOCIETY, monthly.

827. INSTITUTE FOR THE FUTURE, 2740 Sand Hill Road, Menlo Park, CA 94025.

Research and publications on energy policy, alternatives and conservation.

828. INTERNATIONAL CITY MANAGEMENT ASSOCIATION, 1140 Connecticut Avenue NW, Washington, D.C. 20036.

Information on urban energy problems and policies.

829. LEAGUE AGAINST NUCLEAR DANGERS, Route 5, Box 176, Stevens Point, WI 54481.

830. LEAGUE OF WOMEN VOTERS OF THE U.S., 1730 M Street NW, Washington, D.C. 20036.

Information on a variety of contemporary issues and on political action for community problem-solving.

831. LEAGUE OF CONSERVATION VOTERS, 324 C. Street SE, Washington, D.C. 20003.

832. METASTASIS, P.O. Box 128, Marblemount, WA 98267.

Mail order access for hard to get appropriate technology publications, particularly useful for foreign publications.

833. MICHIGAN SAFE ENERGY INITIATIVE, Public Interest Research Group in Michigan, 590 Hollister Building, Lansing, MI 48933.

Information and lobbying for alternatives to nuclear power plants.

834. NATIONAL AIR CONSERVATION COMMISSION, American Lung Association, 1740 Broadway, New York, NY 10019.

835. NATIONAL ASSOCIATION FOR ENVIRONMENTAL EDUCATION, P.O. Box 1295, Miami, FL 33143.

836. NATIONAL ASSOCIATION OF CONSERVATION DISTRICTS, 1025 Vermont Avenue NW, Washington, D.C. 20005.

837. NATIONAL ASSOCIATION OF COUNTIES, 1735 New York Avenue NW, Washington, D.C. 20006.

838. NATIONAL ASSOCIATION OF RECYCLING INDUSTRIES, INC., 330 Madison Avenue, New York, NY 10017.

   Information and consulting services on reuse of solid waste materials.

839. NATIONAL COAL ASSOCIATION, Coal Building, 1130 17th Street NW, Washington, D.C. 20036.

840. NATIONAL CONFERENCE OF STATE LEGISLATURES, Office of Science and Technology, Executive Tower Inn, 1405 Curtis Street, Denver, CO 80202.

841. NATIONAL EDUCATION ASSOCIATION, 1201 16th Street NW, Washington, D.C. 20036.

   Publishes TODAY'S EDUCATION, MAN/SOCIETY/TECHNOLOGY, and other periodicals and materials for the elementary and secondary school teacher.

842. NATIONAL GOVERNOR'S CONFERENCE, 1150 17th Street NW, Washington, D.C. 20036.

843. NATIONAL RURAL ELECTRIC COOPERATIVE ASSOCIATION, 2000 Florida Avenue NW, Washington, D.C. 20009.

844. NATIONAL SCIENCE TEACHERS ASSOCIATION, 1742 Connecticut Avenue NW, Washington, D.C. 20009.

   Publishes SCIENCE TEACHER, and SCIENCE AND CHILDREN.

845. NATURAL RESOURCES DEFENSE COUNCIL, INC., 15 West 44th Street, New York, NY 10036.

   Also offices in Washington, D.C. (1710 N Street NW 20036) and Palo Alto, CA (644 Hamilton Avenue 94301). Promotes environmental protection, education and legal action about environmental protection.

846. NATIONAL WATER RESOURCES ASSOCIATION, 897 National Press Building, Washington, D.C. 20004.

847. NORTH AMERICAN COMMITTEE OF NON-GOVERNMENTAL ORGANIZATIONS FOR THE ENVIRONMENT, c/o Glen Leet, 54 Riverside Drive,

New York, NY 10024.

848. POLLUTION PROBE OTTAWA, 53 Queen Street, Suite 54, Ottawa, Ontario K1P 5C5 CANADA.

Booklets on small scale wind and solar energy systems.

849. RAND CORPORATION, 1700 Main Street, Santa Monica, CA 90406.

Analysis of energy policy issues, with a list of reports available from the Publications Department.

850. RESOURCES FOR THE FUTURE, INC., 1755 Massachusetts Avenue NW, Washington, D.C. 20036.

Non-profit organization for research and education in resource conservation, development and use, and the promotion of environmental quality.

851. SCIENCE FOR THE PEOPLE STUDY GROUP, c/o Progressive Technology Company, P.O. Box 20049, Tallahassee, FL 32304.

Information available on study groups and reading lists in many areas of the people's science movement.

852. SCIENTISTS COMMITTEE FOR PUBLIC INFORMATION, 30 East 68th Street, New York, NY 10021.

Information on technical and scientific issues to promote informed decision-making by the general public. Library, newsletter, speakers, technical advice.

853. SIERRA CLUB, 1050 Mills Tower, San Francisco, CA 94104.

Deals with all aspects of the environment and protection of natural resources. Interested in energy conservation and the environmental impacts of energy use.

854. SMITHSONIAN INSTITUTION, Office of International and Environmental Programs, Washington, D.C. 20560.

Research and information on conservation, ecology and environmental issues.

855. UNION OF CONCERNED SCIENTISTS, P.O. Box 289, MIT Branch Station, Cambridge, MA 02139.

Research on the social consequences of advanced technology on society. Publications on the public health, environmental and national security effects of atomic power.

856. UNION CARBIDE CORPORATION, Nuclear Division, P.O. Box Y, Oak Ridge, TN 37830.

A complete file of material on Annual Cycle Energy Systems, energy conservation and efficiency, home heating and cooling. Material developed by Oak Ridge

National Laboratory.

857. WATER POLLUTION CONTROL FEDERATION, 3900 Wisconsin Avenue NW,
     Washington, D.C. 20016.

858. WORLD ENERGY CONFERENCE/CONFERENCE MONDAILE DE L'ENERGIE,
     5 Bury Street, St. James, London SW1Y 6AB ENGLAND.

     A voluntary international group that collects and
     publishes energy data, and holds the World Energy
     Conference every three years.

GOVERNMENT SERVICES

GOVERNMENT SERVICES

Introduction

There are many U.S. government sources with some type of energy information. This covers a wide range of energy modes from conventional sources such as coal and oil through nuclear energy to alternatives such as solar and wind power.

Inquiries should be directed to the public information officer in a department or agency. House and Senate committees have information on legislation, reports of Congressional hearings, etc. Government agencies provide printed material, films, and many other types of useful materials. If you are not sure which agency or department can answer your questions, write or call your nearest Federal Information Center. The FIC will either answer your questions or refer you to the appropriate official or division of the Federal Government.

President Carter's proposed new national energy policy includes a plan to consolidate most Federal government energy agencies under a Department of Energy to be added to the Cabinet. (See the Introduction for a discussion of his plan based on information available at this writing.) Should this occur, the Federal Information Centers will be able to give you data on the new department, its personnel and duties.

This section also contains a listing of energy information sources in Canada, mostly on the national level, which should be particularly helpful to the Canadian student of energy. A new Council of Planning Librarians Bibliography on Canadian energy questions was published in late 1976. (CPL No. 1188, THE CANADIAN ENERGY CRISIS: FIRST SUPPLEMENTARY BIBLIOGRAPHY, compiled by Eric L. Swanick.) This should provide much useful information to those interested in Canada's energy situation. A brief list of United Nations organizations with energy-related responsibilities is also included.

In addition, a list of at least one state government energy information source in each state is included.

Federal Government Agencies and Departments

859.   APPALACHIAN REGIONAL COMMISSION, 1666 Connecticut Avenue NW, Washington, D.C. 20235.

Data and programs for the economic, physical and social development of the 13-state Appalachian region. Includes energy information (particularly on coal) from the region.

860.   CIVIL AERONAUTICS BOARD, 1825 Connecticut Avenue NW, Washington, D.C. 20420.

Promotes and regulates U.S. civil air transportation, and oversees civil air transportation between the U.S. and foreign countries.

861. CONSUMER INFORMATION CENTER, Pueblo, CO 81009.

Distribution center for Federal government publications for the consumer. Information on home energy conservation, insulation, efficient appliances, and many related areas. Many publications also available in Spanish.

862. COUNCIL ON ENVIRONMENTAL QUALITY, 722 Jackson Place NW, Washington, D.C. 20006.

Develops and recommends to the President national policies that further environmental quality. Analyses changes and trends in the national environment. Assesses energy research and development from an environment and conservation standpoint.

863. DEPARTMENT OF AGRICULTURE, 14th Street and Independence Avenue SW, Washington, D.C. 20250.

Handles all agricultural and farm matters, environment and conservation, food and hunger, rural development, conservation, etc. Includes the Economic Research Service, Rural Electrification Administration, Agricultural Research Service and Co-operative Extension Service.

864. DEPARTMENT OF DEFENSE, The Pentagon, Washington, D.C. 20301.

Information on energy as it relates to military and national defense considerations.

865. DEPARTMENT OF COMMERCE, 14th Street NW, Washington, D.C. 20230.

Promotes and serves U.S. economic development and technological advancement. Business advice and information, statistics, information on science and technology for the economy. Includes the Bureau of Economic Analysis.

866. DEPARTMENT OF HEALTH, EDUCATION AND WELFARE, 330 Independence Avenue SW, Washington, D.C. 20201.

Educational and health programs of the federal government. Includes the Office of Education, National Institute of Education, Food and Drug Administration and National Institute of Health.

867. DEPARTMENT OF HOUSING AND URBAN DEVELOPMENT, 451 Seventh Street SW, Washington, D.C. 20410.

Programs on U.S. housing needs and community improvement. The Office of Policy Development and Research deals with energy conservation in the home.

868.   DEPARTMENT OF THE INTERIOR, C Street between 18th and 19th
       Streets NW, Washington, D.C. 20240.

       Primary conservation agency of the federal government.
       Assesses energy and mineral resources. Includes the
       Bureau of Mines, Office of Minerals Policy Development,
       Ocean Mining Administration and Geological Survey. The
       Office of Research and Development coordinates energy
       and minerals research and development in the department.

869.   DEPARTMENT OF LABOR, 200 Constitution Avenue NW, Washington,
       D.C. 20210.

       Development and promotion of the welfare of wage earners
       promotion of employment and improvement of working con-
       ditions. Collects statistics on labor and employment.

870.   DEPARTMENT OF STATE, Bureau of Economic and Business Affairs,
       Office of Fuels and Energy, 2201 C Street NW, Washington
       D.C. 20520.

       Formulates and implements foreign policy on energy matter

871.   DEPARTMENT OF STATE, Bureau of Intelligence and Research,
       Office of Resources Policy, Washington, D.C.

       Collects and analyzes information on foreign energy
       developments to assist in developing U.S. policy on
       international energy matters.

872.   DEPARTMENT OF STATE, Bureau of International Scientific and
       Technical Affairs, Office of Atomic Energy Affairs,
       Washington, D.C. 20520.

       Deals with the international implications of the de-
       velopment of peaceful uses of atomic energy.

873.   DEPARTMENT OF TRANSPORTATION, 400 Seventh Street SW, Washing-
       ton, D.C. 20590.

       Federal transportation policy, safety and planning. As-
       pects of this affect energy conservation and the use of
       energy resources. Includes the Federal Aviation Admin-
       istration, Federal Highway Administration, Federal Rail-
       road Administration, and Urban Mass Transport Admin-
       istration. The Office of Transportation Energy Policy
       considers the energy implications of DOT policies and
       programs.

874.   DEPARTMENT OF TRANSPORTATION, Transportation Systems Center,
       Kendall Square, Cambridge, MA 02142.

       Research and publications on analysis of social and
       behavioral impacts of energy shortages. Publications
       available from National Technical Information Service.

875. DEPARTMENT OF THE TREASURY, Office of the Assistant Secretary for Trade, Energy and Financial Resources Policy, Washington, D.C. 20220.

Financial and tax policy as it affects the production, distribution and use of energy.

876. ENERGY RESEARCH AND DEVELOPMENT ADMINISTRATION, 20 Massachusetts Avenue NW, Washington, D.C. 20545.

Consolidates federal government energy activities in energy research and development, conservation, self-sufficiency, energy efficiency and the reliability of energy sources. Material on nuclear power, fossil energy, solar and geothermal energy, environmental impacts, safety, conservation, etc. Films, speakers and publications available.

877. ERDA TECHNICAL INFORMATION CENTER, P.O. Box 62, Oak Ridge, TN 37830.

878. ENERGY RESOURCES COUNCIL, Executive Office Building, Washington, D.C. 20500.

Co-ordinates energy policy matters at the Presidential level, facilitates inter-agency communication on energy matters. Concerned with broad national policy formulation, and the development of policy for managing energy resources and intitiatives.

879. ENVIRONMENTAL PROTECTION AGENCY, 410 M Street SW, Washington, D.C. 20460.

Protiection of natural resources, the control and abatement of pollution, and the protection and enhancement of the environment.

880. FEDERAL ENERGY ADMINISTRATION, 12th Street and Pennsylvania Avenue NW, Washington, D.C. 20461.

Regulates energy allocation and pricing, promotes energy conservation. Attempts to ensure adequate U.S. energy supplies, sets priorities for energy use if shortages develop, and tries to ensure equity in bearing the burden of energy shortages. Office of Communications and Public Affairs, Office of Conservation and Environment, and Office of Resource Development are of particular interest to the student of energy.

881. FEDERAL ENERGY ADMINISTRATION, Division of Coal, Nuclear and Advanced Energy Systems Statistics, 2000 M Street NW, Washington, D.C. 20461.

882. FEDERAL ENERGY ADMINISTRATION REGIONAL OFFICES.

Region I. 150 Causeway Street, Boston, MA 02114.
Region II. 26 Federal Plaza, New York, NY 10001.

Region III. 1421 Cherry Street, Philadelphia, PA 19102.
Region IV. 1720 Peachtree Street NW, Atlanta, GA 30309.
Region V. 175 West Jackson Boulevard, Chicago, IL 60604.
Region VI. P.O. Box 2263, Dallas, TX 75221.
Region VII. 811 Grand Avenue, Kansas City, MO 64106.
Region VIII. P.O. Box 26247, Belmar Branch, Lakewood, CO 80226.
Region IX. 111 Pine Street, San Francisco, CA 94111.
Region X. 909 First Avenue, Seattle, WA 98104.

883.   FEDERAL INFORMATION CENTERS.

Information clearing-houses for the federal government. Provide information or refers to experts. Provide some government publications. Cities listed by name only have tie-line telephone communication with Information Centers in nearby cities.

ALABAMA--Birmingham, Mobile.
ARIZONA--Little Rock.
CALIFORNIA--Los Angeles, Federal Building, 300 North Los Angeles Street 90012; Sacramento, Federal Building, 650 Capitol Mall 95814; San Diego, 202 C Street 92101; San Francisco, 450 Golden Gate Avenue 94102; San Jose.
COLORADO--Colorado Springs, Pueblo; Denver 1961 Stout Street 80202.
CONNECTICUT--Hartford, New Haven.
DISTRICT OF COLUMBIA--7th and D Streets SW, 20407.
FLORIDA--Fort Lauderdale, Jacksonville, Tampa, West Palm Beach; Miami, 51 SW 1st Avenue 33130; St. Petersburg, 1441 1st Avenue South 33701.
GEORGIA--Atlanta, 275 Peachtree Street NE 30303.
HAWAII--Honolulu, 335 Merchant Street 96813.
ILLINOIS--Chicago, 219 South Dearborn Street 60604.
INDIANA--Indianapolis, 575 North Pennsylvania Street 46204.
IOWA--Des Moines.
KANSAS-- Topeka, Wichita.
KENTUCKY--Louisville, 600 Federal Place 40202.
LOUISIANA--New Orleans, 701 Loyola Avenue 70113.
MARYLAND--Baltimore, 31 Hopkins Plaza 21201.
MASSACHUSETTS--Boston, JFK Federal Building, Government Center 02203.
MICHIGAN--Detroit, 447 Michigan Avenue 48226.
MINNESOTA--Minneapolis, 110 South 4th Street 55401.
MISSOURI--Kansas City, 601 East 12th Street 64106; St. Joseph; St. Louis, 1520 Market Street 63103.
NEBRASKA--Omaha, 215 North 17th Street 68102.
NEW JERSEY--Newark, 970 Broad Street 07102; Trenton,
NEW MEXICO--Albuquerque, 500 Gold Avenue SW 87101; Santa Fe.
NEW YORK--Albany, Roshester, Syracuse; Buffalo, 111 West Huron Street 14202; New York, 26 Federal Plaza 10007.
NORTH CAROLINA--Charlotte.
OHIO--Akron, Columbus, Dayton, Toledo; Cincinnati, 550 Main Street 45202; Cleveland, 1240 East 9th Street 44194.
OKLAHOMA--Oklahoma City, 201 NW 3rd Street 73102; Tulsa.

109

OREGON--Portland, 1220 SW 3rd Avenue 77204.
PENNSYLVANIA--Philadelphia, 600 Arch Street 19106; Pittsburgh,
    1000 Liberty Avenue 15222.
RHODE ISLAND--Providence.
TENNESSEE--Chattanooga, Nashville; Memphis, 167 North Main
    Street 38103.
TEXAS--Austin, Dallas, San Antonio; Fort Worth, 819 Taylor
    Street 76102; Houston, 515 Rust Avenue 77002.
UTAH--Ogden; Salt Lake City, 125 South State 84138.
WASHINGTON--Seattle, 915 2nd Avenue 98174; Tacoma.
WISCONSIN--Milwaukee.

884. FEDERAL POWER COMMISSION, 825 North Capitol Street NE,
      Washington, D.C. 20426.

      Regulates the interstate aspects of the electric power
      and natural gas industries.

885. GENERAL ACCOUNTING OFFICE, 441 G Street NW, Washington, D.C.
      20546.

      The Comptroller General oversees verification of energy
      data developed by private business under the Energy
      Policy and Conservation Act of 1975. The GAO regional
      suboffice in Houston collects and stores the data.

886. LIBRARY OF CONGRESS, 10 First Street SE, Washington, D.C.
      20540

887. NATIONAL ACADEMY OF SCIENCES, 2101 Constitution Avenue NW,
      Washington, D.C. 20418.

      Programs to further science and its use for the general
      welfare. Includes the National Academy of Engineering
      and the National Research Council, which stimulates
      scientific and technological research and its application
      for public benefit.

888. NATIONAL AERONAUTICS AND SPACE ADMINISTRATION, 400 Maryland
      Avenue SW, Washington, D.C. 20546.

      Research in energy systems, including solar power.

889. NATIONAL AGRICULTURAL LIBRARY, 10301 Beltimore Boulevard,
      Beltsville, MD 20705.

      Operated by the Department of Agriculture to serve
      government agencies, agricultural colleges and univer-
      sities, agricultural associations, industry, scientists,
      farmers and the public with information on agriculture
      and related subjects.

890. NATIONAL BUREAU OF ECONOMIC RESEARCH, 1750 New York Avenue
      NW, Washington, D.C. 20006.

      Publishes conference reports, etc., on energy in relation
      to the economy.

891. NATIONAL BUREAU OF STANDARDS, U.S. Department of Commerce, Washington, D.C. 20234.

Publications on standards for room air conditioners, etc. Data needed to determine energy efficiency of appliances.

892. NATIONAL ENERGY INFORMATION CENTER, Room 1404, 12th Street and Pennsylvania Avenue NW, Washington, D.C. 20461.

Central location for the information resources of the Federal Energy Administration.

893. NATIONAL REFERRAL CENTER, SCIENCE AND TECHNOLOGY DIVISION, Library of Congress, Washington, D.C. 20540.

Information or referrals to information sources for persons with science or technology-related questions.

894. NATIONAL SCIENCE FOUNDATION, 1800 G Street NW, Washington, D.C. 20550.

Promotes scientific progress through support of research and education in the sciences. COURSE AND CURRICULUM DEVELOPMENT MATERIALS, available through the U.S. Government Printing Office, lists films, books and instructional equipment, in science and social science for elementary, intermediate and secondary schools.

895. NATIONAL SCIENCE FOUNDATION, Division of Science Education Development and Research, 1800 G Street NW, Washington, D.C. 20550.

896. NATIONAL SCIENCE FOUNDATION, Energy-Related General Research Office, Research Directorate, 1800 G Street NW, Washington, D.C. 20550.

Research on resource allocation, energy scarcity, social implications of energy scarcity, energy and economic growth.

897. NATIONAL SOLAR HEATING AND COOLING INFORMATION CENTER, P.O. Box 1607, Rockville, MD 20850.

Government-funded information source on solar equipment and installers. Toll-free hotline, (800) 523-2929.

898. NATIONAL TECHNICAL INFORMATION SERVICE, Information and Sales Center, 425 13th Street NW, Room 620, Washington, D.C. 20230.

A division of the Department of Commerce, the NTIS acts as a clearing-house for scientific and technical information from federal agencies and contractors. On-line computer search service, catalog of publications, Weekly Government Abstracts in many fields, including energy.

899. NUCLEAR REGULATORY COMMISSION, 1717 H Street NW, Washington,

D.C. 20555.

The NRC's duty is to license and regulate the use of nuclear energy to protect public health and safety and the environment.

900. OFFICE OF SCIENCE AND TECHNOLOGY POLICY, Executive Office Building, Washington, D.C. 20500.

Advises the President on science, engineering and technological matters for federal government policies, plans and programs and on scientific and technological considerations in matters of national concern. Assists the President in co-ordinating research and development activities in the federal government.

901. OFFICE OF SOLID WASTE MANAGEMENT PROGRAMS, U.S. Environmental Protection Agency, 1835 D Street NW, Washington, D.C. 20460.

902. SOLID WASTE INFORMATIONAL MATERIALS CONTROL SECTION, U.S. Environmental Protection Agency, Cincinnati, OH 45268.

Information on solid waste and recycling problems and projects. List of publications, and names of solid waste officials at the local level.

903. SUPERINTENDENT OF DOCUMENTS, U.S. Government Printing Office, Washington, D.C. 20402.

Mail orders of U.S. Government Publications, except for those obtained directly from the issuing agency or through the National Technical Information Service. The Superintendent of Documents Office is the primary source for U.S. Government publications.

U.S. Congress

Committees of the Senate and House of Representatives. These bodies conduct hearings and investigations relating to legislation before the Congress, and issue reports on their findings.

904. COMMITTEE ON AGRICULTURE, U.S. House of Representatives, 1301 Longworth House Office Building, Washington, D.C. 20515.

Concerned with agriculture, crops, rural electrification, soil conservation, etc.

905. COMMITTEE ON AGRICULTURE,·NUTRITION AND FORESTRY, U.S. Senate, 324 Russell Senate Office Building, Washington, D.C. 20510.

Subcommittees on Agricultural Credit and Rural Electrification.

906. COMMITTEE ON APPROPRIATIONS, U.S. House of Representatives, Room H-218, Capitol Building, Washington, D.C. 20515.

Subcommittees on Agriculture, Environment and Consumer Protection, Housing and Urban Development, Labor, Health, Education and Welfare, Public Works, Transportation.

907. COMMITTEE ON APPROPRIATIONS, U.S. Senate, 1235 Dirksen Senate Office Building, Washington, D.C. 20510.

Matters relating to funds and revenue appropriations for support of government activities.

908. COMMITTEE ON BANKING, HOUSING AND URBAN AFFAIRS, U.S. Senate, 5300 Dirksen Senate Office Building, Washington, D.C. 20510.

Fiscal policy, price controls, foreign trade, export, economic stabilization, urban development and mass transit.

909. COMMITTEE ON COMMERCE, SCIENCE AND TRANSPORTATION, U.S. Senate, 5202 Dirksen Senate Office Building, Washington, D.C. 20510.

Science, engineering and technology research, development and policy. Interstate and foreign trade, conservation, transportation, highway safety, fisheries and wildlife.

910. COMMITTEE ON ENERGY AND NATURAL RESOURCES, U.S. Senate, Dirksen Senate Office Building, Washington, D.C. 20510.

Concerned with energy policy, regulation, conservation, research and development, supply and demand. Deals with oil and gas, solar energy, nuclear power, mining, fossil fuels and hydroelectric power. Subcommittees: Energy Conservation and Regulation; and Energy Production and Supply.

911. COMMITTEE ON ENVIRONMENT AND PUBLIC WORKS, U.S. Senate, 4204 Dirksen Senate Office Building, Washington, D.C. 20510.

Regulation and control of non-military nuclear energy, flood control, dams, water power, economic development. Subcommittees: Nuclear Regulation; Resource Protection; Environmental Pollution; Transportation; Regional and Community Development.

912. COMMITTEE ON INTERIOR AND INSULAR AFFAIRS, U.S. House of Representatives, 1324 Longworth House Office Building, Washington, D.C. 20515.

Public lands, mining, petroleum supply, demand and conservation, geological surveys, etc. Subcommittees: Energy and Environment, Water and Power Resources, Mines and Mining, Public Lands.

913. COMMITTEE ON INTERIOR AND INSULAR AFFAIRS, U.S. Senate, 3106 Dirksen Senate Office Building, Washington, D.C. 20510.

Duties similar to House committee. Subcommittees: Minerals, Materials and Fuels, Public Lands, Water and Power Resources.

914. COMMITTEE ON INTERNATIONAL RELATIONS, U.S. House of Representatives, 2170 Rayburn House Office Building, Washington, D.C. 20515.

Concerned with international trade, foreign business, international financial organizations, etc.

915. COMMITTEE ON INTERSTATE AND FOREIGN COMMERCE, U.S. House of Representatives, 2125 Rayburn House Office Building, Washington, D.C. 20515.

Concerned with petroleum and natural gas, electric power, transportation and air pollution among other subjects. Subcommittees: Communications; Transportation and Commerce; Energy and Power; Health and Environment.

916. COMMITTEE ON PUBLIC WORKS AND TRANSPORTATION, U.S. House of Representatives, 2165 Rayburn House Office Building, Washington, D.C. 20515.

Concerned with economic development, pollution, flood control, transportation, etc. Subcommittees: Economic

Development; Energy Investigation and Review; Surface
Transportation; Water Resources; Urban Mass Transit.

917. COMMITTEE ON SCIENCE AND TECHNOLOGY, U.S. House of Representatives, 2321 Rayburn House Office Building, Washington,
D.C. 20515.

Energy research, environmental research, scientific
research and development, NASA, NSF. Subcommittees:
Advanced Energy Technological and Energy Conservation
Research, Development and Demonstration; Science,
Research and Technology; Transportation, Aviation and
Weather; Fossil and Nuclear Energy Research, Develop-
ment and Demonstration.

State Government Energy Agencies

Many of these agencies offer posters, films, teaching aids,
newsletters and other materials. Publications and information on
energy conservation and efficiency are also available. New laws and
executive orders may change some offices or addresses, but energy
information in a state should be available through most, if not all,
of these sources.

918. ALABAMA, Energy Management Board, Room 203, Executive
Building, 312 Montgomery Street, Montgomery 35104.

919. ALASKA, Alaska Energy Office, 5th Floor, MacKay Building,
338 Denali Street, Anchorage 99501.

920. ARIZONA, Arizona Office of Economic Planning and Development,
1645 West Jefferson, Phoenix 85007.

921. ARKANSAS, State Energy Office, 325 National Old Line Building, Little Rock 72201.

922. CALIFORNIA, Energy Resources Conservation and Development
Commission, 455 Capitol Mall, First Floor, Sacramento
95814.

923. COLORADO, Governor's Energy Policy Council, Office of the
Governor, State Capitol, Denver 80203.

924. CONNECTICUT, Department of Planning and Energy Policy, 20
Grand Street, Hartford 06113.

925. DELAWARE, Division of Emergency Planning and Operations,
Department of Public Safety, Delaware City 19706.

926. FLORIDA, State Energy Office, 108 Collins Building, Tallahassee 32304.

927. GEORGIA, State Energy Office, 7 Hunter Street, Room 145, Atlanta 30334.

928. HAWAII, Department of Planning and Economic Development, Kamamalu Building, P.O. Box 2359, Honolulu 96804.

929. IDAHO, Office of Energy, 300 North 6th Street, Boise 83720.

930. ILLINOIS, Division of Energy, Department of Business and Economic Development, 222 South College Street, Springfield 62706.

931. ILLINOIS, Energy Resources Commission, 2070 State Office Building, Springfield 62706.

932. INDIANA, Indiana Energy Office, 803 State Office Building, Indianapolis 46204.

933. IOWA, Energy Policy Council, 300 Fourth Street, Des Moines 50319.

934. KANSAS, Kansas Energy Office, 503 Kansas Avenue, Room 241, Topeka 66603.

935. KENTUCKY, Kentucky Energy Office, Capitol Plaza Tower, Frankfort 40601.

936. LOUISIANA, Division of Natural Resources and Energy, Department of Conservation, P.O. Box 44156, Baton Rouge 70804.

937. MAINE, Fuel Allocation and Conservation Office, State House, Augusta 04330.

938. MARYLAND, Energy Policy Office, 219 West Hoffman Street, Baltimore 21201.

939. MASSACHUSETTS, State Energy Policy Office, 294 Washington Street, Boston 02108.

940. MICHIGAN, Energy Administration, Department of Commerce, Fourth Floor, Law Building, Lansing 48913.

941. MINNESOTA, Minnesota Energy Agency, 740 American Center Building, St. Paul 55101.

942. MISSISSIPPI, Fuel and Energy Management Commission, 1307 Woolfolk Building, Jackson 39205.

943. MISSOURI, Missouri Energy Agency, P.O. Box 1309, Jefferson City 65101.

944. MONTANA, Energy Advisory Council, c/o Lieutenant Governor, State Capitol, Helena 59601.

945. NEBRASKA, Tax Commissioner, State Capitol, Room 1103, Lincoln 68509.

946. NEVADA, Public Service Commission, 198 South Carson Street, Carson City 89701.

947. NEW HAMPSHIRE, Governor's Council on Energy, 3 Capitol Street, Concord 03301.

948. NEW JERSEY, State Energy Office, 101 Commerce Street, Newark, 07102.

949. NEW MEXICO, Energy Resources Board, P.O. Box 2770, Santa Fe 87501.

950. NEW YORK, Emergency Fuel Office, Tower Building, Empire State Plaza, Albany 12223.

951. NORTH CAROLINA, Energy Policy Council, 215 East Lane Street, Raleigh 27611.

952. NORTH DAKOTA, Governor's Policy Advisor, Governor's Office, State Capitol, Bismarck 58505.

953. OHIO, Ohio Energy and Resources Development Agency, State Office Tower, 30 East Broad Street, Columbus 43215.

954. OKLAHOMA, Department of Energy, 4400 North Lincoln Boulevard, Suite 251, Oklahoma City 73105.

955. OREGON, Department of Energy, 528 Cottage Street NE, Salem 97310.

956. PENNSYLVANIA, Energy Council, 903 Payne Shoemaker Building, Harrisburg 17120.

957. RHODE ISLAND, State Energy Office, State House, Providence 02903.

958. SOUTH CAROLINA, Energy Management Office, 1429 Senate Street, Columbia 29201.

959. SOUTH DAKOTA, Office of Energy Policy, State Capitol, Pierre 57501.

960. TENNESSEE, Tennessee Energy Office, 250 Capitol Hill Building, Nashville 37219.

961. TEXAS, Governor's Energy Advisory Council, 411 West 13th Street, Austin 78701.

962. UTAH, Department of Natural Resources, 438 State Capitol Building, Salt Lake City 84114.

963. VERMONT, State Envergy Office, State Office Building, Montpelier 05602.

964. VIRGINIA, State Energy Office, 823 East Main Street, Richmond 23219.

965. WASHINGTON, Department of Emergency Services, 4220 East Martin Way, Olympia 98504.

966. WEST VIRGINIA, Fuel and Energy Office, 1262½ Greenbrier Street, Charleston 25311.

967. WISCONSIN, Office of Emergency Energy Assistance, 4510 Regent Street, Madison 53702.

968. WYOMING, Department of Economic Planning and Development, 720 West 18th Street, Cheyenne 82002.

969. PUERTO RICO, Office of Fuel Affairs, P.O. Box 9447, Santurce 00908.

Canadian Government Information Sources

970. CANADIAN GOVERNMENT PROGRAMS AND SERVICES, C.C.H. Canadian Ltd., Don Mills, Ontario CANADA. 2/year.

    Information on government organization and functions. Department listings and addresses.

971. CANADIAN GOVERNMENT PUBLICATIONS, Publishing Centre, Printing and Publishing, Supply and Services Canada, Ottawa, Ontario K1A 0S9 CANADA. Monthly.

    Checklist of Canadian government publications. Bilingual, English and French.

972. ORGANIZATION OF THE GOVERNMENT OF CANADA, Information Canada, 171 Slater Street, Ottawa, Ontario K1A 0S9 CANADA.

    Charts and descriptions of Canadian governmental organization. French edition available.

973. ADVANCED CONCEPTS CENTRE, Office of the Science Advisor, Dept. of the Environment, Ottawa, Ontario K1A 0H3 CANADA.

    Information on renewable energy and energy alternatives.

974. AGRICULTURE CANADA, Information Division, Canada Department of Agriculture, Ottawa, Ontario K1A 0C7 CANADA.

975. ATOMIC ENERGY OF CANADA, LTD., Congill Building, 20th Floor, 275 Slater Street, Ottawa, Ontario K1A 0S4 CANADA.

    Crown corporation for research on and marketing of nuclear power. Publications in English and French, many for grades 8-13.

976. ENERGY, MINES AND RESOURCES, 588 Booth Street, Ottawa, Ontario K1A 0E4 CANADA.

    Supply, demand, production and conservation of energy and natural resources. General and technical information, charts, school materials, etc., for grades 7 and up.

977. ENVIRONMENT CANADA, Fontaine Building, Ottawa, Ontario K1A 0H3 CANADA.

    Environment, pollution and environmental impacts,

with energy-related information.

978. INDUSTRY, TRADE AND COMMERCE, Place de Ville, Tower B,
Room 401, 112 Kent Street, Ottawa, Ontario K1A OH5
CANADA.

Information on energy as it affects Canada's economic
situation.

979. INFORMATION CANADA, 171 Slater Street, Ottawa, Ontario
K1A OS9 CANADA.

Most Canadian government publications are available
through Information Canada. Bookshops in Halifax,
Montreal, Toronot, Vancouver and Winnipeg.

980. NATIONAL RESEARCH COUNCIL OF CANADA, Montreal Road,
Ottawa, Ontario K1A OR6 CANADA.

Films, and the bi-monthly general science magazine
SCIENCE DIMENSION.

981. NATIONAL LIBRARY OF CANADA, 395 Wellington Street, Ottawa,
Ontario K1A ON4 CANADA.

982. OFFICE OF ENERGY CONSERVATION, Department of Energy, Mines
and Resources, 588 Booth Street, Ottawa, Ontario
K1A OE4 CANADA.

983. SCIENCE COUNCIL OF CANADA, Information Canada, 171 Slater
Street, Ottawa, Ontario K1A OS9 CANADA.

Reports on Canadian energy conservation, alternatives
and opportunities.

984. STATISTICS CANADA, Ottawa, Ontario K1A OT6 CANADA.

Census data and most other types of statistics collected by the Canadian government.

985. TRANSPORT CANADA, Place de Ville, Tower C, 26th Floor,
330 Sparks Street, Ottawa, Ontario K1A ON5 CANADA.

Transportation planning and policy, with information
on energy as it relates to these areas.

986. URBAN AFFAIRS CANADA, Ministry of State, Ottawa, Ontario
K1A OP6 CANADA.

Energy-related matters pertaining to cities and
urban areas.

United Nations Information Sources

987. INFORMATION CANADA, 171 Slater Street, Ottawa, Ontario
      K1A 0S9 CANADA.

      Canadian distribution of publications of the U.N.
      system, including FAO, UNESCO, International Atomic
      Energy Agency, General Agreement on Tariffs and Trade,
      International Trade Centre, World Meteorological
      Organization.

988. FOOD AND AGRICULTURE ORGANIZATION (FAO), Publications avail-
      able through Unipub, Box 433, 650 First Avenue, New
      York, NY 10016.

      Food, agriculture, nutrition, fisheries, and economic
      statistics in these fields.

989. FAO DOCUMENTATION: CURRENT BIBLIOGRAPHY, Unipub, Inc., P.O.
      Box 433, 650 First Avenue, New York, NY 10016. 11/year
      and annual cumulation.

990. INTERNATIONAL ATOMIC ENERGY, publications available through
      Unipub, P.O. Box 433, 650 First Avenue, New York, NY
      10016.

      Promotes the peaceful use of atomic energy and nuclear
      power. Nuclear techniques in agriculture, life sciences,
      earth sciences, environmental sciences; environmental
      protection, law and waste management. Film catalogue
      available.

991. INTERNATIONAL BANK FOR RECONSTRUCTION AND DEVELOPMENT (WORLD
      BANK), 1818 H Street NW, Washington, D.C. 20433.

992. INTERNATIONAL LABOUR ORGANIZATION, ILO Branch Office,
      666 Eleventh Street NW, Washington, D.C. 20001.

993. LIST OF UNESCO DOCUMENTS AND PUBLICATIONS, Unipub, Inc.,
      P.O. Box 433, 650 First Avenue, New York, NY 10016.
      6/year.

      Publications in education, science, culture, infor-
      mation services, etc.

994. UNIPUB, INC., P.O. Box 433, 650 First Avenue, New York,
      NY 10016.

      U.S. distribution of publications of the U.N. system,

including FAO, UNESCO, International Atomic Energy
Agency, International Trade Centre, General Agreement
on Tariffs and Trade, World Meteorological Organization.

995.   UNITED NATIONS, Sales Section, New York, NY 10017.

Sales of many U.N. documents in various fields.

EDUCATION, COURSES, WORKSHOPS, CONFERENCES

EDUCATION, COURSES, WORKSHOPS, CONFERENCES

Introduction

Since new courses and programs in energy-related areas are
constantly being developed, this listing cannot be comprehensive.
In particular, community colleges are developing courses and
certificate programs in energy, energy alternatives and energy
conservation. In many colleges and universities, energy courses
are found in departments of Engineering, Sociology, Natural
Resources, and environment or technology-related programs.
The School of Engineering at your state university should be
able to provide current information on energy programs in your
state.
.Workshops and conferences.listed in this section are ongoing
ones that meet each year for several years, or are repeatedly
sponsored by organizations. Many.energy workshops and conferences
are one-time events, and information on these can be found in
the magazines and newsletters in the Periodicals section. ACORN,
MOTHER EARTH NEWS, and PEOPLE AND-ENERGY are among those that
publish up-to-date conference information.

Education, Courses, Workshops, Conferences

996. ARIZONA STATE UNIVERSITY, Tempe, AZ 85281.

Bachelor's degrees in Environmental Design and in
Engineering.

997. BARNARD COLLEGE (COLUMBIA UNIVERSITY), 606 West 120th Street,
New York, NY 10027.

Bachelor's degree program in Environmental Conservation
and Management.

998. CALIFORNIA INSTITUTE OF THE ARTS, School of Design,
24700 McBean Parkway, Valencia, CA 91355.

BFA and MFA degrees in Environmental Design, including
solar heating and cooling, energy conservation, wind
power, etc.

999. CALIFORNIA INSTITUTE OF TECHNOLOGY, 1201 East California
Boulevard, Pasadena, CA 91109.

Bachelor's, Master's and Ph.D. concentrations in
Environmental Engineering Science. Conducts much
energy-related research.

1000. CALIFORNIA STATE POLYTECHNIC UNIVERSITY, San Luis Obispo,

CA 93401.

Bachelor's degree in environmental engineering.

1001. CARNEGIE-MELLON UNIVERSITY, Program in Technology and
Humanities, Pittsburgh, PA 15213.

Studies in the impacts of technological development
on the economic, political, social and physical environment.

1002. CASE WESTERN RESERVE UNIVERSITY, 10900 Euclid Avenue,
Cleveland, OH 44106.

Course and degree programs in Engineering and Environmental Design.

1003. CENTER FOR ENVIRONMENTAL AWARENESS, INC., Naples, NY 14512.

Sponsors seminars and workshops on many subjects,
including solar heating.

1004. CORNELL UNIVERSITY, Department of City and Regional Planning,
106 West Sibley Hall, Cornell University, Ithaca,
NY 14853.

1005. CORNELL UNIVERSITY, Program on Science, Technology, and
Society, 620 Clark Hall, Ithaca, NY 14853.

1006. DREXEL UNIVERSITY, 32nd and Chestnut Streets, Philadelphia,
PA 19104.

Master's and Ph.D. concentrations in Environmental
Engineering and Science.

1007. FARALLONES INSTITUTE, Rural Center: 15290 Coleman Valley
Road, Occidental, CA 95465. Urban Center: 1516
Fifth Street, Berkeley, CA 94710.

Research and instruction in urban and rural agriculture,
building design and construction, ecosystem management,
and energy systems design. Offers short courses,
degree programs and apprentice programs.

1008. THE GEORGE WASHINGTON UNIVERSITY, Graduate Program in
Science, Technology and Public Policy, Washington,
D.C. 20052.

Graduate courses on impacts of science and technology
on society and on public policy making. Some are
energy-related.

1009. GODDARD COLLEGE, Social Ecology Program, Plainfield, VT
05667.

Includes work in energy alternatives, energy and
agriculture, ecology and environmental sciences.

B.A. and M.A. degrees. Summer intensive program
for students of other colleges and universities
carries B.A. and M.A. credit.

1010. GOVERNORS STATE UNIVERSITY, Park Forest South, IL 60466.

Works in alternative energy and conservation, head-
quarters of the Midwest Energy Alternatives Network.
Bachelor's and Master's programs in Environment and
Applied Sciences.

1011. GRAND VALLEY STATE COLLEGE, Allendale, MI 49401.

Bachelor's degree in Environment, courses offered
in alternative energy and conservation.

1012. HUMBOLDT STATE UNIVERSITY, Arcata, CA 95521.

Bachelor's degree in Environmental Resources Engineering.

1013. ILLINOIS INSTITUTE OF TECHNOLOGY, Department of Mechanics
and Mechanical Aerospace Engineering, 3100 South
State Street, Chicago, IL 60616.

Courses in solar heating and cooling of buildings
for engineers and architects. IIT offers M.S. and
Ph.D. programs in architecture, environmental engineering and gas engineering.

1014. JOHNS HOPKINS UNIVERSITY, Baltimore, MD 21218.

Bachelor's, Master's and Ph.D. degrees in Geographical
and Environmental Engineering offer energy-related work.

1015. MASSACHUSETTS INSTITUTE OF TECHNOLOGY, 77 Massachusetts
Avenue, Cambridge, MA 0 139.

Programs in engineering, architecture, planning and
related fields. MIT conducts many energy-related
research programs with technological and social
applications.

1016. MIAMI UNIVERSITY OF OHIO, Oxford, OH 45056.

Bachelor's degree in Environmental Design.

1017. MICHIGAN STATE UNIVERSITY, Project Entropy, Science and
Math Teaching Center, McDonel Hall, East Lansing,
MI 48824.

An energy education program, which organizes and
sponsors energy workshops for teachers and students.
Other activities include a weekly newsletter, film-
making, and a travelling energy display. Serves as
an energy information center and provides assistance
in developing energy education programs.

1018. MONTANA COLLEGE OF MINERAL SCIENCE AND TECHNOLOGY, Butte,

Montana 58701.

Programs include a Bachelor's degree in Environmental Engineering.

1019. MONTANA STATE UNIVERSITY, Department of Mechanical Engineering, Bozeman, MT 59715.

1020. NEW MEXICO INSTITUTE OF MINING AND TECHNOLOGY, Socorro, NM 87801.

Bachelor's degree program in Environmental Engineering.

1021. NEW MEXICO STATE UNIVERSITY, LAS CRUCES CAMPUS, Las Cruces, NM 88001.

Bachelor's degree in Environmental and Resources Economics.

1022. NORTH CAROLINA STATE UNIVERSITY, Raleigh, NC 27607.

Engineering programs, and a Bachelor's degree in Environmental Design.

1023. NORTHRUP UNIVERSITY, Helioscience Institute, 1155 West Arbor Vitae Street, Inglewood, CA 90306.

Research and instruction in solar energy, with conferences and workshops.

1024. OKLAHOMA STATE UNIVERSITY, Engineering Energy Lab, College of Engineering, Stillwater, OK 74074.

1025. OREGON MUSEUM OF SCIENCE AND INDUSTRY, Energy Center, 4025 SW Canyon Road, Portland, OR 97221.

Classes, workshops, conferences, displays. Information sheets and abstracts on energy alternatives.

1026. OREGON STATE UNIVERSITY, Geography Department, Corvallis, OR 97331.

Research in environmental assessment, and local participation in decision-making. Includes environmental impacts of energy production and extraction activities.

1027. PENNSYLVANIA STATE UNIVERSITY, University Park, PA 16802.

Bachelor's degree in environmental engineering. Bachelor's, Master's and Ph.D. concentrations in Fuel Science.

1028. PRINCETON UNIVERSITY, Princeton, NJ 08540.

Degree programs in architecture, urban planning, engineering, nuclear engineering, public affairs and policy contain energy-related courses.

1029. PURDUE UNIVERSITY, Science, Technology and Public Policy Program, Department of Political Science, West Lafayette, IN 47907.

1030. RENSSELAER POLYTECHNIC INSTITUTE, Science, Technology and Values Program, Human Dimensions Center, Troy, NY 12181.

An interdisciplinary program on the impacts of science and technology on society and culture, which offers the M.S. degree. RPI also offers Bachelor's, Master's and Ph.D. programs in environmental engineering.

1031. SONOMA COLLEGE, Solar Heating Program, Alternative Energy Building, 1801 East Cotati Avenue, Rohnert Park, CA 94928.

Instruction in solar heating and cooling, and solar technology.

1032. SOUTHERN METHODIST UNIVERSITY, Dallas, TX 75222.

Master's and Ph.D. programs in Environmental Engineering.

1033. STANFORD RESEARCH INSTITUTE, Energy Technology Department, 333 Ravenswood Avenue, Menlo Park, CA 94025.

1034. STANFORD UNIVERSITY, Institute for Energy Studies, Stanford, CA 94305.

1035. SYRACUSE UNIVERSITY, Syracuse, NY 13210.

Master's and Ph.D. concentrations in environmental engineering.

1036. TRINITY COLLEGE, Hartford, CT 06106.

Bachelor's degree in Environmental and Urban Studies.

1037. UNIVERSITY OF CALIFORNIA, Energy and Resources Progam, Corey Hall, Berkeley, CA 94720.

1038. UNIVERSITY OF COLORADO, Builder, CO 80302.

Courses in energy alternatives and appropriate technology.

1039. UNIVERSITY OF DELAWARE, Institute of Energy Conversion, Newark, Delaware 19711.

1040. UNIVERSITY OF FLORIDA, Energy Center, 309 Weil Hall, Gainsville, FL 32611.

1041. UNIVERSITY OF ILLINOIS--CHICAGO CIRCLE, P.O. Box 4348, Chicago, IL 60680.

B.S. and M.S. degrees in Energy Conversion Engineering.

129

Also offers degree programs in Transportation Systems Engineering and Urban Systems Engineering.

1042. UNIVERSITY OF IOWA, Iowa City, IA 52240.

Varied programs, including M.S. and Ph.D. degrees in Environmental Engineering.

1043. UNIVERSITY OF LOUISVILLE, Louisville, KY 40208.

Degree programs include a B.S. in Environmental Engineering.

1044. UNIVERSITY OF MASSACHUSETTS, Amherst, MA 01002.

Varied degree programs include B.S., M.S. and Ph.D. in Environmental Engineering.

1045. UNIVERSITY OF MINNESOTA, School of Architecture, 110 Architecture Building, Minneapolis, MN 55455.

Ouroboros East and Ouroboros South, projects on energy conserving urban dwellings, solar power, etc.

1046. UNIVERSITY OF MISSOURI, Engineering Extension Division, 1020D Engineering Building, Columbia, MO 65201.

Building design for low energy use, solar storage, geothermics, natural cooling, etc.

1047. UNIVERSITY OF MISSOURI, Rolla, MO 65401.

M.S. in Energy Conversion, B.S. and M.S. in Environmental and Planning Engineering.

1048. UNIVERSITY OF NORTH CAROLINA, Chapel Hill, NC 27515.

Master's and Ph.D. programs in Environmental Engineering.

1049. UNIVERSITY OF OKLAHOMA, Norman, OK 73069.

Programs in engineering, petroleum engineering, and environmental design.

1050. UNIVERSITY OF OREGON, School of Architecture and Allied Arts, Eugene, OR 97403.

Courses in energy and building design, with particular interest in solar energy.

1051. UNIVERSITY OF TEXAS, Austin, TX 78712.

Bachelor's degree program in Energy Conversion, as well as degrees in Petroleum Engineering and Architectural Engineering.

1052. UNIVERSITY OF UTAH, Salt Lake City, Utah 84112.

Bachelor's, Master's and Ph.D. programs in Fuels Engineering.

1053. UNIVERSITY OF WASHINGTON, Seattle, WA 98105.

Courses and programs in architecture, environmental design, engineering and mining engineering.

1054. UNIVERSITY OF WISCONSIN, Engineering Program, Madison Extension Wisconsin Center, 702 Langdon Street, Madison, WI 53706.

Solar energy technology, solar heating and cooling of buildings.

1055. UNIVERSITY OF WISCONSIN-MADISON, Institute for Environmental Studies. 120 WARF, 610 Walnut Street, Madison, WI 53706.

1056. UNIVERSITY OF WISCONSIN--MILWAUKEE, Milwaukee, WI 53201.

Bachelor's degree program in Energy Conversion, and a program in Transportation Engineering.

1057. VIRGINIA POLYTECHNIC INSTITUTE AND STATE UNIVERSITY, Blacksburg, VA 20461.

Bachelor's, Master's.and Ph.D. programs in Environmental Design. Also offers programs in architecture, planning, engineering, mining engineering and nuclear engineering.

1058. WASHINGTON UNIVERSITY, Department of Technology and Human Affairs, School of Engineering and Applied Science, P.O. Box 1106, St. Louis, MO 63130.

Degree programs concerned with the application of technology to social problems and with assessing the impacts of technology and technological change on society. Washington University also offers Bachelor's, Master's and Ph.D. degrees in Environmental Engineering.

1059. WILLIAM RAINEY HARPER COLLEGE, Architecture Technology Program, Algonquin and Roselle Roads, Palatine, IL 60067.

Course in solar energy and architecture design.

1060. WORCESTER POLYTECHNIC INSTITUTE, Worcester, MA 01609.

Offers programs in science and technology, urban studies and nuclear engineering.

1061. WORLD ENERGY CONFERENCE/CONFERENCE MONDIALE DE L'ENERGIE, 5 Bury Street, St. James's, London SW1Y 6AB ENGLAND.

International voluntarily sponsored conference for

the exchange of energy information, held every three years.

1062. YOUNGSTOWN STATE UNIVERSITY, Department of Electrical Engineering, 410 Wick Avenue, Youngstown, OH 44503.

Undergraduate and master's level concentrations in solar energy.

PROGRAMS, CENTERS AND RESEARCH PROJECTS

PROGRAMS, CENTERS AND RESEARCH PROJECTS

Introduction

This section contains a sampling of the many investigations being conducted in the general energy field. There are, however, many institutions and centers with new energy research projects, or projects still in the planning stages that are not included in this listing. The National Technical Information Service provides information on federally-sponsored energy research (see Government Organizations). Many major universities now conduct energy research, as do many non-government organizations and companies. The chapter on Non-government Organizations gives addresses and descriptions of many such organizations.

1063. ALTERNATIVE AGRICULTURE·RESOURCES PROJECT, Department of Applied Behavioral Science, Universtiy of California, Davis, CA 95616.

Research in appropriate technology, land use, energy, farming, nutrition, cooperatives.

1064. AMERICAN ENTERPRISE INSTITUTE, National Energy Project, 1150 17th Street NW, Washington, D.C. 20036.

Research on U.S. energy needs and supplies with information on trends and prospects for the future.

1065. ARGONNE NATIONAL LABORATORY, 9700 South Cass Avenue, Argonne, IL 60439.

Research in progress on the socio-economic consequences of coal-related energy development in differing regions of the United States. Various other energy-related projects may be conducted in the future.

1066. THE BRACE RESEARCH INSTITUTE, P.O. Box 400, MacDonald Campus of McGill University, Ste. Anne de Bellevue 800, Quebec, CANADA.

Research in appropriate technologies for rural and third world dwellers. Plans available for solar stills, wind pumps, solar driers, etc.

1067. CENTER FOR ENERGY STUDIES, University of Texas at Austin, Engineering Science Building 143, Austin, TX 78712.

Energy-related research, education and public service.

1068. CENTER FOR ENVIRONMENTAL QUALITY, 239 Administration Building, Michigan State University, East Lansing, MI 48824.

1069.   CENTER FOR ENVIRONMENTAL RESEARCH, School of Architecture
        and Allied Arts, University of Oregon, Eugene, OR 97403.

        Research and publications in solar energy.

1070.   CENTER FOR GROWTH ALTERNATIVES, 1785 Massachusetts Avenue
        NW, Washington, D.C. 20036.

1071.   CENTER FOR PHILOSOPHY AND PUBLIC POLICY, University of
        Maryland, College Park, MD 20742.

        Research and curriculum development on the evaluation
        of social and other scientific research as it relates
        to public policy. Concern with the ethical aspects of
        public policy formation.

1072.   CENTER FOR POLICY PROCESS, 1755 Massachusetts Avenue NW,
        Washington, D.C. 20036.

        Social analysis and forecasting, social policy.

1073.   CENTER FOR POLICY RESEARCH, 475 Riverside Drive, New York,
        NY 10027.

        Research in public understanding of the sciences,
        and patterns and forces in contemporary society.

1074.   CENTER FOR RESEARCH ON THE ACTS OF MAN, 4025 Chestnut Street,
        Philadelphia, PA 19104.

1075.   CENTER FOR SCIENCE IN THE PUBLIC INTEREST, Energy Project,
        1757 S Street NW, Washington, D.C. 20009.

        Working for public participation in energy planning
        and policy. Publishes a monthly newsletter, PEOPLE
        AND ENERGY, and a series of citizens' handbooks on
        oil, nuclear energy, solar energy, strip mining, etc.
        Research focuses on the social, environmental and
        economic aspects of energy policy development.

1076.   CITIZEN AND SCIENCE PROJECT, Indiana University, Sycamore
        Hall 217, Bloomington, IN 47401.

        Videotapes, reader and undergraduate course on science
        and the public, scientific advisory committees,
        controls on scientific research, etc.

1077.   COLORADO ENERGY RESEARCH INSTITUTE, P.O. Box 366, Golden,
        CO 80401.

1078.   COLORADO STATE UNIVERSITY, Solar Applications Laboratory,
        Fort Collins, CO 80521.

1079.   EARTH RESOURCES DEVELOPMENT RESEARCH INSTITUTE, Hearst
        Hall, Wisconsin Ave. & Woodley Rd. NW, Washington,
        D.C. 20016.

International nonprofit organization looking for long-range solutions to problems of human living conditions and world hunger.

1080. ECOLOGY ACTION/COMMON GROUND, 2225 El Camino Real, Palo Alto, CA 94306.

Intensive agriculture with low energy input, energy and the food system.

1081. ECOTOPE GROUP, 747 15th East, Seattle, WA.

Consulting group with experience in the design and building of renewable energy devices and systems.

1082. ECONOMIC DEVELOPMENT LABORATORY, Engineering Experiment Station, Georgia Institute of Technology, Atlanta, GA 30332.

Research, publications and cataloging of information on intermediate technology.

1083. ENERGY CONSERVATION PROJECT, Environmental Law Institute, 1346 Connecticut Avenue NW, Washington, D.C. 20036.

Research on energy conservation laws and regulations at state and local levels. Assessing and examination of current regulations, proposals for new policies.

1084. ENERGY RESOURCES CENTER, University of Illinois, Chicago Circle, Box 4348, Chicago, IL 60680.

1085. FORD FOUNDATION ENERGY POLICY PROJECT, 1776 Massachusetts Avenue NW, Washington, D.C. 20036.

Research and reports on America's energy future and suggested energy policies.

1086. HELION, Box 4301, Sylmar, CA 91342.

Renewable energy design, research and consulting group, with experience in wind and solar power.

1087. HUDSON INSTITUTE, Quaker Ridge Road, Croton-on-Hudson, NY 10520.

Energy policy research for government agencies and private corporations.

1088. INDEPENDENT ENERGY SYSTEMS, 11 Independence Court, Concord, MA 01742.

1089. INSTITUTE FOR MINING AND MINERALS RESEARCH, 213 Bradley Hall, University of Kentucky, Lexington, KY 40506.

1090. INSTITUTE FOR RESEARCH ON LAND AND WATER RESOURCES, Pennsylvania State University, University Park, PA 16802.

Bimonthly newsletter on institute activities.

1091. INSTITUTE FOR SOCIAL SCIENCE RESEARCH, University of California at Los Angeles, 11250 Bunche Hall, Los Angeles, CA 90024.

Analysis of the relationship between energy and economic growth, the effects of the consumption and supply of energy on economic growth and the quality of life.

1092. INSTITUTE FOR THE FUTURE, 2740 Sand Hill Road, Menlo Park, CA 94205.

Studies of technological, environmental and societal changes and their long-range consequences. Publishes reports and working papers.

1093. INSTITUTE OF SOCIAL, ECONOMIC AND GOVERNMENT RESEARCH, University of Alaska, College, Alaska 99701.

Research on business, economic conditions, etc. in Alaska.

1094. INTERMEDIATE TECHNOLOGY DEVELOPMENT GROUP, 9 King Street, Covent Garden, London WC2 8HN ENGLAND.

1095. JOHN B. PIERCE FOUNDATION LABORATORY, 290 Congress Avenue, New Haven, CT 06519.

Research in heating, ventilation and sanitation, energy conservation and efficiency. Affiliated with Yale University.

1096. LOS ALAMOS SCIENTIFIC LABS, Solar Energy Group, Mail Stop 571, Los Alamos, NM 87545.

1097. MIT ENERGY LABORATORY, Headquarters, Room E40-139, Massachusetts Institute of Technology, Cambridge, MA 02139.

Research on energy technology and energy impacts on environment and society, publishes a series of working papers and bibliographies.

1098. MATHEMATICA POLICY RESEARCH, 2101 L Street NW, Suite 416, Washington, D.C. 20037.

1099. MICHIGAN STATE UNIVERSITY, Institute of Public Utilities, 6-H Berkey Hall, East Lansing, MI 48824.

1100. NATIONAL CENTER FOR COMMUNITY ACTION, Network Services: Energy, 1711 Connecticut Avenue NW, Washington, D.C. 20009.

1101. NATIONAL CENTER FOR ENERGY MANAGEMENT AND POWER, Towne Building/D3, Room 260, University of Pennsylvania,

Philadelphia, PA 19174.

1102. NATIONAL OPINION RESEARCH CENTER, University of Chicago, 6030 South Ellis Avenue, Chicago, IL 60637.

The Continuous National Survey obtains information on public attitudes toward issues pertinent to both short-term and long-term policy planning. Reports on this research are used by government agencies, social scientists and policy planners to assess public opinion. Several reports on the energy crisis have been published.

1103. OIL INFORMATION CENTER, University of Oklahoma, 1808 Newton Drive, Room 116, Norman, Oklahoma 73069.

1104. PENNSYLVANIA STATE UNIVERSITY, Coal Research Section, 513 Deike Building, University Park, PA 16802.

1105. POLICY STUDIES ORGANIZATION, 361 Lincoln Hall, University of Illinois at Urbana-Champaign, Urbana, IL 61801.

Research in energy policy and planning.

1106. PROGRAM OF POLICY STUDIES IN SCIENCE AND TECHNOLOGY, The George Washington University, 2130 H Street NW, Washington, D.C. 20052.

1107. RODALE PRESS RESEARCH CENTER, John Haberern, Vice President, 33 East Minor Road, Emmaus, PA 18049.

Testing and developing low-impact tools, solar panels, methane digesters, etc. Specializes in alternatives, conservation, and low-impact lifestyles.

1108. SCIENCE AND PUBLIC POLICY PROGRAM, University of Oklahoma, 601 Elm Avenue, Room 432, Norman, OK 73069.

Technology assessments, research on societal impacts of science and technology.

1109. SURVEY RESEARCH CENTRE, York University, 4700 Keele Street, Downsview, Ontario M3J 1P3 CANADA.

Research projects on Canadian public reaction toward future generation of electricity by nuclear power plants. Suggestions for policy alternatives, and identification of areas for information programs.

1110. TECHNOLOGY APPLICATION CENTER, University of New Mexico, Albuquerque, NM 87131.

1111. INSTITUTE FOR GOVERNMENT RESEARCH, University of Arizona, Tucson, AZ 85721.

Improving communication in energy decision-making. Publications on Arizona energy questions.

1112. UNIVERSITY OF CALIFORNIA, Institute of Geophysics and Planetary Physics, Riverside, CA 92502.

Geothermal Resources program studies geothermal energy in the western U.S.

1113. UNIVERSITY OF CALIFORNIA, Lawrence Berkeley Laboratory, Energy and Environment Division, Berkeley, CA 94720.

Geothermal, solar, other nonnuclear energy technologies and their environmental impacts.

1114. UNIVERSITY OF CALIFORNIA, Sanitary Engineering Research Laboratory, 1301 S. 46th Street, Richmond, CA 94804.

Biogas production from wastes, solar energy.

1115. UNIVERSITY OF CALIFORNIA, SAN DIEGO, Center for Energy Production Techniques and Energy Policy, La Jolla, CA 92037.

1116. UNIVERSITY OF DELAWARE, Newark, Delaware 19711.

Research in equipment and principles for use of solar-electric power systems.

1117. UNIVERSITY OF FLORIDA, Solar Energy and Energy Conversion Laboratory, Gainesville, FL 32601.

1118. UNIVERSITY OF MASSACHUSETTS, Department of Civil Engineering, Amherst, MA 01002.

Research and instruction in solar and wind power.

1119. UNIVERSITY OF UTAH, Architectural Psychology, Building 403, University of Utah, Salt Lake City, UT 84112.

Building design for pleasant and energy-efficient living, publications in solar power.

1120. WATER RESOURCES RESEARCH CENTER, Purdue University, Lilly Hall of Life Sciences, West Lafayette, IN 47907.

1121. WATER RESOURCES RESEARCH CENTER, University of Minnesota, Minneapolis, MN 55455.

Research on the relationship between energy and water resources.

1122. WEST VIRGINIA UNIVERSITY, Coal Research Bureau, 219 White Hall, Morgantown, West Virginia, 26506.

1123. WORLDWATCH INSTITUTE, 1776 Massachusetts Avenue NW, Washington, D.C. 20036.

Nonprofit research organization for the anticipation of global problems and social trends. Publishes research reports on energy conservation, shortages and nuclear power.

ENERGY ALTERNATIVES AND SELF-SUFFICIENCY

ENERGY ALTERNATIVES AND SELF-SUFFICIENCY

Introduction

Interest in unconventional and low-impact energy systems is increasing with public awareness of shortages in our traditional energy sources. Many organizations and authors have available materials on such sources as: solar energy, wind power, geothermal power and wood heat. Many of these sources are also concerned with conserving energy, energy efficiency, and practical information for individuals on constructing small-scale energy systems. Home or farm wind and/or solar power systems are encouraged in an effort to use less of such scarce or environmentally questionable resources as fossil fuels and nuclear power. Many sources can give instructions on how to build solar collectors, windmills, Savonius rotors and other appropriate technology items.

Alternative energy periodicals are listed in the chapter on PERIODICALS, and some books on the subject are to be found in the chapter on TEXTS, READERS MANUALS. Films and other instructional aids on alternative energy are listed under INSTRUCTIONAL AIDS.

Energy Alternatives

Organizations, directories and reference sources on solar energy, wind, biogas, geothermal and water power, energy conservation and efficiency. Periodicals in this area are listed under PERIODICALS.

1124. ALBERTA RESEARCH COUNCIL, 11315 87th Avenue, Edmonton, Alberta CANADA.

Research in solar flux and solar energy applications.

1125. ALPHA ENERGY CONSULTANTS, Suite 125-EN, 7715 Chevy Chase, Austin, TX 78752.

Independent engineering consultants, providing non-technical reports on practical applications of solar heating and cooling and wind power.

1126. ALTERNATE ENERGY DIRECTORY, Synergy, P.O. Box 4790, Grand Central Station, New York, NY 10017.

Directory to over 1200 publications, products and facilities in solar, geothermal, electrical, water and wind power, heat transfer and energy storage. Periodic supplements.

1127. ALTERNATE ENERGY RESOURCES CO., Box 106, Sigourney, IA 52591.

1128. ALTERNATIVE ENERGY CENTER, 120 Oak Avenue, Ithaca, NY 14850.

Information on energy alternatives, conducts seminars on alternative energy and energy conservation.

1129. ALTERNATIVE ENERGY INSTITUTE, P.O. Box 3100, Estes Park, CO 80517.

Research in various alternative energy areas.

1130. ALTERNATIVE ENERGY RESOURCES ORGANIZATION, 417 Stapleton Building, Billings, MT 59101.

A non-profit group promoting and encouraging development of alternative energy sources, especially for Montana and the Northern Plains. Publishes SUN-TIMES, a newsletter, and distributes alternative energy material.

1131. ALTERNATIVE ENERGY SEARCH GROUP, 1421 State Street, Santa Barbara, CA 93101.

Works mostly in solar energy.

1132. ALTERNATIVE TECHNOLOGY INFORMATION PROJECT, UMC Room 331a-c, University of Colorado, Boulder, CO 80302.

Information and classes on energy alternatives, alternative technology, and alternative energy systems.

1133. AMERICAN WIND ENERGY ASSOCIATION, 21243 Grand River, Detroit, MI 48219, or 1919 14th Street 401, Boulder, CO 80302.

Research, publications and programs on wind power and energy self-sufficiency. Sponsors wind energy conferences. Alternate address, 54468 CR31, Bristol, IN 46507.

1134. APPROPRIATE TECHNOLOGY SOURCEBOOK, Volunteers in Asia, P.O. Box 4543, Stanford, CA 94305.

Listings of tools, plans and publications for alternative energy systems.

1135. A-Z SOLAR PRODUCTS, Dept. ME, 200 E. 26th Street, Minneapolis, MN 55404.

Twenty page Solar Energy Catalog of equipment for solar energy systems.

1136. BIOMASS ENERGY INSTITUTE, 310-870 Cambridge Street, Winnipeg, Manitoba R3M 3H5 CANADA.

1137. BOSTON WIND, 307 Centre Street, Jamaica Plain, MA 02130.

Non-profit alternative energy center for research
and information on wind power, solar and methane
power, shelter design and food production. The center
concentrates on means by which individuals can become
energy self-sufficient.

1138. BRACE RESEARCH INSTITUTE, c/o McDonald College of McGill
University, Ste. Anne de Bellevue, Quebec H9X 3M1
CANADA.

Large list of publications, including do-it-yourself
leaflets. Research on energy alternatives, particularly solar and wind energy.

1139. THE BUY WISE GUIDE TO SOLAR HEAT, Arlor Co., P.O. Box 419,
Scituate, MA 02066.

Helps choose the optimum solar heating/cooling
system for your home. Easy to understand discussions
of various types of solar systems, cost calculations,
how to get a home improvement loan for solar installations.

1140. CENTER FOR RURAL AFFAIRS, Walthill, NE.

Research and demonstration projects on low-energy
agriculture for the family farm, solar energy, wind
power and biogas.

1141. CENTRAL ILLINOIS SOLAR ENERGY SOCIETY, Box 171, Rochester,
IL 62563.

Establishing information library on alternative energy
for members' use.

1142. THE DELPHIAN FOUNDATION, Route 2, Box 195, Sheridan, OR 97378.

Research programs on solar energy and methane power.

1143. EARTHMIND, Josel Drive, Saugus, CA 91350.

Nonprofit research in alternative sources of energy,
ecological farming and energy conservation.

1144. EDNOVA INSTITUTE, Berry Creek, CA 95916.

Postal courses on solar energy and energy alternatives.

1145. ENERGY FLASHES, Alternative Energy Hotline, THE MOTHER
EARTH NEWS, P.O. Box 70, Hendersonville, NC 28739.

Special feature on recent developments in alternative
energy and national energy policy, and reviews of
alternative energy publications in each bi-monthly
issue of THE MOTHER EARTH NEWS.

1146. ENERGY INFORMATION SOURCES, 229 7th Avenue, New York,
NY 10011.

Information on alternative energy research and publications.

1147. A FARMERS GUIDE FOR FUEL INDEPENDENCE, Box 7E, Howard Peterson, Benson, MN 56215.

Written by Leslie Grove, this provides do-it-yourself plans for methane power and methane production on the family farm.

1148. GERMAN ORGANIZATION FOR WIND ENERGY RESEARCH, 2330 Ostsee-bad Eckernforde, Postfach 1444, WEST GERMANY.

Information on research and development of wind energy systems in Germany and Western Europe.

1149. GEOTHERMAL INFORMATION RESOURCES, Center for Science in the Public Interest, 1757 S Street NW, Washington, D.C. 20009.

Lists and discusses over 50 groups, industries, individuals and publications concerned with geothermal energy research and issues.

1150. GEOTHERMAL RESOURCES COUNCIL, P.O. Box 1033, Davis, CA 95616.

Educational society, publishes bulletin on applications and potential of geothermal power.

1151. GREAT PLAINS WINDUSTRIES, INC., 3802 South Topeka Avenue, Topeka, KS 66609.

Non-profit organization to promote wind power through written material, slide presentations, etc.

1152. INDEPENDENT POWER DEVELOPERS, INC., P.O. Box 1467, Noxon, MT 59853.

Development and sales of alternative energy hardware, water, wind, solar, methane and other types of energy.

1153. INFORMAL DIRECTORY OF THE ORGANIZATIONS AND PEOPLE INVOLVED IN THE SOLAR HEATING OF BUILDINGS, William A. Shur-cliff, 19 Appleton Street, Cambridge, MA 02138. 1976.

Directory of governmental agencies, professional societies, foundations, solar engineers, inventors, planners, writers, etc. working in solar technology.

1154. INSTITUTE FOR ALTERNATIVE ENERGY SOURCES, c/o General Conference, Mennonite Church, 722 Main Street, Newton, KS 67114.

1155. INTERNATIONAL SOLAR ENERGY SOCIETY, U.S. SECTION, 12441 Parklawn Drive, Rockville, MD 20852.

Research and development in solar energy, promotion of solar energy concepts and use.

146

1156. LIVING SYSTEMS, Route 1, Box 170, Winters, CA 95654.

Consultants on design of energy conserving buildings and solar energy systems. Research on energy conservation.

1157. MIDAMERICA COALITION FOR ENERGY ALTERNATIVES, 5130 Mission Road, Shawnee Mission, KS 66205.

1158. MIDWEST ACCESS CATALOG, Midwest Energy Alternatives Network, Governors State University, Park Forest South, IL 60466.

Access to information, publications and organizations in the Midwest involved in alternative energy.

1159. MIDWEST ENERGY ALTERNATIVES NETWORK, Governors State University, Park Forest South, IL 60466.

Information and communication network for people, organizations, schools, governments, business, etc. in the Midwest interested in energy alternatives, conservation, planning and many related issues.

1160. MOTHER EARTH NEWS HANDBOOK OF HOMEMADE POWER, Bantam Books, Inc., 666 Fifth Avenue, New York, NY 10019. 1974.

Compilation of articles and features from THE MOTHER EARTH NEWS, featuring energy conservation and alternatives, particularly for the householder and homesteader. Also includes reprints from other sources. An excellent basic introduction to the concept of alternative energy.

1161. NATIONAL SOLAR HEATING AND COOLING INFORMATION CENTER, P.O. Box 1607, Rockville, MD 20850.

Government-funded information source on solar equipment and installers. Toll-free hotline, (800) 523-2929.

1162. THE NEW ALCHEMY INSTITUTE, P.O. Box 432, Woods Hole, MA 02543.

Alternatives, efficiency, self-sufficiency and low-impact living. Canadian Branch on Prince Edward Island. Publishes JOURNAL OF THE NEW ALCHEMISTS.

1163. NEW ALCHEMY INSTITUTE-WEST, Box 376, Pescadero, CA 94060.

1164. NEW LOW COST SOURCES OF ENERGY FOR THE HOME, P. Clegg, Garden Way Publishing, Charlotte, VT, 1975.

Descriptions of products and suppliers.

1165. NEW MEXICO SOLAR ENERGY ASSOCIATION, P.O. Box 2004, Santa Fe, NM 87501.

Solar energy and equipment research, solar heating and cooling.

1166. NORTHERN CALIFORNIA SOLAR ENERGY ASSOCIATION, c/o Dr. K.L. Coulson, Department of Agricultural Engineering, University of California, Davis, CA 95616.

1167. PRODUCING YOUR OWN POWER: HOW TO MAKE NATURE'S ENERGY SOURCES WORK FOR YOU, Carol Hupping Stoner (ed.), Rodale Press, Emmaus, PA. 1974. Paperback edition from Random House, 1975.

Information, instructions and equipment descriptions on solar, wind, biogas and water power, wood heat and energy conservation. Advice on adapting alternative energy to existing structures.

1168. RENEWABLE AND DECENTRALIZED ENERGY AND RESOURCES GROUP, c/o Harvey Eder, Route 1, Box 240, Glen Arbor Road, Ben Lomond, CA 95005.

Citizen organization using waste resources to manufacture solar energy collectors and other alternative energy systems. Kits and licensed plans available.

1169. THE RENEWABLE ENERGY HANDBOOK, Richard Fine, Energy Probe, 43 Queen's Park Crescent East, Toronto, Ontario M5S 2C3 CANADA.

Information for Canadian energy users on energy alternatives for efficiency, equity and environmental soundness.

1170. SANTA CRUZ ALTERNATIVE ENERGY COOPERATIVE, P.O. Box 66959, Scotts Valley, CA 95066.

1171. SOCIAL ECOLOGY PROGRAM, Goddard College, Plainfield, VT 05667.

Intensive 12-week program in social ecology and environmental sciences, for B.A. and M.A. credit. Includes alternative technology, the politics of ecology, no-growth economy, and practical work in wind, solar and methane-powered energy production.

1172. SOLAPIC, Franklin Institute Research Labs, 20th and Race Streets, Philadelphia, PA 19103.

Information on applied solar energy.

1173. SOLAR APPLICATION AND RESEARCH, LTD., 1729 Trafalgar Street, Vancouver, B.C. V6K 3R9 CANADA.

Solar energy bibliography with commentary and ordering information.

1174. SOLAR DIRECTORY, Ann Arbor Science Publishers, P.O. Box 1425, Ann Arbor, MI 48106.

Directory of information on solar energy development projects, corporations, manufacturers and distributors of solar equipment, directory of funding sources, and list of persons involved in solar technology. Formerly published by Environmental Action of Colorado.

1175. THE SOLAR DIRECTORY, WHO IS DOING AND SELLING WHAT IN SOLAR ENERGY IN THE U.S.A., available in Canada from: Renouf Publishing Company Ltd., 2812 Ste. Catherine Street West, Montreal, Quebec H3H 1M7 CANADA.

1176. SOLAR ENERGY BIBLIOGRAPHY/BOOK CATALOG, International Compendium, 10762 Tucker Street, Beltsville, MD 20705.

1177. SOLAR ENERGY DIRECTORY, Centerline Press, 401 South 32nd Street, Phoenix, AZ. 1975.

Listing of manufacturers and suppliers involved in using and controlling solar energy.

1178. SOLAR ENERGY HANDBOOK, Time-Wise Publications, P.O. Box 4140, Pasadena, CA 91106.

Reference book on solar energy and solar systems, with definitions, charts and tables.

1179. SOLAR ENERGY INDUSTRIES ASSOCIATION, 1001 Connecticut Avenue NW, Washington, D.C. 20036.

Newsletters: SOLAR ENERGY WASHINGTON LETTER and SOLAR ENERGY INDUSTRY REPORT.

1180. SOLAR ENERGY RESEARCH AND INFORMATION CENTER, INC., 1001 Connecticut Avenue NW, Washington, D.C. 20036.

1181. SOLAR ENERGY SOCIETY OF AMERICA, P.O. Box 4264, Torrance, CA 90510.

Not connected with International Solar Energy Society. Promoting solar and related energy knowledge and management.

1182. SOLAR ENERGY SOCIETY OF CANADA, INC., P.O. Box 1353, Winnipeg, Manitoba R3C 2Z1 CANADA.

Canadian branch of the International Solar Energy Society, quarterly newsletter. Alternate address: P.O. Box 129, Postal Station C, Winnipeg, Manitoba R3M 3S7 CANADA.

1183. SOLAR ENERGY UPDATE, The First Ozark Press, Box 1137-E, Harrison, Arkansas 72601.

Guide to solar power for the homesteader, small farmer and householder, recently revised to include material through January 1, 1977.

1184. SOLAR HEATED BUILDINGS: A BRIEF SURVEY, William A. Shurcliff, 19 Appleton Street, Cambridge, MA 02138. 1977.

This will be the last edition of this useful directory
as the compiler feels there are now too many solar
heated buildings to be discussed in one volume.
Description of important solar heated buildings and
systems.

1185. SOLAR REVIEW, Deerbrook, WI 54424.

Guide to manufacturers of all types of solar equipment
and solar energy system components.

1186. SOLAR USAGE NOW, INC., Department ME, Box 306, Bascom, OH
44809.

Thirty-two page catalog on solar collectors and other
equipment for solar heating.

1187. SOUTHERN OREGON ALTERNATIVE ENERGY EXCHANGE, Route 1, Box 7,
Jacksonville, OR 97530.

1188. SPECTRUM: AN ALTERNATIVE TECHNOLOGY EQUIPMENT DIRECTORY,
special issue of ALTERNATIVE SOURCES OF ENERGY, Route 2,
Box 90A, Milaca, MN 56353.

Equipment for solar, wind, water and biogas systems,
including small-scale systems.

1189. SYNERJY, Box 4790, Grand Central Station, New York, NY 10017.

Alternate energy directories listing over 3,500 publications, products and facilities for solar, geothermal,
electrical, water, wind energy, heat transfer and
storage. Annotations and ordering information.

1190. TOTAL ENVIRONMENTAL ACTION, INC., Old Cheshire Boarding House,
Church Hill, Harrisville, NH 03450.

Workshops for consumers and professionals in solar
energy, wind power, wood heat, water power, and integrated energy systems.

1191. UPLAND HILLS ECOLOGICAL AWARENESS CENTER, 481 Lake George
Road, Oxford, MI 48051.

Programs in solar energy, wind power and methane power.

1192. THE WALDEN FOUNDATION, James B. DeKorne, P.O. Box 5, El Rito,
NM 87530.

Solar heating related to an ecosystem approach to food
production at home.

1193. WIND ENERGY BIBLIOGRAPHY, Windworks, Box 329, Route 3
Mukwonago, WI 53149.

1194. WIND ENERGY DIRECTORY, Conserver, Box 36, Rockville Centre,
NY 11571.

Comprehensive listing of plans, parts, catalogs, manufacturers and distributors of wind energy systems and
components.

1195. WIND ENERGY SOCIETY OF AMERICA, 1700 East Walnut Street,
Pasadena, CA 91106.

Promotion of wind systems as an alternative to conventional power systems. Information and research on wind
systems and applications.

1196. WIND ENERGY UTILIZATION BIBLIOGRAPHY, Technology Application
Center, University of New Mexico, Albuquerque, NM
87131. 1975.

Annotated, and indexed by topic, author, title, keyword.

1197. WIND POWER, P.O. Box 233, Mankato, MN 56001.

Research and publications on wind-driven electric power
systems.

1198. WINDWORKS BIBLIOGRAPHY, Windworks, Box 329, Route 3, Mukwonago,
WI 53149. 1974.

Comprehensive bibliography on all aspects of wind power,
including catalog listings and an annotated source list.
Emphasis on small-scale systems and do-it-yourself.

1199. WOOD ENERGY INSTITUTE, Box 1, Fiddlers Green, Waitsfield,
VT 05673.

Information on efficient uses of wood for home heating,
etc., and promotion of wood as a renewable energy source.

1200. WOODBURNERS ENCYCLOPEDIA, The Fire Place, P.O. Box 173,
Oberlin, OH 44074.

Comprehensive guide to wood heating, with test results,
cost analyses, specifications for 400 stoves, and list
of 150 manufacturers of wood heating equipment.

1201. ZOMEWORKS, Steve Baer, P.O. Box 712, Albuquerque, NM 87103.

Innovative solar consulting group which sells plans for
solar water heaters and other solar heating equipment.
Available for professional consultation.

SOURCES FOR THE VISUALLY HANDICAPPED

SOURCES FOR THE VISUALLY HANDICAPPED

Introduction

This section lists producers and distributors of Braille, large-print and Talking Book materials. Also included are some of the main sources of information on new materials for the visually handicapped. The New York Times Large Type Weekly, listed in this section, provides current events material from the Times regular news coverage. The Library of Congress can give the most up-to-date listings of books and periodicals dealing with energy that have been reproduced in forms accessible to the blind or partially sighted.

1202. AMERICAN FOUNDATION FOR THE BLIND, 15 West 16th Street, New York, NY 10011.

1203. AMERICAN PRINTING HOUSE FOR THE BLIND, 1839 Frankfort Avenue, Box 6085, Louisville, KY 40206.

1204. BASIC SCIENCE EDUCATION SERIES, Row, Perterson, Inc.

> Available from National Association for the Visually Handicapped, 305 East 24th Street, New York, NY 10010.

1205. BRAILLE BOOK REVIEW, U.S. Library of Congress, Division for Blind and Physically Handicapped, Washington, D.C. 20540. Bi-monthly. Monthly and annual indexes.

> Annotated list of Braille materials and library services, fiction and non-fiction, juvenile and adult.

1206. BRAILLE TRANSCRIBER'S GUILD, 1807 Upas Street, San Diego, CA 92103.

1207. COMMUNICATION CENTER FOR THE MASSACHUSETTS ASSOCIATION FOR THE BLIND, 88 Stephen Street, Boston, MA 02115.

1208. FOR YOUNGER READERS: BRAILLE AND TALKING BOOKS, U.S. Library of Congress, Division for Blind and Physically Handicapped, Washington, D.C. 20540. Annual.

1209. FOUNDATION FOR BLIND CHILDREN, 3720 North 75th Street, Scottsdale, AZ 85251.

1210. JOHANNA BUREAU FOR THE BLIND AND VISUALLY HANDICAPPED, INC., 22 West Madison Street, Chicago, IL 60602.

1211. JOHN MILTON SOCIETY FOR THE BLIND, 366 Fifth Avenue, New York, NY 10001.

1212. LARGE TYPE BOOKS IN PRINT, R.R. Bowker, 1180 Avenue of the
      Americas, New York, NY 10036.

      Non-fiction and text books for levels from beginning
      readers through adult. Fiction is also listed.

1213. NATIONAL ASSOCIATION FOR THE VISUALLY HANDICAPPED, 305 East
      24th Street, New York, NY 10010.

1214. NEW YORK TIMES LARGE TYPE WEEKLY, P.O. Box 2570, Boulder,
      CO 80302.

      Coverage from regular editions of the New York Times,
      and a review of the week's major news events from the
      Sunday Times.

1215. RECORDING FOR THE BLIND, INC., 215 East 58th Street, New York,
      NY 10022.

      Produces audio cassettes and tapes, and raised line
      drawings from primary through senior high levels, and
      for college students and adults.

1216. SOURCES OF READING MATERIAL FOR THE VISUALLY HANDICAPPED,
      American Foundation for the Blind, 15 West 16th Street,
      New York, NY 10011.

      Lists of sources for Braille, large-type and talking
      books, in a variety of subjects.

1217. STUDY LESSONS IN GENERAL SCIENCE, Gross and Kopilow. Follett,
      1968.

      In 18 point type, for grades 7-12. Unit I: Intro-
      duction to Matter and Energy; Unit II: Work and Energy.
      Available from American Printing House for the Blind,
      1839 Frankfort Avenue, Box 6085, Louisville, KY 40206.

1218. TALKING BOOK TOPICS, American Foundation for the Blind,
      15 West 16th Street, New York, NY 10011. Bi-monthly.

      Book reviews and ordering information for disc, tape
      recorded, Braille and large-type books. Fiction and
      non-fiction, for children and adults. November issue
      has annual author-title index. Also available from the
      Library of Congress.

1219. TALKING BOOKS: ADULT, U.S. Library of Congress, Division
      for Blind and Physically Handicapped, Washington, D.C.
      20540.

      Guide to Talking Books available from the Library of
      Congress or state distribution centers, with ordering
      information.

1220. U.S. LIBRARY OF CONGRESS, Division for Blind and Physically
      Handicapped, Washington, D.C. 20540.

Administers Braille and talking book services. List of regional libraries available.

1221. VOLUNTEER TRANSCRIBING SERVICES, 205 East Third Avenue, Suite 201, San Mateo, CA 94401.

1222. VOLUNTEERS SERVICE FOR THE BLIND, Nevel Building for the Blind, 919 Walnut Street, Philadelphia, PA 19107.

1223. VOLUNTEERS WHO PRODUCE BOOKS, BRAILLE AND LARGE TYPE, Library of Congress, Division for Blind and Physically Handi-capped, Washington, D.C. 20540.

Listing of individuals and groups transcribing reading material. Arranged alphabetically by state, with a "special talent" index.

RECENT SOCIAL SCIENCE ENERGY STUDIES:
AN ANNOTATED BIBLIOGRAPHY

RECENT SOCIAL SCIENCE ENERGY STUDIES:

AN ANNOTATED BIBLIOGRAPHY

Frederick Frankena
Frederick H. Buttel
Denton E. Morrison

The studies summarized below have been distilled from two
extensive bibliographic searches which culminated in: Energy: A
Bibliography of Social Science and Related Literature and Energy II:
A Bibliography of 1975-1976 Social Science and Related Literature,
compiled by Denton E. Morrison and others and published by Garland
Publishing Co., respectively, in 1975 and 1977. Every effort was
made to find and annotate the empirical studies they cite. The
reference list in each such study was also checked for relevant
citations. The reader is directed to the preface of the first volume and the appendix of the second for an account of the method and
materials used in the literature search.

These summaries represent a substantial portion of the studies
conducted between 1972 and mid-1976 on energy and society, especially those aimed at examining behavioral reactions to the 1973-1974
energy crisis. As such they are a baseline for continued research
in this increasingly important field of study. Within constraints
of space and time as much information as possible has been included
for each citation via the simple format of method, variables, and
findings. However, the reader would do well to consult the original work once he has selected the appropriate items using this
bibliography.

Acknowledgement is due Sally Cook Lopreato and Marian Meriwether
for their assistance in acquiring and annotating many of these
studies. Support for this work was provided by the National
Academy of Sciences, National Research Council. An earlier draft
was prepared for the Committee on Nuclear and Alternative Energy
Systems.

1224.

Albrecht, Stan L., "Socio-Cultural Factors and Energy Resource Development in Rural Areas of the West," unpublished manuscript, Department of Sociology, Brigham Young University, 1976.

> Method: A theoretical model of the socio-cultural impacts of boom growth communities based upon social and demographic data from several such communities in Wyoming and Montana which face extensive population growth due to large scale energy resource development. Secondary data, mostly U.S. Bureau of Census, for the years 1960, 1970, and 1974.

> Variables: The effect of energy resource development upon population growth and social change in adjacent communities.

> Findings: Data from the impacted communities suggest that they will experience interpersonal, family, and community social problems; problems in the delivery of social services; and impacts on the physical environment that have social or quality of life implications.

1225.

Angell and Associates, Inc., A QUALITATIVE STUDY OF CONSUMER ATTITUDES TOWARD ENERGY CONSERVATION, Chicago: Bee Angell and Associates, 1975.

> Method: A marginal frequency analysis of public attitudes and conservation behavior, with respect to the energy situation, involving interviews with a series of ten focus groups of 8-10 per group from four different regions of the U.S. Participants were given a cash incentive and were selected from a heterogeneous cross-section of the population. Study is ongoing.

> Variables: Attitudes and conservation behaviors.

> Findings: Respondents were willing to make sacrifices in energy consumption only if the need is severe and responsibility shared by all. They generally reacted to energy shortage with frustration and sense of helplessness, felt the general public to be exploiting the situation, and tended to blame the oil companies, public utilities, "business," and the government--not the Arabs or the OPEC countries. Based on perceived U.S. technological "know-how," respondents felt optimistic about the future. Since the energy situation was not regarded as critical, they were generally skeptical of suggestions for large environmental sacrifices.

1226.

Barnaby, David J., and Richard C. Reizenstein, "Profiling the Energy Consumer: A Discriminant Analysis Approach," Knoxville: University of Tennessee, 1975.

Method: Multivariate discriminant analysis of behavioral and attitudinal responsiveness to the energy crisis and consumer segments willing to reduce energy consumption, based on a survey conducted February, 1974 and repeated October, 1974. Data were gathered by mail questionnaire from a random sample (N=2500) of Columbus, Georgia; Charlotte, North Carolina; and Chattanooga, Tennessee.

Variables: The effect of the energy crisis on consumer groups and home heat preference groups, in terms of attitudes and behaviors.

Findings: Profiles of high, medium, and low gasoline consumer groups and home heat preference groups. The major factor which seems to identify the energy conscious consumer (for both gasoline and heat) is exposure to media and sources of personal information. Income also was an effective discriminator. A negative attitude toward energy conservation and pollution abatement exists among those respondents who desire to maintain the status quo. Major changes February to October, 1974 seem to be increased awareness that energy resources are running short; greater agreement that rationing will become necessary; and increased agreement with controlling home temperature by law. Also, fewer respondents agreed that oil companies which advertise their efforts to develop new energy sources are more concerned with public relations than with resource development.

1227.

Bartell, Ted, "The Effects of the Energy Crisis on Attitudes and Lifestyles of Los Angeles Residents," University of California, Los Angeles; presented at the 69th Annual Meeting of the American Sociological Association, Montreal, August, 1974.

Method: A multiple regression analysis of a February-March 1974 area probability sample (N=1069) survey of Los Angeles County adults to determine the behavioral and attitudinal effects of the energy crisis and the likely impacts on general political orientations and public policies.

Variables: The effect of the energy crisis on beliefs about its severity and duration, feelings about who is to blame, general perceptions of governmental institutions and actors, preferences among alternate energy policies, and expectations concerning future economic conditions and employment.

Findings: The only significant predictor of personal energy conservation
appeared to be an anticipated effect on one's future employment.
Although some changes in basic life style were reported, these were
generally perceived as causing minimal personal difficulties. Certain socio-demographic characteristics and energy-related expectations were significantly related to beliefs about who was responsible
for the energy crisis. Blacks, women, and persons of lower socioeconomic status tended to blame the President; men and non-Blacks
tended to blame the oil companies. Energy policies having a negative effect on the environment were most often supported by persons
more highly integrated into the social order, and the findings of
this study would predict increasing support for environmentally
detrimental activities if the crisis worsens.

1228.

Barth, Michael, et al., THE IMPACT OF RISING RESIDENTIAL ENERGY PRICES ON THE LOW-
INCOME POPULATION: AN ANALYSIS OF THE HOME-HEATING PROBLEM AND POLICY
ALTERNATIVES, Washington D.C.: U.S. Department of Health, Education and
Welfare, Office of the Assistant Secretary for Planning and Evaluation,
Office of Income Security Policy, Technical Analysis Paper #3, December, 1974.

Method: A study of the effect of rapidly rising residential energy prices,
specifically for home-heating fuels, on the lower income population,
along with an analysis of various policy alternatives to ameliorate
this impact. Home heating is discussed with respect to climate,
housing characteristics, fuel type, and fuel prices. Regional
variations in home-heating cost increases and the problems faced
by low-income households are given special attention.

Variables: The effect of increased energy costs on the low income population in the U.S.

Findings: There are wide variations in heating cost increases as a result
of regional differences in energy price levels and in price
changes, coupled with variations in climate and type of fuel used.
Low income households spend an average of more than 11% of their
income on natural gas and electricity. This compares with less
than 2% for households with annual incomes over $16,000. Yet
the poor consume only 56% as much electricity as the non-poor
and 82% as much natural gas. Home-heating needs of the poor
are lower than other income classes because low-income households are generally in warmer climates, involve smaller sized
homes and are less likely to be single-unit dwellings. But they
also have fewer energy-saving features. The net effect is that
low income households pay in dollar amounts about three-fourths
of what is spent by other households for home heating. However,
while actual dollar increases will be somewhat smaller for the
poor, the increases must be covered out of considerably smaller
incomes.

165

1229.

Berman, M.B., et al., THE IMPACT OF ELECTRICITY PRICE INCREASES ON INCOME GROUPS: WESTERN UNITED STATES AND CALIFORNIA, Santa Monica, California: The Rand Corporation, 1972. Document #R-1050-NSF/CSA.

    Method: An analysis of the effects of increased prices of electricity on residential consumers of different income classes, with the objective of estimating how a reduction in the growth rate of consumption of electricity (through increased prices for electricity) might be distributed among the various socio-economic groups in the residential sector. Western U.S. data are from the Bureau of Labor Statistics and the Federal Power Commission for the years 1960-61. Data for California for the year 1970 were obtained by Los Angeles area utilities.

    Variables: The effect of increased prices of electricity on residential consumers of different income classes in conjunction with stock of appliances, size of household, size and volume of the housing unit and the quality of its insulation, variance in the outside temperature, price of fuels, and amount of time spent away from the home.

    Findings: Consumers in the $5,000 and over category (60% of the population in the year studied) consumed 80% of the electricity demanded by the residential sector, whereas those earning less than $3,000 (17% of the population) consumed only 6% of the total electricity demanded. For Los Angeles, 1970, the ability of low income groups to reduce consumption of electricity was found to be lower than had been predicted by previous research which had used highly aggregated data to predict average reduction. This suggests that the ability to reduce consumption increases with income.

1230.

Berman, M.B., and M.J. Hammer, THE IMPACT OF ELECTRICITY PRICE INCREASES ON INCOME GROUPS: A CASE STUDY OF LOS ANGELES, Santa Monica: The Rand Corporation, 1973. Document #R-1102-NSF/CSA

    Method: A study basically dealing with the likely effect of electricity price increases on income groups in the residential sector of the City of Los Angeles. A model of residential electricity consumption is utilized and fitted to data provided by the L.A. Department of Water and Power for the period 1970-71. Data on population are from U.S. Bureau of Census tract reports, and for climate from the U.S. Department of Commerce.

    Variables: The effect of residential energy price increases on eight income level groups in Los Angeles.

<u>Findings</u>: Residential consumption appears to be largely dependent on
household income and number of household members when the price
of fuels is constant across households. Consumption of electricity was determined to be influenced most by household income,
the influence increasing exponentially with income levels. Relative to income, then, the burden of electricity price increases
was found to fall most heavily on the lowest income groups. Low-
income groups (below $5,000 per annum) constituted 31% of all
L.A. households at the time of the study, but only accounted for
17% of total electricity consumption. For high-income groups
(over $15,000) the respective figures are 21% and 41%. The
evidence is interpreted to indicate that low-income groups
have limited ability to reduce electricity consumption, by contrast with high-income groups.

1231.

Blevins, Audie L., Jr., "Public Response to Municipally Owned Utilities in Wyoming,"
LAND ECONOMICS, 52, 2 (May, 1976), 241-245.

<u>Method</u>: A 1972 survey of 215 randomly selected households in five communities
with municipally owned electrical distribution systems and two
communities with privately owned electrical systems.

<u>Variables</u>: Attitudinal perceptions of municipally owned power systems.

<u>Findings</u>: Residents in the communities with municipally owned utilities favor
public power, are satisfied with the cost of electricity, and believe
that public power is an equitable way to raise revenue. Respondents
in communities with private power generally favor municipally owned
power and are equally divided over the issue of their community
entering the power business.

1232.

Blevins, Audie L., Jr., James G. Thompson, and Carl B. Ellis, "Assessing the Social
Impact of Energy Related Growth in Wyoming," Paper presented at the Annual
Meeting of the Society for the Study of Social Problems, Montreal, August,
1974. (Department of Sociology, University of Wyoming).

<u>Method</u>: A January, 1973, random sample survey of 219 persons, representing a
cross section of individuals in Campbell County, Wyoming, were
questioned about their attitudes toward coal development in the
county.

<u>Variables</u>: Attitudinal perceptions of social impacts of coal development.

<u>Findings</u>: A large percentage of the respondents are fearful of the damage
strip-mining will do to the physical environment and their lifestyles.
They would like to see strict reclamation controls instituted.

167

1233.

Bloom, Martin, et al., THE EFFECT OF RISING ENERGY PRICES ON THE LOW AND MODERATE INCOME ELDERLY, Washington, D.C: Federal Energy Administration, March, 1975.

Method: A study of the effects of energy cost charges on the income and expenditures of the low and moderate income elderly. Expenditure data are from the 1973 Washington Center for Metropolitan Studies Nationwide Sample (N=1455) and its subsample (N=115) of poor households where the age of the head is 65 or over. Secondary data on household consumption patterns and prices were taken from U.S. Bureau of Labor Statistics documents. The climatic data came from an atlas put out by the U.S. Department of Commerce.

Variables: The effects of increasing energy costs on the elderly in the United States, particularly as related to age, income, climate and type of fuel, at the national, regional and SMSA levels.

Findings: Nationally, the elderly poor consume less energy than any other age-income group. Energy expenditures increase gradually as income level rises for all ages combined, but for the age group 65 and over the increase is dramatic from the lower middle income level to the upper middle income level. There were smaller differences in expenditures across income levels for natural gas relative to electricity and gasoline. Of the three energy sources, the energy gap was greatest for gasoline. For all U.S. regions, lower income elderly couples spent a disproportionate amount of their budget on fuel and utilities, compared to similar intermediate or higher budget households. The reverse was found regarding expenditures on transportation. Elderly households spent a much higher portion of their budget for energy in colder than in warmer regions. Energy price inflation hit hardest in the New England and Middle Atlantic States, and least in the South and Southwest. Overall, the rapid rise in energy prices was found to have imposed a severe economic strain on the elderly.

1234.

Bullard, Clark W., III, and Robert A. Herendeen, "Energy Impact of Consumption Decisions," INSTITUTE OF ELECTRICAL AND ELECTRONIC ENGINEERS PROCEEDINGS, 63, 3 (March, 1975), 484-493.

Method: An attempt to determine the energy cost of goods and services, largely based upon a 360-sector input-output analysis of the U.S. economic system. The model is applied to illustrative problems, including (1) total energy cost of an automobile and an electric mixer, (2) energy impact of urban bus and auto transportation, (3) total energy impact of a family's expenditures, (4) energy and labor impacts of government spending, (5) industrial energy dependence, (6) national import-export energy balance, and (7) an energy conservation tax. Secondary data are used and are taken from various statistical sources for the year 1963.

Variables: The direct and indirect effects of consumption decisions in selected sectors of the economy on energy consumption.

Findings: A set of tables is provided which summarize the results of the analyses of the seven problems listed above. Regarding the energy impact of a family's expenditures, for the lowest income group, energy purchases account for 2/3rds of the total purchases, while for the highest income group, the fraction drops to 1/3. Estimates of the impact of direct energy use only might therefore be misleading.

1235.

Bultena, Gordon L., PUBLIC RESPONSE TO THE ENERGY CRISIS: A STUDY OF CITIZENS' ATTITUDES AND ADAPTIVE BEHAVIORS, Ames: Iowa State University Department of Sociology, Sociology Report 130, 1976.

Method: A random sample interview survey of 190 persons from different socioeconomic groups in Des Moines, Iowa. Questions focused on attitudinal and behavioral responses to the 1974 energy crisis. Differences between the three social-class groups were tested for statistical significance using Chi Square.

Variables: Attitudinal perceptions of the crisis, impact of shortages on behavioral patterns, socioeconomic effects, and sociopolitical actions of respondents, all referenced to upper (N=56), middle (N=74), and lower (N=60) class groups.

Findings: Most respondents attributed shortages to the actions of large oil companies, not to dwindling energy reserves. Middle and lower-class respondents more often blamed activities of large oil companies and concomitant government favoritism. Upper-class respondents tended to perceive the energy shortage in terms of dwindling energy reserves. More upper class, than middle or lower class, persons reported taking energy conservation measures. Upper class emphasized environmental quality goal, lower class interested in keeping energy prices down.

1236.

Burdge, Rabel J., et al., "Public Opinion on Energy," unpublished manuscript, Department of Sociology, University of Kentucky, 1976.

Method: Marginal frequency analysis of opinions on various energy conservation and utilization measures based on a statewide survey taken in Kentucky (N=3,438).

Variables: Energy use for transportation, home consumption, new energy sources, government regulation of energy use.

Findings: Respondents were willing to accept energy conservation measures in personal transportation and home use, and to support the development of new energy sources with government funding.

1237.

Buttel, Frederick H., "Social Structure and Energy Efficiency: A Preliminary
Cross-National Analysis," Unpublished manuscript, Department of Sociology,
Michigan State University, East Lansing, 1976.

Method: Data for circa 1965 are taken from UN-type data sources. The
cross-national analysis includes 118 nation-states. A ratio of
gross national product in $ U.S. to total inanimate energy con-
sumption (kg coal equivalent) is used as a measure of energy
efficiency.

Variables: Effect of level of production (GNP per capita), division of labor
outside of the agricultural sector (percentage of gross domestic
product from the agricultural sector--an inverse indicator), urbanization, level of defense expenditures, territorial size, and
population density on energy efficiency, using multiple regression/
correlation analysis.

Findings: Level of production, division of labor outside of the agricultural
sector, and population density exhibit substantial inverse relationships with energy efficiency. Territorial size bears little
bivariate relationship to cross-national patterns of energy efficiency, but proves to have a discernible inverse relationship at
the multivariate level. Level of defense expenditures and urbanization have substantial bivariate relationships with energy efficiency; these variables, however, have only small multivariate
relationships with the dependent measure.

1238.

Carter, Lewis F., "Interactive Monitoring System for Evaluating Energy Policy Effects
on Private Nonindustrial Consumption," Pullman: Washington State University
Social Research Center, on-going.

Method: The establishment of a continuously updated interactive data retrieval
system to monitor consumer energy conservation and the effects of
energy shortages and policies involving a rotating panel design with
six panels selected each year from a random area stratified sample
(N=3100) of Washington state residents. An examination is made of
differences in matched time-lag changes, displacement of time series
data, and pertubations within specific periods. Data are from utilities, interviews, and questionnaires.

Variables: Changes in consumer conservation attitudes and behaviors pursuant
to changes in energy policy and availability.

Findings: Not yet reported.

1239.

Cohen, Reuben, "Setting Equitable National Goals for Household Energy Conservation," Paper presented at the Annual Meeting of the American Sociological Association, New York, August, 1976. (Available from Response Analysis Corporation, Princeton, New Jersey.)

Method: A study of two specific conservation levels, or targets, for electricity and natural gas. These conservation targets are based on an analysis of the distribution of energy consumption by households in the U.S., data being obtained through personal interviews from a May-June, 1973 national probability sample (N=1,500) of households. Low income households were over-sampled and weighting procedures were used to compensate for the disproportionate sampling. Data were also obtained from utilities for 1/3 of the sampled households. A multiple regression analysis was employed to determine the major factors which affect energy use by households.

Variables: The effects of household and climatic characteristics on consumption of natural gas and electricity. Also the potential for energy conservation in relation to specific targets based on the effects established.

Findings: About one-third of the variation among households was explained by factors including size of household, use of fuels for such essentials as hot water and cooking, and climatic conditions. The top income group used about 50% more natural gas and 160% more electricity, on a per household basis, than the lowest. Author relates these findings to target #1 (that U.S. households consume no more energy than the average reported in 1972-73 for households with their characteristics) and finds that 18% of electricity and 13% of natural gas consumption could be conserved. Overall, the biggest per-household share of the savings would have to come from upper income groups. Target #2 (that households occupy no more than the median number of rooms reported for households of the same numbers of persons, and consume no more energy than the average reported for households of that type) would entail a similar savings, requiring a disproportionate reduction by the upper income groups relative to lower because of the more discretionary expenditure for living space at upper income levels.

1240.

Corr, Michael, and Dan MacLeod, "Getting It Together," ENVIRONMENT, 14, 9 (November, 1972), 2-10.

Method: A 1972 study of energy and lifestyle using a questionnaire on energy consumption habits, administered to twelve communes in the Minneapolis area totaling 116 members.

Variables: The effect of commune living on consumption of natural gas, electricity, and gasoline and on energy use in appliances and automobiles.

Findings: Communal lifestyle would appear to make a pronounced difference
in personal energy consumption compared with the average for
households nationally and in some cases for the Minneapolis area.

1241.

Cunningham, William, and Sally Cook Lopreato, "Energy Consumption and Conservation:
Attitudes and Beliefs in the Southwest," Austin: The University of Texas,
Center for Energy Studies (published report not yet available).

Method: Statistical analysis of a fall, 1975, random sample (N=10,000) of
five Southwest cities, drawn by mail questionnaire and billing records
and utilizing a subsample of 801 all-electric users in Austin, Texas
(Spring, 1976), to identify energy attitudes and behavior across
diverse groups of individuals and to relate those to conservation
practice incentives.

Variables: Energy attitudes and behavior with respect to socioeconomic
variables.

Findings: Not yet reported.

1242.

Curtin, Richard T., "Consumer Adaptation to Energy Shortages," Ann Arbor: University
of Michigan Survey Research Center, 1975 (unpublished manuscript).

Method: A multiple classification analysis of conservation behavior, attitudes,
and motivations based upon a fall, 1974 random sample (N=1400) interview survey of family heads or spouses drawn from the 48 contiguous
states of the U.S.

Variables: The effect of the energy crisis on conservation behavior with respect
to the consumption of gasoline, electricity, and home heating.

Findings: Widespread conservation did occur, but there was an almost equally
widespread prospect of difficulty in making future adjustments. Fur-
thermore, differences in past experience and expected difficulty were
further highlighted by the substantial numbers of respondents who
either report patterns of adaptive or maladaptive adjustments in their
energy consumption: while fully one-third of all respondents said
they have conserved in the past and could do so again without difficulty, yet another one in four said they did not conserve and could
not do so without great difficulty.

1243.

Doering, O.C., et al., INDIANA'S VIEWS ON THE ENERGY CRISIS, CES Paper No. 6,
West Lafayette, Indiana: Cooperative Extension Service, Purdue University,
1974.

Method: Marginal frequency analysis of 670 randomly selected Indiana residents responding to a questionnaire concerning public attitudes
toward the 1973-74 energy crisis.

<u>Variables</u>: Attitudinal perceptions; behavioral patterns.

<u>Findings</u>: Although the results indicate substantial adjustments in the home and some changes in personal transportation habits due to the energy shortages, only 36% of the respondents indicated that the crisis had any "real effect" on their lifestyles.

1244.

Doner, W. B., Inc., and Market Opinion Research, CONSUMER STUDY: ENERGY CRISIS ATTITUDES AND AWARENESS, Detroit: W.B. Doner, Inc., 1975.

<u>Method</u>: A marginal frequency study of awareness, attitudes, behavioral changes, and perceived future effects of the energy crisis, based on a stratified area sample (N=525) of the state of Michigan. Data were collected between February 27, 1975 and March 10, 1975 by telephone interview.

<u>Variables</u>: Perceptions of and attitudes toward the energy crisis, behavioral changes due to shortages, and socioeconomic impacts.

<u>Findings</u>: Half of sample perceived that there was an energy crisis, up 9% since a similar survey one year earlier (50%, February, 1975 versus 41%, February, 1974). Media attention the major reason for the increase. Three-fourths claimed to have changed their behavior in response to the energy crisis, even though only half really believe it exists. Sixty-one percent report conservation, the principal behavioral changes being cutting down on the use of gasoline, lowering home temperatures, and using less electricity, mainly by reducing use of lights. One motive for conservation measures is clearly because "conserving energy saves money."

1245.

Donnermeyer, Joseph F., "Social Status and Attitudinal Predictors of Intentions Toward Practicing Energy Conservation Measures and Energy Consumption Behavior," Lexington: Department of Sociology, University of Kentucky (Ph.D. dissertation in progress).

<u>Method</u>: An analysis of the consistency between attitudes, intention, and behavior via an examination of the social status and attitudinal predictors of willingness to practice energy conservation measures and the actual energy consumption in the home. Data are from a statewide (Kentucky) random sample survey (N=3438) employing a mailed questionnaire. The survey determined respondents' attitudes toward a number of issues, including the environment. A subsample involving Fayette County, in conjunction with data from utilities, was used to study energy consumption. Data analysis employs simple and partial regression techniques.

Variables: The effect of income, education, and occupation; favorable
attitudes toward a series of environmental issues; and willingness to practice energy conservation measures, on energy consumption.

Findings: Not yet reported.

1246.

Dunlap, Riley E., and Kenneth R. Tremblay, Jr., "Hard Times and Human Concerns:
Assessing Probable Reactions to Scarcity," Paper presented at the Joint
Session of the Rural Sociological Society and the Society for the Study
of Social Problems at their Annual Meetings, New York, August, 1976.

Method: Panel survey (summers of 1970 and 1974) of a sample of 3,101
Washington State residents to determine any changes in their
priorities for funding government programs.

Variables: Changes from 1970 to 1974 in attitudes toward the allocation
of government funds for government programs in personal security,
public services, social justice, and environmental quality.

Findings: There was a trend toward increased support for personal security
programs, e.g., retirement benefits, health and medical care, and
social security benefits, but a decline in concern for social
justice, environmental quality, and the public good.

1247.

Early, John F., "Effect of the Energy Crisis on Employment," MONTHLY LABOR
REVIEW, 97, 8 (August, 1974), 8-16.

Method: Marginal frequency analysis of the impact on employment of the
energy shortage during November, 1973, to March, 1974, using
data from the payroll survey of the Current Employment Statistic
program, an analysis of its monthly employment estimates and
labor turnover data for manufacturing, and unemployment estimates from the current population survey of households.

Variables: The effects (direct, negative indirect, positive indirect and
tertiary) of the energy crisis on employment in the U.S. economy.
The four types of effects relate, respectively, to the in-
ability of establishments to obtain the power needed for operation, to reduction of goods and services output, to increased
demand for alternative fuel sources and equipment needed for
extraction, and to reductions in aggregate demand due to layoffs.

Findings: Most obvious direct effect was gasoline service station
closings and reduced hours. Other direct effects were well
scattered, but involved an estimated 150,000 to 225,000 jobs
lost from November, 1973 - March, 1974. For the same period
indirect effects entailed a total employment decline of
310,000, more than half of this in the manufacture of automobile parts. Increased unemployment heaviest among adult
men, especially the 20-24 age group. The employment decline
was smaller than those in major employment slowdowns and was
also more concentrated in a few industries.

1248.

Eastman, Clyde, Peggy Hoffer, and Alan Randall, A SOCIOECONOMIC ANALYSIS OF ENVIRONMENTAL CONCERN: CASE OF THE FOUR CORNERS ELECTRIC POWER COMPLEX, Las Cruces: New Mexico State University Agricultural Experiment Station, Bulletin 626, 1974; also reported in "How Much to Abate Pollution," PUBLIC OPINION QUARTERLY, 38 (Winter, 1974-75), 574-584.

Method: A study to determine which socioeconomic characteristics are associated with concern for environmental quality as measured by willingness to pay for pollution abatement. Five bidding games were designed to obtain monetary estimates of willingness to pay for pollution abatement, and utilized in interviews of a target sample (N=760) of reservation and non-reservation residents, and out-of-region recreationists, conducted during the summer of 1972 and January, 1973. The sample was drawn from the four-state air-quality control region in the southwest U.S.

Variables: Willingness to pay for pollution abatement as determined by bidding games and as related to demographic and socioeconomic factors.

Findings: A clear majority of respondents were willing to pay for pollution abatement. A large majority also preferred that companies bear responsibility for financing the costs of abatement. Few consistent relationships were found between concern for environment and socioeconomic characteristics such as age, occupation, income, ethnicity, and organizational participation. Aesthetic concern had little association with membership in any particular social stratum.

1249.

Eichenberger, Mary Ann, "A Comparison of Ownership of Selected Household Appliances and Residential Energy Use by Employed and Nonemployed Homemakers in the Lansing, Michigan, Area," unpublished M.A. thesis, Michigan State University, 1975.

Method: 1974 self-administered questionnaire and interview survey of families in the Lansing S.M.S.A. to assess residential energy use. Data were drawn from a random sample (N=187) and analysis of covariance was the technique used to analyze data.

Variables: The effects of employment status and income on direct residential energy consumption and appliance use by function and quantity.

Findings: No significant differences was found among full-time, part-time and nonemployed homemakers on total quantity of appliances and of major appliances owned by households. The test of a hypothesis concerning total direct residential energy revealed no significant difference among these three employment status groups of homemakers. A non-significant finding but one that was considered interesting was that households with a fully employed homemaker used 8% less, and part-time 6% less, residential energy than nonemployed homemakers.

175

1250.

Frankel, Michael L., MANAGING THE SOCIAL AND ECONOMIC IMPACTS OF ENERGY DEVEL-
OPMENTS, Washington, D.C.: U.S. Energy Research and Development Administration, 1976.

Method: A handbook for local, regional, state, and federal officials,
which sets forth the types of energy developments, and the
assessment of their impacts as well as the institutional settings and organizational designs to manage the impacts. It is
concerned primarily with changes in the demographic or economic
characteristics of an area, including employment, personal income, transportation, housing, waste treatment and disposal,
water supply, education, recreation, safety, and health care.
The handbook describes the scope of concern, the parameters to
be measured, the information required, the relevant methodologies,
standards, and techniques, and references which are available.

Variables: Effects of energy developments on the demographic and economic
characteristics of an area.

Findings: A summary guide for assessing the social and economic impacts
of energy developments.

1251.

Freudenberg, William R., "The Social Impact of Energy Boom Development of Rural
Communities: A Review of Literature and Some Predictions," Paper
presented at the 71st annual meeting of the American Sociological
Association, New York, 1976.

Method: Summary of the largely fugitive literature on the social impacts
of energy boomtown development, and development of hypothesis
concerning the nature and severity of these impacts.

Variables: Size of host community, size and suddenness of development
rate, proportion of jobs going to "locals," skill requirements
of new jobs, number of new (unemployed) persons entering a
region, the unemployment rate outside the region, and notoriety
of the project outside of the region, in relation to the amount
of social disruption caused by energy development of rural
communities.

Findings: No concrete findings are reported, but the following hypotheses
guide the author's ongoing study of energy boom-town development:
(1) Size of host community being held constant, social disruption
will be directly related to both the size and the suddenness of
development. (2) Given a particular development, the lower the
population density of the host region, the greater the disruption.
(2a) Impact will be inversely proportional to the local unemployment rate. (3) The higher the proportion of jobs going to
persons already living within the area, the lower the disruption.
(3a) The higher the skill requirements, the greater the disruption. (4) Impact will be directly proportional to the number
of new (unemployed) persons entering a region, and will vary
directly with (4a) the unemployment rate outside the region, and
(4b) the general notoriety of the project outside the region.

176

The author is conducting a questionnaire study (N=800) of energy growth/potential growth towns of Colorado, with plans to employ a panel design (re-interview) at a later time. This questionnaire is the primary methodological device to be used to test the hypotheses given above.

1252.

Gilmore, John S., "Boom Towns May Hinder Energy Resource Development," SCIENCE, 191 (February 13, 1976), 535-540.

Method: A qualitative appraisal, based on the author's socioeconomic impact study of coal and oil shale boom towns, of the effects of rapid growth associated with energy resource development. A typology of the boom town is used to assess its functions and problems.

Variables: The socioeconomic effects of the rapid growth accompanying energy resource development.

Findings: The boom town is a major source of social tension in an area or a region. Both litigation and legislation result, with confrontation between state and federal governments a likely outcome. When communities are unable to furnish the services and facilities to accomodate rapid growth or to maintain the amenities of life, productivity declines, projects over-run time and cost schedules, and operating outputs fall behind.

1253.

Gollin, Albert E., et al., ENERGY CONSUMERS' AWARENESS AND PREFERENCES IN NEW HAMPSHIRE: A COMPARATIVE ASSESSMENT, Washington, D.C.: Bureau of Social Science Research, Inc.,,1976.

Method: A marginal frequency analysis of a random sample of New Hampshire households (N=256) surveyed by telephone interview between April 30 and May 2, 1976 to determine energy consumers' awareness and preferences with an eye toward establishing the degree of comparability to the relationship between residents and energy consumption in neighboring states.

Variables: Population, housing, climatic conditions, appliance saturation, consumer concern and awareness, household routines and time-of-day pricing, and acceptance of time-of-day pricing.

Findings: Respondents were found to be concerned about energy, especially for home heating and electrical appliance use. They were usually aware of the main aspects of the pricing system now in use in the state; and a substantial number seemed prepared to consider significant changes in their household routines in order to take advantage of a favorable alternative pricing scheme.

1254.

Gottlieb, David, "Sociological Dimensions of the Energy Crisis," Austin: The State
   of Texas Governor's Energy Advisory Council, 1974. Project E/S-5.

   Method: Statistical analysis (frequencies, crosstabs, x^2) of a random sample
            of housing units from urban (Houston, Amarillo) and rural (Colorado
            County, Deaf Smith County) areas of Texas to discern perceptions,
            attitudes, behavior, and expectations in response to the energy crisi
            A pre-embargo sample from South Texas (April-May 1974) and a post-
            embargo sample from North Texas (June-July, 1974). Urban sample base
            on year-round housing units from census block data tapes, rural deriv
            from names and addresses from county tax rolls. Data were gathered
            from heads of household by hand delivered questionnaires.

   Variables: The effects of the energy crisis on the communities sampled with
            respect to three categories of socioeconomic status, an energy know-
            ledge scale, and a measure of energy consumption.

   Findings: The only major difference found between the two regional samples
            was a greater concern about anticipated escalating costs of energy
            expressed by the post-embargo (North Texas) sample. Both samples
            failed to see the energy crisis as of long-term consequence; showed
            distrust of energy producers and distributors, and government officia
            connected with energy policies and programs; felt citizens are energy
            wasteful; and did not blame environmentalists. Lack of knowledge
            about energy sources and appliance energy consumption characteristics
            were found to be correlated with lack of belief in the crisis. Poore
            people seem to be affected most because they have the fewest alter-
            natives. Consensus about waste was not accompanied by voluntary con-
            servation sentiments. Respondents believed that the more real the
            perception of the crisis or emergency, the more responsible the pop-
            ulace would become, and that the shortage was more of a political
            contrivance than the result of the world running out of fuel.

1255.

Gottlieb, David, and Marc Matre, "Conceptions of Energy Shortages and Energy Conserving Behavior," Paper presented at the Annual Meeting of the American
   Sociological Association, San Francisco, August, 1975. (University of Housto

   Method: Marginal frequency analysis of randomly selected heads of household
            (N=782) in four different geographic areas of Texas, via question-
            naires administered during and shortly after the Arab oil embargo
            of Spring, 1974.

   Variables: Attitudinal conceptions toward energy crisis; behavioral patterns
            concerning energy conservation.

   Findings: A large percentage of the respondents expressed scepticism regard-
            ing the reality of the energy crises and a high level of distrust of
            energy producing corporations and of leadership in the national
            government. Those of lower socioeconomic status more often reported
            conservation efforts, especially in response to rising utility
            costs, than those of higher socioeconomic status.

1256.

Gottlieb, David, and Marc Matre, "Sociological Dimensions of the Energy Crisis--
A Follow-up Study," Houston: The University of Houston Energy Institution,
1976.

Method: Statistical analysis of a follow-up questionnaire, administered
April-June, 1975, on the sample described above under Gottlieb, 1974,
to determine the extent of change in energy conservation behavior,
attitudes, and values from those in the 1974 study.

Variables: The effects of the energy crisis on the communities sampled with
respect to three categories of socioeconomic status, an energy knowledge scale, and a measure of energy consumption.

Findings: The majority of respondents came to accept the proposition that the
world is running out of fuel and that Americans are wasteful, but
there was only a slight increase in belief in a serious, long term
energy crisis. No positive relationship was found between belief and
energy consuming behavior. The main motivation of those who conserved was cost. Thus, while higher socioeconomic status persons
were more likely to believe in the crisis, lower and middle status
people were more likely to reduce energy usage. As in 1974, the
majority was not energy and conservation knowledgeable, was only willing
to endure policies which would cause the least disturbance in lifestyle, and largely blamed big oil companies for the crisis.

1257.

Grier, Eunice S., "Changing Patterns of Energy Consumption and Costs in U.S. House-
holds," Paper presented at Allied Social Science Association Meeting, Atlantic
City, September, 1976. (Available from Washington Center for Metropolitan
Studies.)

Method: A report on the findings of two consecutive national surveys, conducted
by the Washington Center for Metropolitan Studies, which examine the
responses of U.S. households to increasing energy costs. Each was a
random sample cross-section survey, the first (N=1600) having been done
in the spring of 1973 and the second (N=3200) during the spring of
1975.

Variables: The effect of increased energy costs on householders' behaviors and
perceptions in conjunction with energy-related practices.

Findings: An energy conservation ethic is beginning to take hold among U.S.
households, but efforts to conserve are as yet meager. Although residential energy costs have risen rapidly, they remain a relatively small
portion of the average U.S. household's budget. However, for certain
categories of households--e.g., the poor and the elderly--this rising
cost is a serious and growing burden.

1258.

Hannon, Bruce, "Energy Conservation and the Consumer," SCIENCE, 189, 4197 (July 11, 1975), 95-102.

Method: Data evaluation in connection with three conservation "dilemmas:" (1) the substitution of energy for labor; (2) the relation between personal income and energy use; and (3) the respending of saved dollars as a function of energy use. Secondary data from U.S. Department of Commerce, Edison Electric Institute, and other sources for various years from 1925-1975.

Variables: The effect of economic activities on the energy-intensity of dollar flows.

Findings: (1) When wages increase relative to costs, then energy use increase through the process of mechanization. (2) Energy use and income are linearly connected such that the spending of an average additiona dollar of income demands nearly the same amount of energy, regardless of one's income level. (3) Saving energy usually means saving money--the respending of which reduces, if not eliminates, the energy first thought saved. Given the interactions shown for these three "dilemmas," it is argued that there are probably no popularly acceptable solutions to energy conservation.

1259.

Hannon, Bruce, "Energy, Employment, and Transportation," FORENSIC QUARTERLY, 49, 4 (September, 1975), 497-511.

Method: An estimate of the impact of transportation systems on energy use and on employment, using an input-output model. U.S. data for 1963 1967 are used in this study.

Variables: Dollar flow values from 362 sectors of the U.S. economy transformed into energy flow values.

Findings: In general, the slower the mode of transportation, the less energy intensive it is. Cars and airplanes are more energy-intensive than buses, and trucks more so than trains.

1260.

Harris, Louis, and Associates, A SURVEY OF PUBLIC AND LEADERSHIP ATTITUDES TOWARD NUCLEAR POWER DEVELOPMENT IN THE UNITED STATES, New York: Ebasco Services, 1975.

Method: A study designed to measure attitudes of the public and their leaders toward the development of nuclear energy in the United States, based on a nationwide random sample (N=1537) of households conducted by in-person interviews between March 21 and April 3, 1975. In addition, 301 interviews were conducted with neighbors of three nuclear power plants: 195 in San Onofre, California; 93 in Morris, Illinois; and 103 in Indian Point, New York. Finally, between March 31 and April 12, 1975 in-person interviews were conducted with 201 leaders nationwide: 51 political, 51 business, 47 regulators, and 52 environmental.

<u>Variables</u>: Public and leadership attitudes toward nuclear power development in the U.S., with reference to respondents' socioeconomic background, political interests, and concerns over environmental and health issues.

<u>Findings</u>: The public sample believed strongly in the prospect of a serious energy shortage that will not disappear overnight. Four in five hoped the U.S. would become independent of foreign energy sources. Nuclear energy was viewed by them as a viable alternative to fossil fuels as a source of electric power. The biggest drawback (registered by 63%) in the public's mind is the disposal of radioactive waste materials, followed by escape of radioactivity into the atmosphere (49%), chance of an explosion in the case of an accident (47%), thermal pollution (47%), the threat of sabotage (39%), giving off polluting fumes (36%), and the possibility of theft of plutonium (34%). However, 26% regarded nuclear power plants as "very safe" and 38% as "somewhat safe," with only 13% believing they are "not so safe" and 5% believing that they are "dangerous " ; 18% were undecided on this issue. Neighbors of nuclear power plants indicated that they had learned to live with them. The public identified some apparent advantages of nuclear energy over coal and oil, and were prepared to live with the risks involved if proper safeguards and precautions are taken. Leaders, especially those in politics, seriously underestimated public concern about environmental quality and public support for building more nuclear plants. Both the public and leaders regarded scientists as more credible than any other group (e.g., government leaders, the media, environmentalists). Although the public expected government to regulate nuclear energy development, it harbored deep distrust of government control of private industry or intrusion into the private sector as the agent of development.

1261.

Hass, James W.,et al., "Coping with the Energy Crisis: Effects of Fear Appeals Upon Attitudes Toward Energy Consumption," JOURNAL OF APPLIED PSYCHOLOGY, 60, 6 (1975), 754-756.

<u>Method</u>: A 2 X 2 factorial experiment conducted in 1975 which examines the persuasive effect of two communication variables—(a) the magnitude of noxiousness of a threatened event and (b) the probability of its occurrence—in connection with an energy crisis. The subjects were 60 students enrolled in undergraduate business courses. Analysis of variance was used for main and interaction effects.

<u>Variables</u>: The effect of two between-subjects experimental manipulations: high versus low magnitude of noxiousness of a potential energy crisis and high versus low probability of that event's occurrence.

Findings: Although increases in the perceived likelihood of an energy
shortage had no effect, increments in the perceived noxiousness
or severity of an energy crisis strengthened intentions to reduce energy consumption.

1262.

Heberlein, Thomas A., "Conservation Information: The Energy Crisis and Electricity
Consumption in an Apartment Complex," ENERGY SYSTEMS AND POLICY, 1, 2 (1975),
105-118.

Method: Time-series experiment to determine the effect of informational
material designed to either increase or decrease the amount of
electricity use in an apartment complex near Madison, Wisconsin,
March and April, 1973.

Variables: Electricity consumption and three types of information inputs.

Findings: Neither the attempt to "engineer" a behavior change nor the
energy crisis influenced electricity consumption in these apart-
ments.

1263.

Herendeen, Robert A., "Affluence and Energy Demand," MECHANICAL ENGINEERING, 9,
6 (October, 1974), 18-22.

Method: Input-output analysis of Bureau of Labor Statistics data for
368 sectors of the U.S. economy (aggregated to 97) in order to
evaluate direct and indirect energy needs of three income classes.

Variables: The effect of income (measured by three "classes) on seven
consumption categories, i.e. direct energy purchase, food and
water, housing and clothing, auto purchase and maintenance,
medical and education, transportation and recreation (besides
auto), and investment.

Findings: Increasing importance of indirect energy impact with income.
2/3 of energy indirect for highest income classes, 1/2 for
all consumers. A flat rate energy tax would be less regressive
than one only on direct uses.

1264.

Herendeen, Robert A. and Jerry Tanaka, ENERGY COST OF LIVING, Urbana: University of Illinois, Center for Advanced Computation, Document 171, 1975.

Method: Evaluation of energy requirements of household expenditures for
all products from the 1960-61 Consumer Expenditure Survey of the
Bureau of Labor Statistics (N=13,000), using input-output analysis.

Variables: Socioeconomic variables, e.g. income, number of members,
location, and age of family head, as related to household
energy requirements and expenditures.

Findings: Within error bounds one "universal" curve shows the dependence of energy impact of expenditures for households of 2 through 6 members. A typical poor household exerts about 65% of its energy requirements through purchases of residential energy and fuel. This fraction drops to 35% for an affluent household.

1265.

Herendeen, Robert A. and Anthony Sebald, "Energy, Employment and Dollar Impacts of Certain Consumer Options," in Robert H. Williams, (ed.), FORD FOUNDATION ENERGY POLICY PROJECT REPORT: THE ENERGY CONSERVATION PAPERS, Washington, D.C.: Ford Foundation, 1975.

Method: An examination of energy conservation opportunities in switching from one transport mode to another, using input-output analysis. Energy and dollar costs are calculated, along with employment impacts for both intercity and urban transport modes. Secondary data are taken from various statistical sources for the years 1963 and 1971.

Variables: Per miles values for dollars, BTU's, and man-years.

Findings: The more labor-intensive, less energy-intensive, and more economical transportation modes were rail for intercity travel and buses for urban travel. For intercity travel the modes in order of increasing energy-intensiveness were train, car, and plane, although car and train were sometimes nearly equal. Urban bus travel costs 52% more money, used 42% less energy, and was twice as labor-intensive as urban car travel on a per-passenger-mile basis when total actual user costs are compared.

1266.

Hirst, Eric, and John C. Moyers, "Efficiency of Energy Use in the United States," SCIENCE, 179, (March, 1973), 1299-1304.

Method: A review of 1970 energy use in transportation, space heating, and air conditioning to ascertain possibilities for conservation. Secondary data gathered from various sources, e.g. Stanford Research Institute, Edison Electric Institute, and U.S. Bureau of the Census.

Variables: Effect of energy consumption patterns in transportation, space heating, and air conditioning on efficiency of energy utilization.

Findings: (1) To some extent the current mix of transport modes is optimal, disregarding non-internalized social costs. (2) Electrical resistance heating is more wasteful of primary energy than direct combustion heating. (3) Air conditioning units vary widely in efficiency; an improvement in average efficiency of same would result in appreciable energy savings. Various measures for potential energy savings are suggested pursuant to the data analysis.

1267.

Hogan, M. Janice, "Energy Conservation: Family Values, Household Practices, and Contextual Variables," unpublished Ph.D. dissertation, Michigan State University, 1976.

Method: Determination of differences in the rate of adoption of household energy conservation practices among families with varying husband-wife patterns of congruency and commitment to values. Statistical analysis of 1974 Lansing S.M.S.A. survey (N=157).

Variables: The effect of contextual variables and measured attitudes such as self-esteem, social responsiveness, familism, and eco-consciousness, on energy conservation behavior.

Findings: Those conscious of environmental problems were most likely to report conserving energy. No systematic relationship was found between conservation behavior and contextual variables--education, occupation, employment status of wife, age, family size, income, and urban-rural residence. The same lack of association was true of self-esteem and familism in relation to conservation behavior.

1268.

Hohenemser, Christoph, et al., "The Distrust of Nuclear Power," unpublished manuscri June, 1976 (available from Clark University, Worcester, Massachusetts 01610).

Method: A qualitative study of the safety of nuclear power, particularly to explore how the risk of rare events enters into energy policy decisions of our society.

Variables: Public perceptions of nuclear power safety as they pertain to con-comitant policy decisions.

Findings: The issue of nuclear safety keeps cropping up no matter how many technical problems appear to be solved. This is evident in the fact that many times more per fatality is spent on accident prevention in the nuclear industry than is spent for this purpose in the fossil fuel power plants, even after the catastrophic nature of nuclear accidents is taken into account. The reasons society tends to over-whelm nuclear issues are shown to stem from the social history of nuclear power, the genuine uncertainty and complexity of safety issues the underestimation of the regulatory task, and the rancorous nature of the debate. "Distrust of nuclear power, which begins as a question about technology turns out to be as much a question about the social institutions designed to develop, regulate, and contain that technology."

1269.

Holmes, Cheryl Lynn, "A Socio-Demographic Analysis of the Energy Intensiveness of Food Consumed with Implications for National Energy Conservation," unpublished Master's thesis, Michigan State University, 1975.

Method: An examination of the relationship between food consumption and associated energy costs, based upon a statistical analysis of a 1974 survey of a stratified random sample (N=190) of households in the Lansing S.M.S.A. Family food consumption and socio-economic characteristics were determined via interview. Data on fossil fuel expenditure from agriculture to supermarket were obtained from a variety of sources.

Variables: The energy intensiveness of individual diets, given estimates of the energy cost per pound and per serving of specific food items. Individual diets were posited in terms of family income, occupation of the head, education and working status of the wife, and urban or rural residence.

Findings: The data did not support any hypothesized differences between groups, i.e., there is apparently no one group toward which to direct national energy conservation efforts in connection with shifts in food consumption.

1270.

Holmes, Cheryl Lynn, and Peter Michael Gladhart, "The Energy Cost of Food: The Family Can Now Make Informed Decisions," unpublished manuscript, 1976. (Department of Family Ecology, Michigan State University).

Method: Food consumption data was collected from a 1974 subsample of 190 individuals from 85 families in the Lansing S.M.S.A.

Variables: Food consumption choices; consumption timeframe; energy cost of food consumed.

Findings: Energy intensiveness of individual diets was not found to vary with family income, occupation of household head, wife's education and work status, or residence location. Energy costs in BTU's per serving of selected representative foods are discussed.

1271.

Honnold, Julie A., and L.D. Nelson, "Voluntary Rationing of Scarce Resources: Some Implications of an Experimental Study," paper presented at the Annual Meeting of the American Sociological Association, New York, August 30-September 3, 1976.

Method: A typology of conservation orientations is developed to test commitment to conservation behavior, and tested on a sample (N=485) of undergraduate students surveyed by questionnaire. Hypotheses tested with a partial correlation analysis.

Variables: Scales relating conservationism, necessity, and sufficiency attitudes and perceptions to conservation orientation.

Findings: Zero order correlation between perceived sufficiency and conservation commitment of .41 (p=.001), for the hypothesis that conservationists and cynics have a higher commitment to conservation behavior than do consumerists. Results provided for five other hypotheses.

1272.

Hummel, Carl F., Lynn Levitt, and Ross J. Loomis, PERCEPTIONS OF THE ENERGY CRISIS: WHO IS BLAMED AND HOW DO CITIZENS REACT TO ENVIRONMENT-LIFESTYLE TRADEOFFS? Fort Collins: Colorado State University, Department of Psychology, Working Paper in Environmental Psychology 2, Fall, 1975.

Method: Survey of two representative samples (total N=238) of residents of a Colorado community; one when gasoline was abruptly scarce and the other after the energy problem had been established. Data analyzed by stepwise regression.

Variables: Effect of the 1973 gasoline shortage on support for (1) voluntary, (2) mandatory actions that had benefits for energy and air polution problems but entailed lifestyle costs, and (3) actions with energy benefits but environment costs.

Findings: Relatively inconsistent predictive power across five criteria (dependent variables) of explanatory variables dealing with demographics and perceived personal effects of the energy crisis. But in both samples blaming environmentalists was negatively related to support for mandatory actions that would attack air pollution as well as energy problems, and was a positive predictor for pro-energy actions that would damage the environment. Those blaming individual consumers supported mandatory remedies.

1273.

Hyland, Stanley E., et al., THE EAST URBANA ENERGY STUDY, 1972-1974: INSTRUMENT DEVELOPMENT, METHODOLOGICAL ASSESSMENT, AND BASE DATA, Champaign-Urbana: University of Illinois College of Engineering, 1975.

Method: Marginal frequency analysis of two surveys (Fall 1972, Spring 1973; follow-up in June 1974) of a 10 percent stratified random sample (N=228 for first, N=116 for second) of households in East Urbana, IL, to determine change in behavior and attitudes regarding energy and conservation. Data were gathered by a questionaire administered in personal interviews.

Variables: Behavioral change over time with respect to 382 household and individual variables in the first survey; 182 household and individual variables in the second.

Findings: (Major findings have not yet been published.) Population appears to have responded to energy crisis and concomitant rising costs by using air conditioners, vacuum cleaners, and ovens less. There has been little change in automobile use--perhaps due to respondents' high value emphasis placed on privacy, autonomy, and mobility.

1274.

Johnson, Jean, "Societal and Political Implications of the Energy Crisis," unpublished manuscript, Forecasting International, Ltd., Arlington, Virginia,
1974.

Method: A scenario approach to forecasting alternative lifestyles with
reduced energy, with baseline secondary socioeconomic data
gathered from a variety of sources and empirical studies.

Variables: Effect of alternative lifestyles (referenced to income level)
with reduced energy on energy intensity, level of risk, environment, social cohesiveness, and four dominant forces for changing
energy use: political control, technological breakthrough,
economic allocation, and social adaptation.

Findings: Twenty-four scenarios are created along with a "policy cap-
turing" technique for inferring subject (public opinion) preferences among the scenarios.

1275.

JOURNAL OF PROPERTY MANAGEMENT, "Solar Energy Installations: Trends and Lender
Attitudes," JOURNAL OF PROPERTY MANAGEMENT, 41, 1 (January-February, 1976),
21-28.

Method: A marginal frequency analysis of representatives' of lending
institutions attitudes toward solar heating and cooling of residences and the feasibility of advancing funds for same, based on
a questionaire survey (N=300).

Variables: Lender attitudes toward solar heating and cooling with respect
to fuel savings, reliability, insurability of home, etc., as well
as on their feasibility for purposes of finance.

Findings: Nearly three-fourths believed solar energy would represent a
feasible alternative energy source for heating and cooling of
single family residences during the next ten years. Financiers
indicated a preference for making loans on solar homes. Concern
was expressed about the expected life of solar equipment and
the associated maintenance costs.

1276.

Kasperson, Roger, et al., "Nuclear Energy, Local Conflict, and Public Opposition,"
unpublished manuscript, August, 1976 (available from Clark University,
Worcester, MA 01610).

Method: A qualitative study of the emergence of public concern over the
risks of nuclear power. Appropriate articles appearing in the
New York Times and Reader's Guide between 1945 and 1975 were
surveyed and categorized. Local controversy, the escalation of
conflict to higher societal level, and linkages to the environmental movement are discussed in turn. A review is made of various surveys, conducted in America and abroad, of public attitudes
toward nuclear power. The socioeconomic correlates of public
response are noted, particularly the differences between men
and women (see the Harris survey report above).

<u>Variables</u>: The nature of and change in public concern since 1945 with respect to nuclear power.

<u>Findings</u>: Prior to 1955 there was little concern over the risks entailed in the operation of what were then experimental reactors. A number of accidents were reported and media interest rose between 1955 and 1961. The context of the period 1961-68 was ripe for the growth of public concern, but instead it declined precipitously. Although public interest was low in the 1960's, local controversy increased. From these isolated clashes over individual reactors, a coordinated national compaign of nuclear opposition emerged subsequent to 1968. The evidence is substantial that environmental activists have spearheaded the opposition. The prognosis of the study is that public opposition to nuclear energy at both the local and national level will not dissipate in the near future. Nevertheless, the authors expect the nuclear industry to continue to grow.

1277.

Keck, Carol A., et al., CHANGES IN INDIVIDUAL TRAVEL BEHAVIOR DURING THE ENERGY CRISIS, 1973-74, Albany: New York State Department of Transportation, Planning and Research Bureau, Preliminary Research Report 67, 1974.

<u>Method</u>: Four articles describe and analyze changes in individual travel behavior, as effected by the 1973-74 energy crisis, from the viewpoints of (1) individual responses, (2) amount of gasoline used, (3) car purchase habits, and (4) the effectiveness of car-pooling. These analyses are based on three community-wide surveys conducted by the New York State Department of Transportation during the early months of 1974. In each of the three communities (Oneonta, Gloversville/ Johnstown, and Hudson) a random selection (N=300) was made from available telephone listings, with one person being interviewed from each household.

<u>Variables</u>: The effect of the energy crisis of 1973-74 on travel behavior in terms of individual responses amount of gasoline used, car purchase habits, and car-pooling.

<u>Findings</u>: People did not react strongly to a prospective rationing of 8 gallons per week per licensed driver, notwithstanding precrisis consumption of 15-20 gallons per week average per driver. Publicity about the small number of miles per gallon for new large cars did not cause people to buy small cars so much as to by used ones. The gasoline-saving potential of car pooling was only differentially used by those who had either already shown an awareness by driving a small car or by those for whom many people shared their work destination. Overall, the energy crisis did not induce significant changes in travel habits for most people in the communities sampled.

1278.

Kelley, Tom, "The American Energy Consumer: The Way Some People Live," in
    Dorothy K. Newman and Dawn Day Wachtel, (eds.), FORD FOUNDATION ENERGY
    POLICY PROJECT REPORT: THE AMERICAN ENERGY CONSUMER, Washington, D.C.:
    Ford Foundation, 1975.

Method: A qualitative study of energy and lifestyle which utilizes a
    set of six family vignettes to provide a living frame for the
    facts and figures discussed in other chapters of the volume.
    Data were gathered from selected interviews.

Variables: Lifestyle by income and location, e.g., "David and Gloria M--
    Income $11,000 a year-plus--Near Alexandria, Va." and "Edward
    and Mable A--Income $3,000 or Less--Mid-City, Baltimore,
    Maryland."

Findings: Compared with prior generations nearly all in the six families
    interviewed were materially better off. The rise of affluence
    based on cheap energy is evident in the automobile, in both its
    symbolic and practical value. Nearly all owned or had owned a
    car. The poorest family was content to walk or take the bus.
    Mobility was a major secondary effect imputed to cheap energy
    and the automobile.

1279.

Keyfitz, Nathan, "World Resources and the World Middle Class," SCIENTIFIC AMERICAN,
    235, 1 (July 1976) 28-35.

Method: A largely qualitative study of the feasibility of entry by the
    less developed countries into the resource intensive world
    "middle-class." UN figures are the points of departure.

Variables: Economic development for less developed countries as a
    function of world population growth in relation to dwindling
    world resources.

Findings: Constraints on both production and environmental quality
    limit the growth of the world middle class.

1280.

Kilkeary, Rovena, "The Energy Crisis and Decision-Making in the Family," Springfield,
    Va.: National Technical Information Service Report No. NSF-SOS GY-11543,
    January, 1975.

Method: A statistical analysis of a random sample (N=602) of Bronx and
    Queens, New York households to determine whether family charac-
    teristics and energy-related experiences affect household energy
    knowledge and conservation practices. Data were collected by
    interview during July and August, 1974.

Variables: The effect of the energy crisis on household member character-
    istics, energy knowledge, and actual practices in terms of ex-
    posure to extended blackouts, direct payment of utility bills,
    car ownership, belief that families in the U.S. pulling together
    can influence the energy crisis, family income, educational
    attainment, family composition, age, sex, and recent major appli-
    ance purchase.

189

<u>Findings</u>: Car ownership, education, and family composition (number, ages, and sex) were found to be positively related to energy knowledge scores. Exposure to extended blackouts, direct payment of utility bills, car ownership, the belief U.S. families can together affect the energy crisis, and family composition were positively related to changed practice scores, i.e., a measure of the practice of energy savings. The strongest influence on knowledge and conservation was income, with middle income having the highest scores. Families composed of couples with children also demonstrated high levels of energy knowledge and conservation practices. This study found the strongest influence on energy use to be the pocketbook. Those families who could afford to pay energy price rises did, while moderate income families tended to strive to be energy-saving.

1281.

King, Jill A., THE IMPACT OF ENERGY PRICE INCREASES ON LOW INCOME FAMILIES, Washington, D.C.: U.S. Federal Agency Administration, Office of Economic Impact, 1975.

<u>Method</u>: Econometric analysis of energy price increases on low income families, using an energy data file for a nationally representative sample of 50,000 households in the continental U.S. Energy expenditures for each of six energy types--electricity, piped natural gas, bottled gas, fuel oil, coal, and gasoline-- were imputed for each household, depending on its usage, from this data file. The primary data source was the Public Use Sample of the 1970 Census of Population, supplemented by travel information from the Nationwide Personal Transportation Study. Energy expenditures in 1974 were estimated using figures from a micro-simulation which related energy consumption and disposable income for 1973 data.

<u>Variables</u>: The effect of increasing energy expenditures for electricity, piped natural gas, bottled gas, fuel oil, coal, and gasoline, on low income families.

<u>Findings</u>: A substantial rise in expenditures for energy in the home occurred as a result of 1973-74 energy price increases. Households in New England and the Middle Atlantic regions were hardest hit. Although low-income households spent less on energy and experienced smaller absolute increases in expenditures, these expenditures and increases represented a much larger proportion of their disposable income than for high-income households, by a factor of 10. Single-family homes, larger families, and rural location were associated with larger impact because they use more energy. Impact of higher energy prices for home fuel expenditures did not vary by household characteristics, e.g., race, age, or occupation of head of household. Gasoline expenditures, and their impact, did not exhibit as wide a regional variation.

190

1282.

Kostyniuk, Lidia P., and Wilfred Recker, "Effect of a Gasoline Shortage on
Acceptability of Modes for the Urban Grocery Shopping Trip," JOURNAL
OF ENVIRONMENTAL SYSTEMS, 6, 9 (1976), 1-30.

Method: A study of the differences in perceived acceptabilities, in
relation to the gasoline shortage, of modes for the urban
grocery shopping trip. Data were gathered using a psychological
continuum scale, from a mail-out survey sent to a random sample
of 1500 households in six representative subareas of Buffalo,
New York during December 1973 - March 1974.

Variables: The effect of the gasoline shortage on travel mode to and
place of shopping, opinions on mode choice, and socio-economic
description of households.

Findings: A general increase in acceptability of walking in the middle
of the scale and a decrease in the acceptability of the driver
mode across the subsamples. Taxi, bus, and bicycle were
rated near the bottom end of the scale for all subsamples. An
increase in the acceptability of the bus was most pronounced
among the lower income subsamples; but this was not sufficient to
take this mode into the acceptable category.

1283.

Kruvant, William J., "People, Energy, and Pollution," in Dorothy K. Newman and
Dawn Day Wachtel, (eds.), FORD FOUNDATION ENERGY POLICY PROJECT REPORT:
THE AMERICAN ENERGY CONSUMER, Washington D.C.: Ford Foundation, 1975.

Method: A study of the most likely victims of pollution by examining
pollution estimates for the major part of five metropolitan
areas, and by a detailed look at the relationship between air
pollution and the socioeconomic characteristics of people in
the Washington, D.C. metropolitan area. 1968-70 secondary data
was mostly from U.S. Bureau of Census reports and pollution data
was from the District of Columbia Dept. of Environmental
Services, data from both sources having been prepared by
the Washington Center for Metropolitan Studies.

Variables: The relative income-level effect of pollution on subareas of Washington, D.C.

Findings: The Washington data show that socioeconomic characteristics
associated with disadvantage--poverty, occupations below
management and professional levels, low rent, and high concentrations of black residents--go hand-in-hand with poor air
quality. It is noted that these groups produce little of the
air pollution which affects them. The findings show that anti-
pollution policies have already helped disadvantaged groups,
proving that well-enforced policies can be effective.

191

1284.

Leholm, Arlen, et al., PROFILE OF NORTH DAKOTA'S COAL MINE AND ELECTRIC POWER
PLANT OPERATING WORK FORCE, Agricultural Economics Report No. 100, Fargo:
Department of Agricultural Economics, North Dakota State University, 1975.

Method: Marginal frequency analysis of a questionnaire mailed or handed out
to all (N=416) employees of the four largest coal mines and four
largest electric power plants in North Dakota, to determine the
socioeconomic characteristics of the operating work force in these
mines and plants. Survey was taken during June, 1974.

Variables: Years lived in present community, years worked for the given
company, rates of pay, job satisfaction, commuting distance, education, in-migration from out-of-state to work at the plants or
mines.

Findings: The work force proved to be very stable, having lived an average of 22 years in their present community and having worked an
average of 8.6 years with their present employing company. The
coal industry workers proved to have higher average annual incomes than coal workers average in the state as a whole (median
incomes average between $12,000 to $13,000 per annum), despite
their low levels of formal education (72 percent of employees
had 12 years or less of education). More than half the work
force resided within the county before they were hired. The
workers reported generally high satisfaction with their jobs.
Length of employment is negatively associated with commuting
distance. Income is positively associated with in-migration
from another state.

1285.

Levy, Paul F., "The Residential Demand for Electricity in New England," Report
No. MIT-EL-73-017, Cambridge, Massachusetts: Massachusetts Institute of
Technology, 1973.

Method: An econometric model based on 1970 cross-section data for sixty-
seven New England electric utilities and their service areas.
A two-stage least squares is used to obtain consistent coeffici-
ents in terms of estimated supply price and demand equations.
Elasticities of demand were also calculated. Data are from the
utilities and a number of statistical reports.

Variables: The effect of price on residential electricity demand in
conjunction with various socioeconomic characteristics.

Findings: Residential demand for electricity was found to be significantly
correlated with its average price, family income, family size,
heating degree days, and the ownership (private or public) of
the electric utility--price and income being the most important
determinants. The supply price is correlated with the quantity
of electricity consumed, utility operation and maintenance costs,
total number of customers, degree of urbanization, and the
ownership of the utility. A significant elasticity of demand
with respect to price as well as income was established.

1286.

Little, Ronald L., "Rural Industrialization: The Four Corners Region," In
Lewis Carter and Louis Gray (eds.), SOCIAL IMPLICATIONS OF ENERGY SCARCITY:
SOCIAL AND TECHNOLOGICAL PRIORITIES IN STEADY STATE AND CONSTRICTING
SYSTEMS, Washington, D.C.: National Science Foundation, 1976.

Method: The study team utilized a random sample survey of 407 residents
of five communities (Blanding, Monticello, Kanab, and Escalante,
Utah; and Page, Arizona) in the Four Corners area of the Southwest during the summer of 1974. Each of the five communities
was in the proximity of and/or had experienced "energy resource
development." Over 92 percent of all sampled respondents fur-
nished completed interviews, and the interview schedules were
largely composed of open-ended questions. All persons interviewed
were household heads. Marginal frequency analysis of the survey
results is combined with presentation of relevant U.S. Census
data.

Variables: Attitudes toward energy development in the Four Corners Region.

Findings: Over 80 percent of the respondents were favorably disposed toward
"extant energy developments" (e.g., the Four Corners Power Plant,
Glen Canyon Dam, Black Mesa Coal Mine), and the proposed "Kaiparowits project" (a coal strip-mining venture). Two major reasons
were given by respondents for favoring extant and proposed energy
development projects: (1) the societal need for energy, and
(2) the expected employment and economic benefits of energy development projects for the region. Expected environmental damage and
the belief that there was no overwhelming need for more energy
were the two major reasons for disapproving of energy development
projects. The author speculates that these attitudes which are
highly supportive of energy resource development can be attributed
to the prevailing economic and religious patterns in the communities. For example, Mormon religious beliefs are dominant in the
region, and the author suggests that "Mormon doctrine and practice
provide both stimulus and justification for engaging in economic
activities," and "stresses the active development of resources."
See also Lovejoy (1976).

1287.

Little, Ronald L., "Some Social Consequences of Boom Towns," Logan: Department
of Sociology, Utah State University, 1976.

Method: Summarization of research on boom towns and an analysis of the
boom town experiences of Page, Arizona. The analysis of Page
employs both Census-type data and the survey data gathered in
connection with the Little and Lovejoy paper detailed below.

Variables: The social consequences of boom and bust cycles of community
development.

<u>Findings</u>: The primary result of boom town development is rapid population growth, and rapid population growth typically leads to a breakdown in municipal services and other institutional facets of the community. Because population growth is the major initial facet of the boom town phenomenon, boom towns are seldom manifest in urban areas (since a new industry that adds 10,000 or 20,000 persons will be only a negligible proportion of the population of a large city). Energy resource development in the Western states appears destined to foster boom town problems on a number of small rural communities, and these problems are apparent in the case study of Page (increased crime rate and high community conflict).

While the obvious solution to boom town problems is to slow down and stretch-out the construction process, industries find this solution unacceptable because construction compressed into a short time period is most economical. "The present national mania over energy self-sufficiency would also conflict with this (stretching-out the construction process) solution," in the opinion of the author. The author also argues that the boom town consequences of energy and other natural resource developments are seldom considered in the making of political decisions, and the environmental impact statement process only exacerbates these problems. Boom town phenomena are complex, and EISs are structured so as to direct attention away from questions that <u>need</u> to be answered and re-directs it toward questions that <u>can</u> be answered in a short period of time and with little research effort.

1288.

Little, Ronald L., and Stephen B. Lovejoy, "Employment Benefits from Rural Industrialization," Logan: Department of Sociology, Utah State University, 1976.

<u>Methods</u>: Data are taken from 248 household interviews obtained from residents of one northern Arizona and two southern Utah communities situated in the Four Corners area and near the proposed Kaiparowits power project. The Kaiparowits power project is a combined coal mining and electrical power generation project sponsored by a consortium of utilities. The respondents were selected by simple random sampling and were given open-ended interviews. All respondents are household heads.

<u>Variables</u>: The extent to which employment benefits of the Kaiparowits project might accrue to local residents, based on respondents' characteristics.

194

Findings: Similar to other rural development-industrialization projects in the U.S., the authors suggest that relatively few jobs deriving from the power generation project will go to local residents, and the jobs that local residents will get are largely in the non-skilled categories. These projected benefits are substantially lower than the respondents anticipate. Four factors are seen to account for the meager employment gains resulting from the Kaiparowits project: (1) there is a mismatch between project employment requirements--generally, skilled jobs--and the low level of job skills available in the local population, (2) there is an apparent unwillingness on the part of local residents to be trained or re-trained for employment, (3) there is a lack of desire on the part of local residents to apply for employment with the project, and (4) the communities are a long commuting distance from the project.

1289.

Lockeretz, William, "Growth of Residential Consumption of Electricity: Distribution among Households at Various Consumption Levels," LAND ECONOMICS, 51, 2 (May, 1975), 149-157.

Method: Econometric analysis of Missouri service area (about 580,000 households) of the Union Electric Company to determine how the monthly frequency distributions of residential consumption had changed from 1968 to 1973 for both base load and peak load months.

Variables: Electricity consumption of classes of consumers according to consumption level.

Findings: Only a small fraction of the overall increase in consumption went to those in the lowest consumption levels.

1290.

Lovejoy, Stephen B., "Future Energy Development in the Western United States and Inmigration," Logan: Department of Sociology, Utah State University, 1976.

Method: A random sample survey of four rural communities (ranging in population size from 638 to 2250) in Utah was made during the summer of 1974. An open-ended interview was conducted with 337 household heads. All four communities are in the Four Corners Region of the southwest.

Variables: The effects of the religious composition of inmigration streams on local attitudes toward future energy development in Southern Utah--particularly with respect to the "Kaiparowits project" (a combined coal mining and electrical power generation project sponsored by a consortium of utilities).

195

<u>Findings</u>: Inmigrants are less likely to practice the Mormom religion and less likely to favor energy resource development than "locals." Non-Mormon inmigrants were less in favor of the development of energy resources than either Mormon inmigrants or long-term residents, regardless of long-term residents' religious beliefs. The author concludes by suggesting that inmigration may have a greater impact on local attitudes in other rural areas of the Western United States where religion is not such a primary influence on attitudes toward natural resources.

1291.

Lovejoy, Stephen B., "Local Perceptions of Energy Development: The Case of the Kaiparowits Plateau," Logan: Department of Sociology, Utah State University, 1976.

<u>Method</u>: A random sample survey of 407 household heads in five communities (Blanding, Monticello, Knab, and Escalante, Utah; and Page, Arizona) in the Four Corners area of the Southwest was conducted during the summer of 1974. Each of the five communities was in the proximity of and/or had experienced "energy resource development." The response rate was in excess of 92 percent, and the interview schedules were composed of open-ended questions.

<u>Variables</u>: Opinions on the "Kaiparowits project" (a combined coal mining and electrical power generation project sponsored by a consortium of utility companies) in relation to perceived effects of the project.

<u>Findings</u>: The solid majority of residents of the five rural communities in the Four Corners region favor the Kaiparowits project. The author argues that local residents tend to overemphasize the positive effects of the project while deemphasizing or ignoring the negative consequences. He suggests further that these attitudes reflect a high level of mis-information on the part of the respondents--primarily because local residents received most of their information about the proposed project from the utilities and the news media, who in turn strongly favor the energy development project.

1292.

Mazur, Allan, and Eugene Rosa, "Energy and Life-Style," SCIENCE, 186 (November 15, 1974), 607-610.

<u>Method</u>: Correlation analysis of the 1971 energy consumption patterns in 55 countries in order to estimate some of the long-term effects of reduced energy consumption on life-style. United Nations data.

<u>Variables</u>: Energy consumption (total and electricity) in relation to life-style indicators for health, education and culture, general satisfaction and economic well-being, among all nations and developed market economies.

196

Findings: Nearly all the life-style indicators for all nations sampled correlate highly with the measures of energy consumption. Among nations with developed market economies the majority of correlations drop to insignificance. However, economic indicators generally retain high correlations with the measures of energy consumption.

1293.

Mazur, Allan, and Peter Leahy, "Movements Against Technology," unpublished manuscript, 1976. (Department of Sociology, Syracuse University).

Method: A qualitative, comparative study of citizen movements against three technical innovations: fluoridation, the antiballistic missile system (ABM), and nuclear power plants. Some consideration is also given to the movement against legalized abortion inasmuch as it is a social innovation with technical overtones. Included are graphs of the number of articles appearing in the Reader's Guide indexed under various controversial topics over appropriate timespans.

Variables: The similarities and differences between three movements against technical innovations, with an eye toward finding the general principles of such movements.

Findings: There are similar patterns of leadership and growth in the four movements analyzed. Leaders appear to be knowledgeable, reputable, well-integrated members of society. They oppose technology on grounds of ideology as well as risk. Such leaders are usually recruited by personal associates of a like political philosophy who are already in the movement. Mass media play a crucial role in a regular sequence of rise and fall of controversy. As media coverage increases so does opposition to the technology among the wider public. Coverage rises and falls with the activity of leaders. The authors suggest, based on this comparative study, that without resurgence of opposition leadership the nuclear power controversy will diminish.

1294.

Miernyk, William H., "Regional Economic Consequences of High Energy Prices in the United States," JOURNAL OF ENERGY AND DEVELOPMENT, 1, 2 (Spring 1976), 213-239.

Method: A largely qualitative and future-oriented study of the regional economy of coal, given that petroleum and natural gas are becoming less available, i.e., are rising in price as demand outruns supply. The historical, secondary data used are from various statistical sources.

Variables: Regional patterns of economic activity in the United States as a function of changing energy availability.

Findings: Throughout much of the nation's history, energy-producing regions have "subsidized" the growth of urban areas via an abundant supply of energy at low and stable prices. Pursuant to the energy crisis of 1973-74, the energy producing states have gained an economic advantage relative to the energy consuming states. The former are growing in population and economic activity and have experienced less adversity as a result of high energy prices. Based on these assumptions and trends, the author projects that there will be a regional shift of real income from the energy consumers to the energy producers. Thus, "the coal-producing regions of Appalachia and the Far West could be transformed into relatively prosperous areas. Meanwhile, parts of some of the nation's most prosperous states--such as Michigan and Connecticut--could become chronically depressed areas."

1295.

Morrison, Bonnie Maas, "Socio-Physical Factors Affecting Energy Consumption in Single Family Dwellings: An Empirical Test of a Human Ecosystems Model," unpublished Ph.D. dissertation, Michigan State University, 1975.

Method: Multiple step-wise regression and recursive path analysis were used to test hypotheses relating selected socio-physical determinants with (1) belief in the reality of the energy problem and (2) total direct energy consumption in single family detached dwellings. Datawere gathered by interview, based upon a cross-sectional field survey, and drawn from a May-June 1974 multi-stage probability sample (N=97) of the Lansing S.M.S.A.

Variables: The effect of the energy crisis of 1973-1974 in terms of energy consumption characteristics and the beliefs of household members residing in single-family dwellings.

Findings: Belief in the reality of the energy problem is positively related to mean (husband-wife) educational attainment, agreement (husband-wife)on the availability of electrical energy, and reported total costs of all energy forms used in the dwelling unit (June, 1974 - May, 1974). The number of persons, the number of major appliances, and the number of rooms in a dwelling unit contributed most to the variance explained with respect to energy consumption as a function of lifestyle and behavior. Belief in the reality of the energy problem was not found to effect a change in energy consumption patterns.

1296.

Morrison, Bonnie Maas, and Peter Gladhart, "Energy and Families: The Crisis and Response," JOURNAL OF HOME ECONOMICS, (January, 1976), 15-18.

Method: Overview of a 5-year longitudinal study of the Lansing S.M.S.A. households to determine how family decisions are made about energy use. A multi-stage area probability sample survey was used for urban (N=160) and rural (N=57) areas.

Variables: Energy use as related to attitudes, food consumption, transportation, housing conditions, financial expenditures and resources, and the character and quality of the family's functioning in terms of interaction patterns within the family, with friends, relatives, and the larger community.

Findings: Family income found to be the single best indirect predictor of residential energy consumption. In general, families in the child-rearing stages use more residential energy than families without children, or at the early or later family life-cycle stages. Larger families use more than smaller ones. Single-family homes use more energy than multifamily dwellings or mobile homes. Half of respondents believed in the reality of the 1973-74 energy crisis, but this belief did not diminish in any meaningful way the energy consumed in a household. Eco-consciousness was associated with energy conservation, and tended to be found in higher categories of educational level and occupational attainment. Urban and rural respondents differed on energy policies.

1297.

Muchinsky, P.M., "Attitudes of Petroleum Company Executives and College Students Toward Various Aspects of the Energy Crisis," JOURNAL OF SOCIAL PSYCHOLOGY, 98, 2 (1976), 293-294.

Method: Spring, 1974, survey and statistical analysis of the attitudes of 26 members of the Independent Connecticut Petroleum Association and 328 undergraduates at Iowa State University toward various aspects of the energy crisis.

Variables: Responses on (a) causes, (b) solutions, (c) personal involvement, and, (d) present and future status--all regarding the energy crisis.

Findings: Students generally found companies responsible while companies faulted government for the 1974 energy crisis.

1298.

Murray, James R., et al., "Evolution of Public Response to the Energy Crisis,"
SCIENCE, 184, 4134 (April 19, 1974), 257-263. Also reported in THE
IMPACT OF THE 1973-74 OIL EMBARGO ON THE AMERICAN HOUSEHOLD, Chicago:
University of Chicago, National Opinion Research Center, Report 126, 1974.

Method: An assessment and evaluation of changes in behavior and attitudes
of the public as they encountered energy shortages in 1973, based
on the continuous national panel survey conducted by National
Opinion Research Center. For fuel oil (N=331), electricity and
gasoline (N=1946). The sampling was done from Nov., 1973, to Feb., 1

Variables: Attitudinal and behavioral responses related to fuel oil,
electricity, and gasoline consumption.

Findings: The importance of the energy problem was perceived to be stable.
Respondents generally regarded the government to be responsible
for the energy crisis. Two-thirds of a sample taken during the
gasoline shortage believed it could be solved if individual consumers cut down on gasoline consumption. Opinions were not found
to be significantly related to region, education, income, or area
of residence.

1299.

Nelkin, Dorothy, "The Role of Experts in a Nuclear Siting Controversy,"
BULLETIN OF THE ATOMIC SCIENTISTS, 30, 9 (November, 1974), 29-36.

Method: A qualitative study of the role of academic experts in the
1973 case of organized community opposition to the construction
of a nuclear power plant on the shore of Cayuga Lake, N.Y.

Variables: The influence of academic experts on the controversy over
construction of a nuclear power plant.

Findings: (1) In a controversial situation political values can per-
meate technical material itself, whether or not the experts
intended it. (2) Public sentiment tended to reflect non-
technical considerations. (3) Technical advocacy is likely
to encourage participation in technical decisions, and to
increase the probability of controversy.

1300.

Newman, Dorothy K, and Dawn Day Wachtel, (eds.), "The Energy Gap: Poor to Well
Off," in FORD FOUNDATION ENERGY POLICY PROJECT REPORT: THE AMERICAN
ENERGY CONSUMER, Washington, D.C.: Ford Foundation, 1975.

Method: A description of how poor, middle income, and well off families
use energy, based on data from the Washington Center for
Metropolitan Studies Lifestyles and Energy Surveys, conducted
May-June, 1973 (household interviews) and June-September, 1973
(acquistion of billing data from utilities) on a nationwide
multi-stage area probability sample (N=1455) of heads of
households.

Variables: Energy consumption characteristics relative to income class
characteristics.

Findings: The poor use less energy, pay relatively more for the energy
they must have, and, more than any other American group, suffer
from exposure to the residuals of energy production/consumption.
The energy gaps were found to be greatest in gasoline use.

1301.

Newman, Dorothy K., and Dawn Day Wachtel, (eds.), "Energy in the Home," in FORD
FOUNDATION ENERGY POLICY PROJECT REPORT: THE AMERICAN ENERGY CONSUMER,
Washington, D.C.: Ford Foundation, 1975.

Method: A marginal frequency study of the role of consumer choice
in home energy use (the domain for over half of all personal
energy consumption) based on secondary data from a variety of
sources and on the Washington Center for Metropolitan Studies
Lifestyles and Energy Surveys, conducted May-June, 1973
(household interviews) and June-September, 1973 (acquisition
of billing data from utilities) on a nationwide multi-stage
area probability sample (N=1455) of heads of households.

Variables: Consumer choice in relation to: personal energy use
distribution; type of structure and heating fuel; mean
annual total cooling degree days; size of home, presence of
insulation, and other physical housing characteristics;
energy use characteristics and changes in these for regions
and specific characteristics, e.g., heating fuel use and
square feet of flour space; appliances, water heating, and
air conditioning.

Findings: On the average, space heating is the most important energy
use in the home, accounting for almost a third of all personal
energy use. Water heating uses about one-tenth. Cooking and
refrigeration each use about 3%, with other appliances and
lighting composing the remaining 9%. With regard to consumer
choice this study is more oriented toward the prescriptive
than the descriptive, although numerous data are reported on
actual consumer and housing market behavior.

1302.

Newman, Dorothy K., and Dawn Day Wachtel, "Energy, the Environment, and the
Poor," Paper presented at the Society for the Study of Social Problems,
August, 1974. (Request from Washington Center for Metropolitan Studies.)

Method: A study of the interrelationships between energy, environmental
quality, and poverty, using 1972-73 figures from the Washington
Center for Metropolitan Studies Lifestyles and Energy Surveys.
The survey used is based on a stratified national sample (N=1455)
of households. A second survey (N=142) asked utility companies serving the sample households how much electricity and
natural gas the households used and how much they paid for it
in the most recent 12 months.

201

Variables: The effect of changing patterns of energy consumption on the poor and their environment.

Findings: At the time of the study, currently accepted fuel pricing bore heavily on respondents who were least able to afford it. The price of fuel was found to be higher for those who use it as a necessity, and cheaper for those whose demand is more a matter of lifestyle. Authors conclude from their data analysis that the question of which households use energy and for what purposes is intimately related to the question of how our rapid growth in household energy consumption can be slowed. Further, slowing of the growth of energy consumption is extremely important for slowing the spread of pollution.

1303.

Odum, Howard T., et al., "Net Energy Analysis of Alternatives for the United States," in Hearings Before the Subcommittee on Energy and Power of the Committee on Interstate and Foreign Commerce, House of Representatives, Ninety-fourth Congress, MIDDLE- AND LONG-TERM ENERGY POLICIES AND ALTERNATIVES: PART I, Washington, D.C.: U.S. Government Printing Office, 1976.

Method: Given that energy flows are the basis for organization of matter, information, money, and value, this study uses systems level models to analyze the U.S. economic system in terms of flows of energy from domestic sources, from the environment, and from international exchanges. Termed "energy analysis," this technique produces estimates of net energy, i.e., energy yield minus that needed to collect and process the original energy. Part and parcel of energy analysis is a system of symbols for describing energy flows and storages. The secondary data used were transformed into fossil fuel equivalents and are derived from a variety of statistical sources.

Variables: The net energy values of present and proposed types of energy sources and their current and likely future effects on the U.S. economy.

Findings: In view of the net energy constraints pursuant
to declining stocks of fossil energy resources, it was determined that the present leveling trends in the U.S. economic
system will not be reversed. Moreover, energy analysis dia-
grams suggest that when energy sources decline, the very high
quality sectors of the economy on the end of the energy chain
decrease most. Steady state regimes (leveled economies) are
projected for the U.S. and suggest sharp changes in public
viewpoint and public policy if a smooth transition is to take
place. Net energy analyses are discussed for the following
cases: cooling towers, tertiary treatment, interface ecosystems, environmental technology generally, the harvest of
environmental products, industrialized agriculture, and
housing density. Public policy predictions based upon net
energy analysis are provided for domestic energy sources,
imported petroleum and project independence, deficit financing,
unemployment, military defense, environmental protection, and
energy pricing.

1304.

Passino, Emily M., and John W. Lounsbury, "Sex Differences in Opposition to and
Support for Construction of a Proposed Nuclear Power Plant," in Lawrence
M. Ward, et al., (eds.), THE BEHAVIORAL BASIS OF DESIGN: SELECTED PAPERS,
Shroudsburg, Pennsylvania: Dowden, Hutchinson and Ross, 1976.

Method: Statistical analysis of a 1975 survey of adults (171 males and 179
females) to determine sex differences in views toward the social
impacts of a proposed nuclear power plant for a rural Tennessee
county.

Variables: The effect of gender on perceptions of hazards, economic
growth, social disruption, lower costs, and community visibility.

Findings: 73% of males versus 57% of females answered either "definitely
yes" or "probably yes" to the question of permitting construction.
Results show that females were more opposed than males regardless
of whether respondents were above or below the median age
(46 years) and educational level (12 years), or above the
median level for number of years lived in the county (30).

1305.

Patterson, Arthur H., "The Effect of the Winter 1973-74 Energy Shortage Upon Attitudes
About Preserving the Environment," unpublished manuscript, Pennsylvania State
University, University Park, 1975.

Method: A two-wave telephone questionnaire (December, 1973 and February, 1974)
of a random sample of 60 homeowners in the Philadelphia and
Centre County areas of Pennsylvania.

Variables: The effect of the energy crisis on attitudes about preservation of
the environment, based on a ten-item attitude scale containing 9-point
Likert-type items on, e.g., importance to the person of clean air
and pure water. Data also collected on self-reported energy consumption
patterns.

<u>Findings</u>: A significant difference on post-crisis attitudes between those who
heated their homes with fuel oil, and those who used natural gas or
electricity, the former rating environmental quality less important
than the latter. This suggests that attitudes toward preserving the
environment will become more negative as the costs of those holding
the attitudes increase.

1306.

Peck, A.E., and O.C. Doering, III, "Voluntarism and Price Response: Consumer Reacti
to the Energy Shortage," BELL JOURNAL OF ECONOMICS, 7,1 (Spring, 1976), 287-29

<u>Method</u>: An econometric study of changes in efficiency of household use of two
heating fuels, natural gas (N=174) and liquefied petroleum (LP) gas
(n=279) over the period 1971 to 1974, to test the effectiveness of
the national conservation policy in creating voluntary alterations in
consumption habits. Price data were from two private gas companies
(converted to an index with April 1971 as the base period) for the
towns of Romney and Battle Ground, Indiana. A correction was made
for temperature differences between winters.

<u>Variables</u>: The effect of national conservation policy (and the energy crisis)
on fuel-use efficiency of LP gas and natural gas.

<u>Findings</u>: For LP gas customers, fuel-use efficiency increased some 14.4%,
while natural gas customers increased only 5.8%. The latter increase
was not significant at the .05 level. Authors suggest that among
rural users of the types sampled, voluntarism evidently cannot be
relied upon to reduce consumption substantially. They interpret the
results as reinforcing the need for higher prices to induce fuel-use
efficiency.

1307.

Perlman, Robert, and Roland Warren, "Effects of the Energy Crisis on Households of
Different Income Groups," Paper presented at the Annual Meeting of the
Society for the Study of Social Problems, San Francisco, 1975.

<u>Method</u>: Analysis of a November, 1974, multi-stage probability sample (N=1440
households) of Hartford, Connecticut, Mobile, Alabama, and Salem,
Oregon, to determine the differential income effects of the energy
crisis.

<u>Variables</u>: The effect of the energy crisis on income groups in terms of
energy conservation behavioral patterns and impact of the energy
crisis on attitudes and opinions.

<u>Findings</u>: In some activities, especially home heating, the well-to-do
conserved relatively more energy but did so from a much higher
energy consumption level, and still used more after their adjustments than the poor. This greater absolute usage applies
in all other categories as well, e.g., automobiles, appliances,
and electricity. Well-to-do's appeared to have relatively more
options for making energy-related adjustments.

1308.

Perlman, Robert and Roland L. Warren, "Energy-Saving by Households in Three Metropolitan Areas," Report #1 of the Energy Impact Study, Florence Heller Graduate
School for Advanced Studies in Social Welfare, Brandeis University, 1975.

Method: A study of the impact of energy problems on households of different
income levels and social characteristics, and how these adjustments
vary in areas where the energy situation and the climate differ.
This report is devoted to an analysis of aggregate energy-saving
behaviors in three metropolitan areas--Hartford, Connecticut, Mobile,
Alabama and Salem, Oregon. Interviews were conducted in November,
1974, on households selected from a multi-stage area probability
sample (N's respectively of 658, 483, and 243).

Variables: The effects of energy costs on respondents, particularly in terms
of energy-saving behaviors.

Findings: A high proportion took steps to conserve all forms of energy during
the winter of 1973-74 even though 62% thought the shortage was con-
trived to boost oil and gas company profits. Hartford is in an area
most dependent on imported oil and reported the greatest efforts to
save energy. Heating proved less critical in Mobile. Salem, with
very low electric power rates, made less of an attempt to curtail
electricity consumption. Households reported a reduction of 1.7
degrees in home heating and a drop in the speed of highway driving
from 63 to 55 m.p.h., both compared to the previous winter. Some
activities were cut back less than others, e.g., shopping, visiting,
and recreation were curtailed more than driving children to school
and after-school activities; and the use of dishwashers and clothes
dryers was reduced far more than the use of TVs and freezers.
Car pools and walking, rather than public transportation, tended
to substitute for driving. Price instead of a sense of civic
duty was the most frequent explanation for energy conservation
in driving and home heating.

1309.

Perlman, Robert, and Roland L. Warren, ENERGY-SAVING BY HOUSEHOLDS OF DIFFERENT INCOMES
IN THREE METROPOLITAN AREAS, Waltham, Massachusetts: Florence Heller Graduate
School for Advanced Studies in Social Welfare, Brandeis University, 1975.

Method: Sample survey of 1440 respondents during November, 1974, in Hartford, CT,
Mobile, AL, and Salem, OR.

Variables: Family income in relation to energy-conserving behavior, behavioral
changes in the aftermath of the energy crisis, and perceptions of the
causes of the energy crisis.

Findings: Income is positively related to belief in the reality of the energy crisis, although only moderately, and income differences in these beliefs were less pronounced than regional variations. Upper-income families reported cutting down on heating fuel use more than lower-income families, but there were only small differences among income groups in reported conservation of gasoline and electricity. There were no clear income-related patterns in the reduction of driving. Even though high income families made the greatest reductions in home heating use, their average room temperatures remained higher than those of low income families. Reductions in energy use were most pronounced where rates/costs were highest.

1310.

Pilati, David A., "Energy Savings via Behavioral Changes," INDUSTRIALIZATION FORUM, 7, 2-3 (1976), 103-106.

Method: Computer simulation to determine potential energy savings from several behavioral changes, based on data for a home typical of early 1960's construction.

Variables: The effect of behavior change on energy savings with respect to temperature control settings. Hourly weather for cities also was a variable

Findings: Theoretically, behavioral changes in the use of home space conditioning systems could reduce U.S. energy consumption by about 4.5% with little discomfort.

1311.

Rappeport, Michael, and Patricia Labaw, OPINION RESEARCH CORPORATION ENERGY POLLS, 1974-75. (Available from National Technical Information Service, U.S. Department of Commerce, Sprindgield, VA 22151.)

Method: Public opinion polls on energy were taken to determine ongoing public attitudes and behaviors toward the costs and availability of energy. Surveys were conducted monthly for 20 months, beginning September, 1974, using telephone interviews. The samples (usually N=600-1200 interviews/ month) were randomly drawn on a nationwide basis from selected adults in households having telephones. Analysis techniques used include frequencies and crosstabs (multiple regression in the study on reasons for using mass transit).

Variables: See individual listings below.

Findings: Mostly detailed tables without discussion; see individual listings below.

1312.   1974a   GENERAL PUBLIC ATTITUDES AND BEHAVIOR TOWARD ENERGY SAVING. HIGHLIGHT REPORT VOLUME I. Princeton, New Jersey: Opinion Research Corporation.
         This study is based on 1,213 telephone interviews conducted over a four-week period ending September 6, 1974. Question areas and results include: (1) respondents had come to believe that energy shortages are both a serious and long-term problem; (2) the degree to which respondents think the energy shortage is serious correlated strongly with whom they hold responsible; (3) consumer groups were seen as the most trustworthy source of information. Additional results are presented on energy-related knowledge, solutions to the energy crisis, car pools, and packaging.

1313.   1974b   GENERAL PUBLIC ATTITUDES AND BEHAVIOR TOWARD ENERGY SAVING. HIGHLIGHT REPORT VOLUME II. Princeton, New Jersey: Opinion Research Corporation.
         This report is based on 1,210 interviews conducted September 15 - October 15, 1974. The survey involved the following areas and results: (1) there was a small decline in trust in the Federal Government as an information source between the end of August and the beginning of October; (2) perceptions of reasons for the energy shortage are reported; (3) the majority of respondents thought Congress should legislate a minimum miles per gallon for autos; (4) the majority indicated that public transportation for shopping is available. Five areas having policy implications were also investigated: (1) gasoline tax policy; (2) foreign trade policy; (3) natural resource availability; (4) home lighting; and (5) home heating. For (1) and (3) respectively, results show that most respondents are strongly opposed to any rise in taxes in order to cut down usage, and they appear to hold themselves responsible for doing a poor job of conserving natural resources.

1314. 1974c   ATTITUDES AND BEHAVIOR OF RESIDENTS IN ALL-ELECTRIC HOMES.
               HIGHLIGHT REPORT VOLUME III. Princeton, New Jersey: Opinion
               Research Corporation.
                    This study concentrates on residents of all-electric homes
               and is based upon 100 personal interviews conducted among resi-
               dents in two all-electric communities in West Chester, New
               York. The purpose of the study is to determine in what way
               higher electric rates have affected behavior and whether resi-
               dents are responding to higher rates through organized poli-
               tical action. Results are reported for the following variables:
               construction of the home, cost of heating, amount of yearly
               heating bill, total electric cost during the past 12 months,
               incidence of TV sets, and political action of residents out-
               raged over increased electrical rates.

1315. 1974d   ENERGY CONSUMPTION AND ATTITUDES OF THE POOR AND ELDERLY.
               HIGHLIGHT REPORT VOLUME IV. Princeton, New Jersey: Opinion
               Research Corporation.
                    This study deals with energy consumption and attitudes of
               families with income under $7,000, and those 50 years or more
               in age. Results are reported for the following variables:
               seriousness of the energy shortage; length and severity of the
               energy shortage; the energy shortage as real vs. contrived;
               personal conservation efforts and their impact on total con-
               sumption of energy; attitudes toward specific government policies;
               changes in shopping habits as a result of inflation; cash pay-
               ment vs. charging; means of transportation; and personal effects
               of the energy shortage.

1316. 1974e   TRENDS IN ENERGY CONSUMPTION AND ATTITUDES TOWARD THE ENERGY
               SHORTAGE. HIGHLIGHT REPORT VOLUME V. Princetown, New Jersey:
               Opinion Research Corporation.
                    This study concentrates on energy consumption and
               attitudes toward the energy shortage. Issues that are con-
               sidered and on which results are reported include: seriousness
               of the energy shortage; duration of the energy shortage; per-
               ceived severity of the shortage; the energy shortage as real vs.
               contrived; effect of shortages on the public; satisfaction with
               President Ford's energy measures; effort made to save energy; re-
               sults of the price increases on people's behavior, including
               use of cars influenced by shortages, use of cars inluenced by
               price, leisure activities, and hobbies at home.

1317. 1975a   CONSUMER ATTITUDES TOWARD GASOLINE PRICES, SHORTAGES, AND THEIR
               RELATIONSHIPS TO INFLATION. HIGHLIGHT REPORT VOLUME VI.
               Princeton, New Jersey: Opinion Research Corporation.
                    This study focuses on consumer attitudes toward gasoline
               prices, shortages, and the relationship between the latter two

and inflation.

Respondents were categorized according to whether their cars averaged under 15 miles per gallon, 15-19 miles per gallon, or 20 miles per gallon or more, and they were categorized by their average miles driven per week as follows: under 30 miles, 30-99 miles, 100 miles or more.

Data are reported on the following variables: reasonableness of gasoline prices; efforts made to save energy; concern for gas mileage; attitudes towards rationing vs. higher prices; higher prices for low mileage cars; higher taxes on gas vs. taxes on cars; the environmental costs of producing more energy; environmental threats of energy self-sufficiency; power plants and pollution; water and air pollution; the impact of lowered car usage on rate of inflation; and sponsoring of ads on gasoline mileage.

1318. 1975b CONSUMER ATTITUDES AND BEHAVIOR RESULTING FROM ISSUES SURROUNDING THE ENERGY SHORTAGE. HIGHLIGHT REPORT VOLUME VII. Princeton, New Jersey: Opinion Research Corporation.

This study deals with consumer attitudes and behavior resulting from issues surrounding the energy shortage and is divided into (1) highlights from Opinion Research Corporations energy impact program (Waves 20-21), (2) analysis of the role of education on attitudes and behavior; (3) data on type of fuel used for home heating and its effects on consumer behavior attitudes, and (4) synthesis of available data dealing with the public's willingness to pay for pollution controls and environmental cleanup.

In addition, the report includes data on the rising cost of electricity; rationing; the role of education in attitudes toward strip mining; energy self-sufficiency; power plants and oil refineries as a cause of air pollution; and oil heat users.

1319. 1975c CONSUMER BEHAVIOR AND ATTITUDES TOWARD ENERGY-RELATED ISSUES. HIGHLIGHT REPORT VOLUME VIII. Princeton, New Jersey: Opinion Research Corporation.

This study is concerned with such national problems and issues as: unemployment, inflation, energy shortage, rationing vs. increased prices, increased oil import taxes, pollution control requirements, and nuclear power plants; sensitivity to rising gasoline prices; public awareness of FEA and specific FEA advertisements; certain energy-saving efforts among the general public and lack of public motivation and belief in the existence of an energy crisis; and public attitudes toward nuclear power plants including thermal pollution, radiating discharge, nuclear accident, or disposal of radioactive wastes.

1320.   1975d   GENERAL PUBLIC ATTITUDES AND BEHAVIOR REGARDING ENERGY SAVING.
                  HIGHLIGHT REPORT VOLUME IX. Princeton, New Jersey: Opinion
                  Research Corporation.
                       This study focuses on: seriousness of the energy shortage;
                  methods for solving the energy problem; inflation and increased
                  prices, unemployment, and the rebate plan; the role of rebates
                  to encourage installation of storm windows and insulation; atti-
                  tudes toward gasoline use and gas taxes, including concern with
                  automobile gas mileage; appliance purchases, including the price
                  of appliances and the electricity they consume; and public atti-
                  tudes toward returnable bottles and cans.

1321.   1975e   GENERAL PUBLIC ATTITUDES AND BEHAVIOR REGARDING ENERGY SAVING.
                  HIGHLIGHT REPORT VOLUME X. Princeton, New Jersey: Opinion
                  Research Corporation.
                       A study of energy saving divided in five parts: (1)responsib
                  ity for conservation of natural resources; (2)public awareness of t
                  Federal Energy Administration; (3)attitudes and behavior related to
                  daylight savings time; (4)automobile usage and attitudes toward al-
                  ternatives; and (5) insulation of homes among the general public.

1322.   1975f   THE PUBLIC'S ATTITUDES TOWARD AND KNOWLEDGE OF ENERGY-RELATED
                  ISSUES. HIGHLIGHT REPORT VOLUME XI. Princeton, New Jersey:
                  Opinion Research Corporation.
                       This study concentrates on public attitudes with re-
                  spect to energy-related issues, including: attitudes toward
                  nuclear power plants; the impact of school programs on home
                  energy consumption; factors affecting the public's use of
                  mass transit; company efforts at energy conservation.
                       In connection with these categories the following
                  variables are considered: role of the school in emphasizing
                  energy conservation; efforts of children to conserve at home;
                  efforts of children to recycle; car pooling in relationship
                  to long distance mass transit; availability of public trans-
                  portation; interest in public transit for shopping; drawbacks
                  to using public transportation; likelihood of using buses if
                  special lanes were provided for them; impact of increased
                  travel time; type of mass transit most needed; and money for
                  mass transit vs. highways.

1323.   1975g   GENERAL PUBLIC BEHAVIOR AND ATTITUDES REGARDING VACATION AND
                  BUSINESS TRAVEL, BEVERAGE CONTAINERS, REASONS FOR USING MASS
                  TRANSIT. HIGHLIGHT REPORT VOLUME XII. Princeton, New Jersey:
                  Opinion Research Corporation.
                       A study concerned with vacation and business travel,
                  including vacation; weekend and business travel; attitudes
                  regarding beverage containers; and a regression analysis of
                  the reasons for using mass transit.

The following variables were involved: travel miles anticipated; kinds of trips taken; duration of trips; types of transportation; places visited; number of miles traveled; effect of energy situation on trips; regional differences in availability of containers; type of container preferred and type purchased; reasons for container selection; public reaction to deposit containers; attitudes towards mass transit, and mass transit available as a means of going to work.

1324.   1975h   ENERGY-RELATED ATTITUDES AND BEHAVIOR OF THE POOR AND THE ELDERLY. HIGHLIGHT REPORT VOLUME XIII. Princeton, New Jersey: Opinion Research Corporation.
A study of the energy-related attitudes and behavior of the poor and elderly, divided into three parts: (1) major problems in the U.S. and how they affect the poor and the elderly; (2) plans for 1974 income tax rebates; and (3) tradeoffs in pollution vs. price. Respondents had family incomes of under $10,000 or were 50 years of age and older. Interview items for which results are reported include: problems facing the U.S. today, such as rising unemployment, inflation, energy shortage; looking ahead at the problem of unemployment; impact of inflation; the Federal Government: spend or economize; trend in perceived impact of inflation; anticipated consumer price fluctuation; potential of income to keep pace with prices; fuels used in households;perceived and projected increases in prices of fuels; attitudes toward selling food to other nations; and ways to spend tax rebates.

1325.   1975i   AUTOMOBILE USAGE PATTERNS. HIGHLIGHT REPORT VOLUME XIV. Princeton, New Jersey: Opinion Research Corporation.
This study concentrates on patterns of automobile usage and is based on 1,007 telephone interviews. Variables include: car usage as affected by lifestyle; car usage patterns; planned trips as compared with routine or spontaneous trips; times per week trip is usually made; analysis of trips; the extent to which shopping trips are done by phone instead of by car; willingness to cut out trips; and factors deterring car use. Findings suggest that the primary way that people could cut down automobile use without eliminating leisure time use would be in more careful planning of trips for shopping and errands. Another important finding is a lack of sensitivity to gasoline price increases.

1326.   1975j   HOW THE PUBLIC VIEWS THE NATION'S DEPENDENCE ON OIL IMPORTS; A POSSIBLE NATURAL GAS SHORTAGE THIS WINTER; THE OVERALL NEED TO SAVE ENERGY. HIGHLIGHT REPORT VOLUME XV. Princeton, New Jersey: Opinion Research Corporation.
A study of opinions on these three issues. One general result is that respondents recognized the era of cheap energy to be over, but also believed consumption of foreign oil ought to

be reduced and domestic resources developed. Variables involved perceptions and attitudes related to opposition to increased dependence on foreign oil; the fear of a natural gas shortage this winter; and the concern over the need to save energy.

1327.

Schipper, Lee, and A.J. Lichtenbert, EFFICIENT ENERGY USE AND WELL-BEING: THE SWEDISH EXAMPLE, Berkeley: University of California, Lawrence Berkeley Laboratory, Report 4430, 1976.

Method: A detailed comparison between per capita energy consumption in the U.S. and Sweden, based largely on 1970-72 data from statistical abstracts and various other sources.

Variables: U.S. versus Sweden in connection with: basic economic and social indicators; energy use related to transportation, residences and commerce, industry, and imports and exports.

Findings: Sweden used 55-65% of the per capita energy (with the counting of hydroelectric being problematic) at essentially the same per-capita income as the U.S. This difference was shown to arise both from differences in the mix of economic activities and in the energy consumption per unit output in these activities. In this regard Sweden had higher efficiencies in transportation, materials processing, and space heating. Heavy use of automobiles in the U.S. was a major factor here. The study suggests that institutional and social factors determine how close individual consumers, firms, and society as a whole come to the most economic use of energy, e.g., in U.S. mortgage policies and market considerations constrain developers to minimize first costs, rather than life cycle costs, in contrast to Sweden.

1328.

Schnaiberg, Allan, "Social Syntheses of the Societal-Environmental Dialectic: The Role of Distributional Impacts," SOCIAL SCIENCE QUARTERLY 56, 1 (June, 1975), 5-20.

Method: Summarizes existing empirical research on the distributional consequences of the energy crisis.

Variables: Effects of the energy crisis on consumption, employment, income, and profits.

Findings: Energy crisis (as a simulation of "planned scarcity") had net regressive distributional impacts, e.g., the poor suffered more than the well-to-do in terms of income loss, unemployment, impacts on lifestyles; small businesses were hurt more than large corporations; and the Nixon administration was able to use the energy crisis to justify curtailing "non-essential" federal governmental expenditures such as health, education and welfare.

1329.
Schneider, Alan M., "Elasticity of Demand for Gasoline," ENERGY SYSTEMS AND POLICY, 1, 3 (1975), 277-286.

Method: A study of gasoline sales in California in order to measure elasticity of demand. A time-series analysis was used in conjunction with data from thirteen-plus years (1960-1972). Data for sales were taken from the State Board of Equalization and from reported sales for regular grade from 4,000 major brand retail stations in Los Angeles. An average figure for price was arrived at using the latter.

Variables: Price per gallon and monthly sales of gasoline in the Los Angeles area.

Findings: A 17% increase in the price of gasoline in the Los Angeles area produced no observable change in gasoline consumption for the time period analyzed. Gasoline prices were thus found to be in elastic to demand.

1330.
Schuller, C. Richard, et al., CITIZENS' VIEWS ABOUT THE PROPOSED HARTVILLE NUCLEAR POWER PLANT: A PRELIMINARY REPORT OF POTENTIAL SOCIAL IMPACTS, Oak Ridge, Tennessee: Oak Ridge National Laboratory, 1975.

Method: A marginal frequency analysis of a random sample (N=350) of Trousdale County, Tennessee, surveyed by interview during February, 1975, to determine the potential impact of a large nuclear power plant complex on a rural community.

Variables: Socioeconomic background, demographic characteristics, attitudinal perceptions of the community, the changes respondents anticipate would accompany construction and operation of the plant, and how they evaluate the changes which may be brought about.

Findings: People were apparently residing in the community because they liked it. 65% of respondents favored the plant, 29% opposed, and 10% were undecided. The strongest supporters tended to be involved in business and labor occupations. A small majority of farmers opposed the facility. The most adamant opponents were generally women. No differences between supporters or opponents emerged from other background indicators such as formal education, age, and length of residence in the area. Support was most closely associated with the expectation of positive economic benefits. Opposition stemmed from concern over radiation and the potential for accidents at the facility, even though opponents tended to regard economic growth and development as desirable for the community.

1331.
Schwartz, Timothy P., "Societal Energy Consumption: An Evolutionary Theory and a Preliminary Empirical Analysis," unpublished Ph.D. dissertation, Department of Sociology, University of North Carolina (Chapel Hill), 1975.

Method: A correlation and regression/path analysis of cross-national time-series data (largely collected from UN sources) on 120 societies, in order to test an evolutionary theory of energy consumption. The data are for the years 1929 and 1969.

Variables: The author provides 34 operationalizations of nine theoretical constructs, e.g., urbanization, division of labor, and energy consumption--all of which are macro-social structural charac- teristics of nations. The research views societal energy con- sumption as both a major cause and effect in a complex matrix of socio-demographic-economic forces.

Findings: Societal energy consumption is found to be a major causal element in determining aspects of social structure, e.g. intra- societal contact and economic productivity. These variables appear to have important causal ramifications for urbanization, division of labor, and intersocietal contact, which, in turn, influence energy consumption. The results, while suggestive, are tempered by the limitations of the data-base.

1332.
Schwartz, T.P. and Donna Schwartz-Barcott, "The Short End of the Shortage: On the Self-Reported Impact of the Energy Shortage on the Socially Disadvantaged," Paper presented at the 1974 meeting of the Society for the Study of Social Problems, Montreal.

Method: A study of the self-reported effects of energy shortage, based on a panel survey conducted in July and November, 1973 and March, 1974. A systematic sample (N=200), proportionate to city size, of heads of households was drawn from the city directories of Chapel Hill, Durham and Raleigh, North Carolina. Data were cross-tabulated using a sig- nificance level of .05.

Variables: The differential impact of energy shortage as self-reported by heads of households.

Findings: The energy shortage did not discriminate against socially disadvan- taged groups; it did not discriminate more against groups that have multiple social disadvantages; and such discrimination did not emerge and increase as the shortage endured and worsened.

1333.

Sears, David O., et al., "Political System Support and Public Response to the
    1974 Energy Crisis," paper presented at the Conference on Political
    Alienation and Political Support, Stanford, California, May 27-30, 1976.

    Method: An examination of the role of support for the political system in
            determining compliance to attitudes and actions that government
            defines as in the public interest, specifically in connection with
            the case of responses by Los Angeles County residents to the
            energy crisis of 1974. A multi-stage probability sample (N=1069)
            of Los Angeles residents aged 18 and over was used and interviews
            were conducted February-March of 1974. Data on household electricity
            and natural gas usage was obtained from utility companies. Four
            major hypotheses were tested.

    Variables: Support for the political system as indicated by diffuse
               system support, partisanship, the individual's longstanding
               symbolic loyalties, and personal impact, all as related to
               the 1974 energy crisis in Los Angeles.

    Findings: Diffuse system support was found to be significantly related
              to the official government energy line. Partisanship was also,
              as well as being strongly correlated with system support. The
              personal impact of the crisis had virtually no effects at all
              in terms of citizen's attitudinal response, i.e., it did not
              inspire general conformity to or rebellion against the official
              government interpretation of and response to the energy crisis.
              Neither system support nor partisanship contributed significantly
              to behavioral reductions in energy comsumption; however, the
              personal impact of the crisis did. Overall, attitudinal pre-
              dictors (system support, partisanship, and perceptions of the crisis)
              are the most important predictors of attitudinal response (policy
              support). Personal impact rather than longstanding political atti-
              tudes was the major factor in behavioral compliance.

1334.

Seaver, W. Burleigh, and Arthur H. Patterson, "Decreasing Fuel Oil Consumption Through
    Feedback and Social Commendation," JOURNAL OF APPLIED BEHAVIOR ANALYSIS, 9,
    2 (1976).

    Method: A sample of 180 households was drawn randomly from the list of con-
            tinuing accounts in the area of a university community in central Penn-
            sylvania, and divided into two test groups and a control group to
            assess two methods of facilitating fuel-oil conservation, i.e., infor-
            mational feedback and informational feedback plus commendation. The
            study was conducted from February through May 1974, during an acute
            oil shortage.

    Variables: Impact of the two methods on consumer behavioral patterns of fuel
               oil consumption.

    Findings: The consumption rate of the feedback plus commendation group was
              significantly lower than that of either the group receiving only
              information on rate of oil use, or the no-treatment control group.

1335.
Seligman, Clive, and John M. Darley, "Feedback as a Means of Decreasing Energy Consumption," (Princeton University) Paper presented at the 71st annual meeting
of the American Sociological Association, August 30-September 3, 1976.

Method: July-September, 1975, experimental study of 40 homeowners in a planne
urban development of identical dwellings in Central New Jersey to
determine the effect of consumption feedback on energy consumption
in residential housing. Participants were randomly divided into
control and feedback groups. A baseline relationship between daily
average temperature and daily consumption was established from daily
readings of electric meters for five weeks, with.the use of regressio
analysis. Both groups were told air conditioning is the biggest ener
user and should be reduced. The feedback group was given daily (Tues
Friday) percentage scores indicating the degree to which participants
actual consumption corresponded to predicted consumption. The technique used was analysis of variance.

Variables: The effect of information feedback on the energy conservation
behavior of families in connection with the use of home air condition
ing.

Findings: Both groups used significantly less electricity during the treatment
period compared to the baseline, which was partly the result of
cooler weather during the treatment phase. During treatment, the
feedback group consumed 10.3 percent less than the control group.
Within the feedback group, the lower the initial level of consumption
the greater the amount of conservation during treatment. This suggests that feedback is more successful with moderate users than with
high users of electricity.

1336.
Smith, B.W., and G.R. Frey, "Factors Influencing Spatial Consumption of Energy in th
United States," TIJDSCHRIFT VOOR ECONOMISCHE EN SOCIALE GEOGRAPHIE, 66, 4 (197
246-250.

Method: Correlation and regression of 1971 aggregate U.S. energy consumption
by state, using secondary data from the U.S. Departments of Census
and Interior, the Federal Highway Administrations, and the National
Oceanic and Atmospheric Administration.

Variables: The effect of per capita scores for value added by manufacturing,
value added by minerals production, and value of agricultural output,
income, total miles traveled, and climate,on the spatial consumption
of energy in the U.S.

Findings: The major factors influencing the spatial pattern of energy use of
states are the localization of manufacturing and minerals production.
Income, climatic conditions, and volume of traffic appear to bear
little, if any, relationship to the pattern of aggregate energy use.

1337.

Socolow, Robert H., et al., "Energy Conservation in Housing: Work in Progress and Plans for 1975-76," Center for Environmental Studies Report No. 19, Princeton University, April 1975.

Method: Description of experimentation and analysis of energy conservation opportunities in residential housing underway at Princeton University. Goals of the research are (1) improving the state-of-the-art of single-house modeling by field-validated analyses, (2) identifying the significant behavioral and structural components of the observed variations in gas and electric consumption, (3) documenting, via designed experiments, the energy savings associated with low-cost residential retrofits, and (4) verifying the effects of commitment and feedback on the resident's ability to achieve reduced energy consumption.

Variables: Not yet reported.

Findings: Not yet reported.

1338.

Stearns, Mary D., THE BEHAVIORAL IMPACTS OF THE ENERGY SHORTAGE: SHIFTS IN TRIP-MAKING CHARACTERISTICS, Cambridge, Massachusetts: U.S. Department of Transportation, Transportation Systems Center, December, 1975.

Method: National random sample surveys (N=700), December, 1973 and February, 1974, gathered by home interview and statistically analyzed to contrast aggregate and disaggregate shifts in trip-making characteristics. Data from National Opinion Research Center's Continuous National Survey.

Variables: The effect of the 1973-74 energy shortage on trip-making frequency, modes and purpose for households of different income level.

Findings: In the aggregate, the energy shortage seems to have mildly decreased trip frequency, not changed modal use, and decreased shopping trip incidence. Disaggregation by income level revealed that sub-poverty level respondents apparently did not decrease trip frequency, significantly reduced their use of the auto-driver mode, and reported no significant shifts in their incidence of trip purposes, all by contrast with above poverty level respondents.

1339.

Stearns, Mary D., THE SOCIAL IMPACTS OF THE ENERGY SHORTAGE: BEHAVIORAL AND ATTITUDE SHIFTS, Washington, D.C.: U.S. Department of Transportation, 1975.

Method: A study of selected household responses to the energy shortage, specifically with respect to shifts in behavior or trip-making characteristics, and in attitudes towards the energy shortage and conservation alternatives. Data were drawn from National Opinion Research Center national random sample survey (N=700) collected at the onset and peak of the national energy shortage of Winter, 1973-74.

217

Variables: The effect of the 1973-74 energy shortage on trip making
frequency, mode, and purpose for households of different income
level, and on household attitudes towards the energy shortage
and conservation alternatives.

Findings: Sub-poverty level household members report significant modal
shifts away from auto-driver trips, compared with no change for
above poverty household members. Trip frequency remained the
same for the former but decreased for the latter. Analyses of
attitudes showed that social status is positively correlated
with shortage perception, household evaluation of its financial status is negatively correlated with expected duration
of the energy shortage, and negative evaluations of household energy shortage impacts are positively correlated with
disatisfaction with regard to enacted energy conservation
policies. It was also found that households became less
tolerant of conservation policies as they experienced the
energy shortage.

1340.
Stewart, Charles T., Jr., and James T. Bennett, "Urban Size and Structure and Private
Expenditures for Gasoline," LAND ECONOMICS, 51, 4 (November, 1975)', 365-373.

Method: Correlation and regression analysis of 134 SMSA's with 1970 population
of 200,000 or greater. Data for retail sales of gasoline and lubrican
were obtained from the 1967 Census of Business; population data are
from the U.S. Bureau of Census.

Variables: Effect of urban size, proportion of the population in central citie
population per square mile in the central city and outside the central
city, rate of growth, etc., on per capita retail gasoline sales.

Findings: The predictive power of the regression was generally low. SMSA size
and rate of growth were found to be negatively related to per capita
gasoline consumption, proportion of nonwhite population to be positive
related. Per capita gasoline consumption was much higher in the West
and Northcentral regions and much lower in the Northeast and South.

1341.
Sundstrom, Eric, et al., "Community Attitudes Toward a Proposed Nuclear Power
Generating Facility as a Function of Expected Outcomes," unpublished
manuscript, University of Tennessee, Knoxville, Tennessee, 1975.

Method: A January, 1975 sample survey of 350 residents of a rural
Tennessee county. A factor analysis and simple multiple
regression equation using factors as predictors were used to
analyze variation in attitudes.

Variables: Attitudes about hazards, economic growth, power costs, social
disruption, and community visibility, etc. as related to a proposed nuclear power plant.

Findings: Approximately two-thirds of the respondents expressed favorable
attitudes toward the proposed nuclear plant. The five main
variables listed above accounted for 54% of the variation in
attitudes toward the plant. The strongest predictor--perceived
likelihood of hazards--was inversely related to favoring the proposed nuclear power plant.

1342.

Talarzyk, W. Wayne, and Glenn S. Omura, "Consumer Attitudes Toward and Perceptions
of the Energy Crisis," in Ronald C. Curhan (ed.), COMBINED PROCEEDINGS OF
THE AMERICAN MARKETING ASSOCIATION, 1974 CONFERENCE, Chicago: American
Marketing Association, 1975.

Method: Initial findings from a national survey on consumer attitudes
toward the energy crisis (N=1000 households), administered a
few days after the oil embargo officially lifted (March 1, 1974).
Factor analysis was performed on the survey results.

Variables: The effect of the energy crisis on consumers activities, interests, and opinions (AIO). Also a varimax rotated factor analysis
of the effect of differences in age, income, geographic area,
and other socioeconomic variables on consumer AIO statements.

Findings: Greatest accord among respondents was found in the areas of
attitudinal response to the energy shortage, energy shortage
effect on activities, blame and responsibility for the energy
shortage, rationing of energy resources, and the economic
repercussions of energy resources. Cross-classifications
between socio-economic variables and the AIO statements, as
related to the above six issues, revealed associations primarily
between age versus attitudinal response (older less resistant
to energy conservation) and between age and income versus the
energy shortage affect on activities ($15,000+ more likely to
report a change in activities, middle-range age groups had less
tendency to report a change in miles expended shopping).

1343.

Thompson, Phyllis T., and John MacTavish, "Energy Problems: Public Beliefs,
Attitudes and Behaviors," unpublished manuscript, Urban and Environmental
Studies Institute, Grand Valley State College, Allendale, Michigan, 1976.

Method: A February, 1976 random sample (N=600) survey of the Grand Rapids
metropolitan area drawn to determine the perceptions and beliefs
that might underline energy related behaviors. The data were
collected by interview and subjected to marginal frequency
analysis.

Variables: Beliefs, attitudes, and behaviors in relation to energy use.

Findings: The respondents were distinctly divided on energy questions.
The larger group (over 50%) was cynical and did not trust the
information they had received, did not believe oil and gas
resources could be exhausted, and regarded gasoline shortages
of 1974 as manipulation by industry and government. This
group adopted few or no conservation measures. They tended
to be at lower occupational levels, less educated, and older
than the smaller distinct group (approximately 20%) which
believed we have a real and persistent energy problem. The
latter believed in future exhaustion of oil and gas, and
expected energy shortages with higher development costs and
large price increases. They adopted a variety of conservation
measures. This group tended to be skilled, college educated,
and under 45.

1344.

Tuso, Margaret A., and E. Scott Geller, "Behavior Analysis Applied to Environmental/
Ecological Problems: A Review," Unpublished manuscript, 1976 (Available from
Virginia Polytechnic Institute and State University).

Method: A topical set of summaries of the research designs, procedures, resul
and conclusions of recent behavioral interventions for ecological
rebalance. The topic most germane to the present purpose is "Energy
Consumption" (pp. 42-49) where a number of studies dealing with behav
ioral manipulations to achieve energy conservation are described.

Variables: Effectiveness of behavioral measures, as reported by various studie
to achieve energy and materials conservation.

Findings: Reinforcement procedures for litter control, recycling, and energy
conservation show that cash payments or incentives of monetary value
have proved effective, as have contingencies administered in the form
of large-scale programs of lotteries, group contests, token economies
and individual rewards based on specific levels of performance. Difficulties include transiency of effects and the number of personnel
and amount of time necessary to conduct the projects.

1345.

Walker, Nolan E., and E. Linn Draper, "The Effects of Electricity Price Increases
on Residential Usage of Three Economic Groups: A Case Study," in Texas
Nuclear Power Policies, Volume V: Social-Demographic and Economic Effects,
Policy Study Number 1, Austin: The University of Texas Center for Energy
Studies, 1975.

Method: Marginal frequency analysis based on a July, 1974, survey of a
random sample (N=60) of households in Austin, Texas, to determine
the impact of price increases on income groups, behavior and attitudes, and electricity consumption changes. Data were gathered
by personal interview and electricity consumption records
(from a utility company) for the previous two years.

<u>Variables</u>: The effect of electricity price increases on three economic groups (lower, middle, and upper income) over a two year period.

<u>Findings</u>: The number of lower income households increasing their energy use equalled the number decreasing their energy use. For middle income households, the number decreasing was greater than the number increasing their energy use. For upper income households, the number increasing ran well ahead of the number decreasing electricity consumption--suggesting that upper income groups are the least influenced by price rises. Middle income groups seem to show the greatest price elasticity.

1346.

Warkov, Seymour, "Energy Conservation in the Houston-Galveston Area Complex: 1976," The University of Houston Energy Institute, October, 1976.

<u>Method</u>: A marginal frequency analysis of Houston-area residents' energy conservation and usage practices as related to income level and home ownership, based on a spring/summer 1976 random sample telephone survey (N=3019) of Houston-Galveston metropolitan residents. The survey had the larger purpose of monitoring changes in lifestyles, attitudes, and other behaviors of the population.

<u>Variables</u>: Energy conservation related attitudes and behaviors by household income level.

<u>Findings</u>: During the 12 months preceeding the interviews: (1) 75% of the respondents reported curtailment in the use of electric lights in their homes, with 65% also reporting curtailment in the use of air conditioners; (2) 54% said they or other household members had reduced family or personal driving; (3) 29% reported that they "bought a car that consumes less gas;" (4) 26% indicated that they and/or other household members reduced the amount of driving to and from work by car pooling; (5) 14% had insulated their home or apartment. Virtually no difference was found between the twelve income groups selected with respect to the use of electric lights, but the higher income levels curtailed air conditioning less. Regarding family or personal driving, both the highest and the lowest income level households were least likely to report this mode of energy conservation. This was also true for carpooling. The likelihood of insulating proved to be directly related to income level, the poor being least and the upper income groups most likely to do so. The very lowest income households were least likely to report carpooling. In general, the higher the income level, the greater the likelihood of reporting purchase of a more energy-efficient car.

1347.

Warren, Donald I., INDIVIDUAL AND COMMUNITY EFFECTS ON RESPONSE TO THE ENERGY
CRISIS OF WINTER 1974: AN ANALYSIS OF SURVEY FINDINGS FROM EIGHT DETROIT
AREA COMMUNITIES, Ann Arbor: University of Michigan, Institute of Labor
and Industrial Relations, Program in Community Effectiveness, 1974.

Method: An April-June 1974 random sample survey of 766 households in eight
Detroit area communities, using interviews to determine responses
to and attitudes toward the "energy crisis" in the previous months.
Data were statistically analyzed for individual and socioeconomic
correlates.

Variables: Effects of income level, individual conservation behavior,
employment status, household characteristics and community setting
on attitudes toward the Winter 1973-74 energy crisis.

Findings: The energy crisis of 1973-74 was perceived by respondents as a
failure of U.S. institutions rather than resulting from the actions
of foreign countries. It was experienced most prominently by the
middle class ($10,000+ incomes). Those with incomes below
$10,000 were less likely to report that they had experienced
shortages or had cut back in the use of energy. The vast majority
of respondents indicated some energy conserving behavior. The
individual's social setting was determined to play a major role in
respondents' perceptions and attitudes.

1348.

Warren, Donald I., and David L. Clifford, LOCAL NEIGHBORHOOD SOCIAL STRUCTURE
AND RESPONSE TO THE ENERGY CRISIS OF 1973-74, Ann Arbor: University of
Michigan, Institute of Labor and Industrial Relations, Program in Community
Effectiveness, 1974.

Method: Statistical analysis of an April-June 1974 random sample interview
survey (N=766) of households in eight Detroit area communities to
determine the role of local neighborhood social structure in the
energy crisis of 1973-74.

Variables: The effect of neighborhood typology (six varieties of local
contexts) on individual attitudes and responses to the energy crisis.

Findings: The typology provided an important source of explained variance
in perceptions, reported behaviors, and helpful sources of information. These differential patterns tended to follow closely
those theoretically predicted by the concepts describing each
neighborhood type. "Integral" and "Stepping-Stone" type neighborhoods were highest in perceiving the energy crisis as real,
while "Anomic" type was lowest.

222

1349.

Williams, Robin M., Jr., TESTIMONY BEFORE THE PUBLIC SERVICE COMMISSION OF
NEW YORK, CASE NO. 26806: REPORT ON RECENT DEVELOPMENTS IN THE DESIGN
OF RATES FOR LOW-VOLUME RESIDENTIAL ELECTRIC UTILITY CUSTOMERS, unpublished manuscript, June, 1976 (available from Chemung County Neighborhood Legal Services, Inc., 115 East Church St., Elmira, N.Y. 14901).

Method: A reporting of selected data and findings from the 1975
national household energy use survey carried out for the
Washington Center for Metropolitan Studies by the Response
Analysis Corporation. The survey is basically an update
and expansion of one carried out in 1973 as part of the
Ford Foundation Energy Policy Project (see Newman and Day
papers from THE AMERICAN ENERGY CONSUMER above). The 1975
random sample (N=2952) survey involved personal interviews
of households nationwide, with a subsample (N=221) of New
York households and a subsample (N=569) of Northeastern U.S.
households. Meter data were collected for the households
surveyed.

Variables: The relationship between income and other socioeconomic
characteristics, and the consumption of electricity.

Findings: The correlation between income and electricity usage was
determined to be generally the same for all U.S. households,
for those in the Northeast, and for New York State, i.e., that
the poor use much smaller amounts of electricity than the
average household, and about half or less of the amount
used by the well-off. For New York State the range in
average monthly kilowatt hours consumed is 335 for the poor
to 761 for the well-off. According to the survey, by contrast with the well-off the poor tend to live in smaller
quarters, to use electricity less for air conditioning, and
to have a smaller number of electric appliances. The poor
also spend proportionately more of their income for the
electricity they use. The results of the 1975 survey cor-
roborate those of the 1973 survey.

1350.

Winett, Richard A., and Michael T. Nietzel, "Behavioral Ecology: Contingency
Management of Consumer Energy Use," AMERICAN JOURNAL OF COMMUNITY
PSYCHOLOGY, 1975.

Method: January 31-March 28, 1974 study of two volunteer groups in
Lexington, Kentucky, one receiving monetary incentives (N=16)
and the other just information on how to conserve (N=15), to determine their relative reduction in the use of natural gas and
electricity (monitored by meter). A one-way analysis of
variance technique was used.

Variables: The relative effect of monetary incentives and information
alone on conservation behavior.

Findings: The Incentive group averaged approximately 15% more electricity
reduction than the Information group. This statistically
significant difference was maintained in follow-ups.

1351.

Woodson, Herbert H., _et al._, DIRECT AND INDIRECT ECONOMIC, SOCIAL, AND ENVIRON-
MENTAL IMPACTS OF THE PASSAGE OF THE CALIFORNIA NUCLEAR POWER PLANTS
INITIATIVE, Austin: The University of Texas· Austin,Center for Energy
Studies, 1976.

> Method: A set of scenarios projecting low, medium, and high electric
> energy demand growth rates, in conjunction with different
> electric energy supply alternatives, are used to evaluate the
> likely impacts of the California nuclear power plants initia-
> tive. Analytical models were used to study the interaction of
> the following components: conservation assessment, electrical
> energy demand/supply/projection/cost analysis, long-run economic
> growth assessment, California input-output assessment, energy
> resource assessment, socio-cultural assessment, and environ-
> mental and health impacts assessments. Results are reported
> for years 1977, 1985, and 1995.

> Variables: Projections of the direct and indirect economic, social, and
> environmental impacts of enactment of the California nuclear
> power plants initiative.

> Findings: California apparently will need additional electricity. Large-
> scale supplies may be required in addition to hydro, geother-
> mal, and solar energy resources. Elimination of nuclear as an
> alternative would force increased reliance on other energy
> sources which possess their own impacts, risks, and uncertain-
> ties. Nuclear energy is assumed to provide the lowest cost
> electricity compared to coal and oil, leading the authors to
> conclude that elimination of nuclear energy will cause the price
> of electricity to rise in California. The scenerios show that
> there may be few overall economic or socio-cultural effects
> should nuclear power be phased out, provided that alternatives
> are available. Increased use of coal could have significant
> sociocultural and environmental effects in nearby states,
> especially in terms of air and water quality. Increased use
> of oil could have adverse impacts on California's air quality,
> and would be contrary to the goals of Project Independence. The
> uncertainties related to nuclear waste and the fuel cycle are
> noted.

1352.

Wright, Susan, "Public Responses to the Energy Shortage: An Examination of Social
Class Variables," unpublished Ph.D. dissertation, Iowa State University,
Ames, 1975.

> Method: Interviews from a random sample (N=190) of Des Moines, Iowa,
> residents, stratified by social class criteria, were used to
> investigate relationships between social class and perceptions
> of energy shortages.

<u>Variables</u>: Social status measures in relation to energy shortage response
variables.

<u>Findings</u>: Correlational analysis revealed significant relationships be-
tween each of the energy shortage response variables--e.g.,
attribution of responsibility for the energy crisis--and at
least one of the social status indices (education, income, occupation, and so forth). The strengths of these relationships,
however, were not sufficiently large to indicate a general social
class polarization of interests over the energy crisis issue.

1353.

Viladas, J.M. Company, IMPACT OF THE FUEL SHORTAGE ON PUBLIC ATTITUDES TOWARD
ENVIRONMENTAL PROTECTION, Washington, D.C.: U.S. Environmental Protection
Agency, 1974. (2 volumes).

<u>Method</u>: A study of the impact of the energy crisis on attitudes
toward environmental protection and how these attitudes were
related to how affected respondents were by the fuel shortage.
Telephone interviews were conducted with 500 of 3,012 respondents from a national sample studied in 1973. The follow-up
telephone interviewing was accomplished during May, 1974.

<u>Variables</u>: The effect of the energy crisis on attitudes toward envi-
ronmental protection.

<u>Findings</u>: The energy crisis appeared to have little impact on attitudes
about fighting pollution. The most popular prospective
methods of reducing fuel consumption were improving public
transportation, lowering speed limits on highways, and driving smaller cars. Rationing and fuel and fuel price increases
were among the most unpopular steps to reducing fuel consumption. In addition, five steps which represent various ways
of relaxing environmental control standards so as to reduce
energy shortages were generally unpopular. One of these
anti-environmental strategies--letting air pollution increase
in areas that now have clean air--was the least acceptable
of the entire battery of 18 potential public policy options.
Strategies related to increasing the supplies of energy--e.g.,
increasing coal production through strip mining, building
more atomic power plants, and building the Alaska pipeline--
were generally intermediate in public acceptibility between
the popular conservation measures and the unpopular anti-
environmental measures. In general, people who report being
affected in their lifestyles and consumption patterns by the
energy crisis/fuel shortage (compared to those indicating
they were not affected by the crisis) were most likely to:
(1) favor policies to conserve energy, (2) favor policies to
to expand energy supplies, and (3) believe that these conservation and expansion of energy supply policies would be
effective in alleviating the fuel shortage.

1354.

Young, Jeffery W., et al., "Land Use and Energy Flow at the National Level," SIMULATION, 24, 1 (January, 1975), 113-116.

> Method: Simulation model of the interaction of the agricultural and energy sectors at the national level. The model, SPECULATER, simulates certain hypothetical interactions between national-level-import versus agricultural-export policies and the urban population density-versus-transportation characteristics of U.S. urbanized areas. Runs are reported for 1970, 1975, 1985, and 2000. The secondary data used are from various sources.

> Variables: Per-capita gasoline demand, population size and age-structure, price of agricultural land, acreage harvested, wheat exports, etc.

> Findings: Preliminary simulations demonstrate inherent homeostatic mechanisms. Results of three runs with differing assumptions are given. Although the quadrupling of petroleum prices by OPEC has had a major impact on the U.S. economy, it can be inferred from the model that the overall impact may have certain positive effects, e.g. the boosting of U.S. agricultural production and exports.

1355.

Zucchetto, James, "Energy-Economic Theory and Mathematical Models for Combining the Systems of Man and Nature, Case study: the Urban Region of Miami, Florida," ECOLOGICAL MODELING 1, (1975), 241-268.

> Method: A study of the Miami, Florida urban region with respect to energy flow and the relationship between energy theory and economics. Economic, natural system, and energy data were compiled for this region for the period 1950-1972. These data were analyzed by cross-correlation, i.e. a technique for determining how well two functions track each other in time, and used for a simulation model on an analog computer.

> Variables: The systematic interactions of socioeconomic (e.g., retail sales, food, population, building structure, and taxes) and natural (e.g., rainfall, wind, and pollution assimilated by the environment) energy flows and storages.

> Findings: Cross-correlations showed significant levels of correlation between the rate of change of fossil fuel use and the rates of change of population, budget, sales tax, income, building structure, and number of telephones. It was determined from the simulation that the ratio of natural to fossil fuel energy changed from 1.77 in 1950 to 0.25 in 1972.

1356.

Zuiches, James J., ACCEPTABILITY OF ENERGY POLICIES TO MID-MICHIGAN FAMILIES, East Lansing: Michigan State University Agricultural Experiment Station, Research Report 298, 1976.

Method: Marginal frequency analysis of the attitudes of a 1974 survey of Lansing S.M.S.A. (N=217) families toward the energy crisis.

Variables: Respondent attitudes with respect to energy policies.

Findings: A bare majority of respondents believed the crisis to be real. There was wide divergence in the acceptability of specific energy-saving policies. In general, urban females were most favorable to each policy. Policies that would restrict electrical use, ration meat, increase taxes for large families, and manipulate school seasons, were in the category of limited acceptability (less than 20%). Most respondents were supportive of policies for re-establishing local grocery stores, tax deductions for home insulation and home improvements, increased home gardening, and more food preparation at home.

1357.

Zuiches, James J., "Coercion and Public Acceptance: The Case of Energy Policies," Paper presented at the annual meeting of the Society for the Study of Social Problems, New York, August 1976 (Department of Sociology, Michigan State University, East Lansing, Michigan 48824).

Method: An evaluation model based on Theodore J. Lowi's typology of public policies is used to determine the acceptability of various energy policies that would directly or indirectly affect energy conservation by consumers. Data are from two surveys of the Lansing SMSA, taken during Spring 1974 (N=216) and Spring 1976 (N=259). The model of policy acceptance employs path analysis. Results are compared with a partial regression model of energy policy as affected by sex, urban/rural residence, energy awareness, belief in the energy crisis, and education.

Variables: The effect of socioeconomic characteristics (e.g., urban/rural residence and male/female gender) on attitudes toward four policy types: (1) distributive--policies without negative sanction; (2) constituent-voluntaristic--policies affecting the individual's environment, but entailing no coercion, (3) regulative--policies with explicit negative sanctions; and (4) redistributive--policies which affect individuals through their environment in an involuntary way.

Findings: Regulative and redistributive policies had the lowest levels of support, on the average being acceptable to about ¼ of the respondents in 1974 and 1/3 in 1976. Voluntaristic policies with no value-laden implications scored highest (75 percent in 1974). Distributive policies were acceptable to 43 percent of the respondents in 1974 and 54 percent in 1976. In general, urban women were most favorable to each policy. Urban males, rural females, and rural males, in descending order, found policies less acceptable. The partial regression model was found to do a better job in explaining levels of acceptance of energy policies than the model of coercion.

1358.

Zuiches, James J., ENERGY AND THE FAMILY, East Lansing: Michigan State University, Department of Agricultural Economics, Cooperative Extension Service, Report No. 390, 1975.

Method: Overview of and initial findings from a 5-year logitudinal study of energy and the family. Bench mark cross-section was established May-June 1974 when a multi-stage area probability sample (N=217, 160 urban and 57 rural) of Lansing S.M.S.A. families was surveyed by self-administered questionnaires and personal interviews.

Variables: Energy use as related to attitudes, food consumption, transportation, housing conditions, financial expenditures and resources, and the character and quality of the family's functioning in terms of interaction patterns within the family, with friends, relatives, and the larger community.

Findings: Respondents were evenly divided about the reality of the 1973-74 energy crisis, 30% believing energy shortage will be crucial within 5 to 10 years. Acceptability of specific energy policies varied by sex and location, from most to least: urban females, urban males, rural females, and rural males. Least acceptable policies involved severe restrictions regulation, or rationing. A positive association was found between education, energy awareness, and policy acceptance. Preliminary results are also reported for changes in family nutritional status, household energy use, and the effect of homemaker employment on household energy consumption.

INDEX

INDEX

Alternative energy--general, 100, 116, 151, 243, 244, 317, 325, 349,
351, 352, 358, 382, 393, 406, 413, 415, 422, 459, 460, 475,
489, 509, 585, 590, 604, 617, 619, 623, 658, 659, 661, 662,
664, 666, 671, 673, 674, 675, 676, 677, 678, 680, 690, 692,
697, 700, 701, 709, 719, 722, 729, 730, 744, 749, 772, 776,
782, 796, 799, 810, 821, 827, 832, 917, 973, 983, 1007, 1009,
1010, 1011, 1025, 1038, 1063, 1066, 1080, 1082, 1086, 1088,
1094, 1107, 1114, 1126, 1127, 1128, 1132, 1134, 1136, 1138,
1143, 1144, 1145, 1146, 1152, 1154, 1157, 1158, 1159, 1160,
1168, 1169, 1170, 1171, 1187, 1189, 1320.

Alternative Energy Periodicals, Subsection of Periodicals, see
page 77.

Behavior, lifestyles, attitudes, etc., 211, 292, 351, 472, 544, 567,
601, 605, 664, 673, 719, 778, 796, 800, 819, 874, 896, 1030,
1074, 1102, 1109, 1119, 1162, 1163, 1225, 1226, 1227, 1231,
1232, 1234, 1235, 1236, 1240; 1241, 1242, 1243, 1244, 1245,
1246, 1253, 1255, 1256, 1260, 1261, 1262, 1267, 1270, 1271,
1272, 1273, 1274, 1277, 1278, 1282, 1286, 1290, 1291, 1292,
1293, 1295, 1296, 1297, 1298, 1301, 1304, 1305, 1306, 1307,
1309, 1310, 1311, 1312, 1314, 1315, 1316, 1317, 1318, 1319,
1320, 1321, 1322, 1323, 1324, 1325, 1330, 1334, 1335, 1338,
1339, 1341, 1342, 1343, 1344, 1347, 1348, 1350, 1352, 1353,
1356, 1357, 1358.

Biogas, methane, hydrogen, 460, 486, 660, 672, 674, 690, 744, 1107,
1115, 1136, 1137, 1140, 1142, 1147, 1152, 1167, 1173, 1188,
1189, 1191.

Canada, 11, 12, 13, 29, 36, 73, 93, 94, 95, 96, 136, 160, 162, 220,
221, 222, 332, 224, 231, 232, 269, 280, 287, 289, 312, 362,
381, 428, 499, 519, 520, 555, 584, 633, 634, 647, 661, 671,
706, 810, 848, 970, 971, 972, 973, 974, 975, 976, 977, 978,
979, 980, 981, 982, 983, 984, 985, 986, 987, 1066, 1109, 1138,
1169, 1177, 1182.

Canadian Government, Subsection of Government Services, see page
119. See also Canada.

Children and younger readers, 7, 8, 15, 16, 18, 33, 50, 51, 58, 68,
69, 82, 102, 104, 114, 115, 130, 155, 168, 169, 170, 174, 191,
202, 207, 210, 214, 238, 309, 314, 315, 348, 366, 369, 375,
378, 394, 398, 402, 411, 416, 420, 434, 435, 437, 438, 441,
442, 451, 452, 455, 473, 479, 629, 648, 757, 815, 894, 975,

481, 674, 679, 701, 1125, 1132, 1134, 1138, 1139, 1144, 1147, 1160, 1167, 1168, 1169, 1198.

International relations, foreign policy, 33, 139, 281, 305, 333, 341, 364, 367, 372, 389, 390, 401, 430, 432, 443, 448, 453, 476, 477, 491, 492, 511, 530, 552, 554, 564, 581, 586, 595, 714, 792, 858, 864, 870, 987, 1326.

Natural gas, 86, 228, 417, 501, 502, 522, 553, 616, 733, 760, 824, 884, 910, 915, 1013, 1239, 1302, 1306, 1326, 1337, 1343, 1350.

Newsletters, Subsection of Periodicals, see page 81.

Non-Government Organizations, Associations and Companies, see page 89.

Nuclear energy--controversy, risks, potentials, 82, 100, 106, 114, 11 116, 139, 180, 195, 218, 234, 243, 272, 276, 311, 360, 366, 374, 377, 391, 433, 440, 441, 442, 449, 452, 456, 488, 507, 512, 519, 591, 615, 639, 707, 710, 725, 726, 727, 730, 731, 733, 765, 774, 775, 780, 790, 794, 804, 805, 810, 821, 829, 833, 855, 872, 876, 881, 899, 911, 917, 975, 987, 990, 994, 1028, 1057, 1060, 1075, 1109, 1123, 1260, 1268, 1276, 1293, 1299, 1304, 1319, 1330, 1341, 1351.

Oil, petroleum, gasoline, 88, 148, 184, 341, 342, 364, 368, 371, 414, 448, 453, 467, 476, 478, 492, 501, 522, 553, 616, 656, 733, 758, 766, 824, 876, 910, 912, 913, 915, 917, 1049, 1051, 1075, 1103, 1233, 1240, 1242, 1252, 1277, 1282, 1297, 1298, 1317, 1319, 1326, 1329, 1334, 1340, 1343, 1354.

Periodicals, see page 61.

Policy, politics, law, legislation, planning, 211, 220, 225, 226, 229, 243, 250, 252, 259, 303, 306, 307, 308, 320, 332, 333, 334, 341, 344, 345, 349, 353, 358, 359, 362, 363, 367, 373, 376, 377, 381, 383, 390, 399, 400, 401, 406, 409, 410, 414, 424, 430, 439, 457, 469, 471, 480, 482, 483, 490, 491, 508, 512, 517, 528, 529, 540, 541, 542, 543, 545, 546, 549, 551, 554, 556, 561, 562, 563, 570, 582, 595, 603, 608, 610, 622, 624, 627, 630, 641, 642, 651, 652, 685, 706, 707, 713, 714, 715, 723, 727, 732, 733, 737, 747, 748, 750, 751, 752, 753, 763, 767, 770, 777, 781, 784, 785, 788, 795, 801, 802, 808, 809, 817, 818, 823, 826, 827, 837, 840, 842, 845, 849, 878, 885, 900, 910, 918, 919, 920, 921, 922, 923, 924, 925, 926, 927, 928, 929, 930, 931, 932, 933, 934, 935, 936, 937, 938, 939, 940, 941, 942, 943, 944, 945, 946, 947, 948, 949, 950, 951, 952, 953, 954, 955, 956, 957, 958, 959, 960, 961, 962, 963, 964, 965, 966, 967, 968, 969, 990, 1004, 1008, 1015, 1026, 1028, 1029, 1057, 1070, 1071, 1072, 1073, 1083, 1085, 1087, 1098, 1100, 1101, 1102, 1105, 1106, 1108, 1109, 1111, 1115, 1145, 1172, 1214, 1215, 1238, 1246, 1250, 1260, 1274, 1303, 1313, 1319, 1321, 1328, 1333, 1356, 1357.

Printed in the United States
by Baker & Taylor Publisher Services